FIREPOT
STORIES

The dream of my early years as a deer hunter became reality through management.

FIREPOT
STORIES

Collected writings of a naturalist,
conservationist, wildlife biologist,
sportsman and raconteur

R. Joseph Hamilton

Published by
Evening Post Books
Charleston, South Carolina

First edition

Editor: John M. Burbage
Designer: Gill Guerry

First printing 2017
Printed in the United States of America
A CIP catalog record for this book has been applied
for from the Library of Congress.
ISBN: 978-1-929647-32-3

CONTENTS

CONTENTS

CONTENTS

FOREWORD
By Al Brothers and Larry Marchinton

This book's author, Joe Hamilton, is not only a great storyteller but also a professional wildlife biologist. He has worked for the South Carolina Department of Natural Resources, the Nature Conservancy, Ducks Unlimited, and, of course, the Quality Deer Management Association, which he founded and in the early years provided its leadership and funding out of his own pocket. Joe made notable contributions to the causes of natural resources conservation while with all of these organizations. Under his tutelage, the QDMA teachings and philosophy profoundly changed the way deer are managed and hunted throughout the U.S., Canada, Australia, and other countries that have deer. He has received more national and international awards for his conservation work than anyone we know. These came from a variety of government, private and professional organizations.

From some of his prolific writing through the years, Joe has compiled a classic in *Firepot Stories*. He has a writing style like no other and is the best storyteller you will ever hear or read. The authors of this Foreword were present when some of the stories unfolded and can attest that they were true to the last detail. Joe has an incredible memory of people — their words, mannerisms, colloquialisms, and characters! His book can make you sad and happy at the same time. And for those of us who, to paraphrase Arthur Bentley's poem at the end of the book, are "stirring the embers and throwing in the ends," it evokes memories and is particularly nostalgic. You laugh a lot, cry a little, and learn from his lifetime of experiences and studies, not only of people and white-tailed deer but other game and non-game species as well.

Joe is a naturalist with a wide knowledge of animals and plants. The book contains valuable information for the neophyte deer manager, but also for more advanced practitioners who would like a quality deer herd, quality hunting, and quality habitat. Just as important, Joe has captured the very essence of the hunting experience to include camaraderie and camp life along with the assorted "characters" and events usually associated with it.

Many years ago Al called Joe the "Johnny Appleseed" of proper deer management in the southeastern states. Since that time, his "seedlings" have spread much farther and wider. The fruits of that effort will be enjoyed by many over future decades and beyond.

The wildlife profession in its entirety has a preponderance of the type of individuals anyone would want as friends. Joe has been ours for over 40 years, and we are honored for the opportunity to write this Foreword.

I have his cast antlers, but that's not all, I have seasons of memories.

DEDICATION

Thank you Mr. Whitetail, I am who I am and where I am because of my relationship with you.

For over three million years you have walked this planet. Recently, humans have transposed your habitat into pavement, buildings, golf courses, and other deer "unfriendly" items. We have caused you great pain, inconvenience, and many losses on our highways.

I apologize for those of us who show no respect for you by taking you beyond the limits of hunting season, and particularly at night. There was a time when our kind took you any way any time for sustenance, but now it's done for excitement, and I find this behavior unacceptable.

I thank you for your role in our long-term relationship. Your eyes are positioned more to the side to allow you to detect danger in a broader spectrum — you are a prey species. My eyes are forward facing — the design of a predator.

I am well aware that we, you Mr. Whitetail and I, can't correspond, nor can you talk (as we know it) to your kind or other wild creatures. I'm afraid too many of my kind believe otherwise — this was the result of a famous movie producer driven to entertain my kind regardless of the negative ramifications affecting your well-being.

Your beauty has inspired artists, photographers, and sculptors to "capture" your grace in a woodland habitat. Your ways have inspired biologists to understand how and why you do the things you do. Your mystique as a denizen of the deep forest has inspired hunters, like me, to match wits with you on an even playing field. Your quality as table fare has inspired chefs to create one unique and tasty dish after another. Your ability to alter natural habitats has challenged managers to create a symbiotic relationship with your fellow wildlife and plant species.

Mr. Whitetail, I have no idea of who I would have become without you in my life. I'll do everything possible to prevent that scenario from developing or from your relegation from the status of game animal to a pest. In situations where you've been allowed to outgrow your home at the whims of human emotion and then are referred to as a hooved rat, I apologize for this defamation of character. We must avoid allowing our intelligence from taking second place to our emotions — an unfortunate artifact of urbanism.

You, like me, are mortal and you have millions of years of genetic fine-tuning to ensure longevity for your species. I can only pledge myself to the education of all who may interact with you to ensure that your path into the future is one worthy of the noble quarry you are.

Although I still have the enthusiasm of a nine-year-old deer hunter from well over a half century ago, I realize that youngsters of that age look to me for guidance now. I shoulder this responsibility with conviction, honor, and pride.

Even after more than 60 years of deer hunting experience I am more excited now than in the beginning because I know so much more to get excited about. Back then, my excitement level was based purely on speculation and false hope. I had always hoped for that magazine-cover buck to walk into view within gun's range, but didn't realize that there was probably not a buck like that in the entire county. Now, I know there are mature bucks a plenty — we find cast antlers, see them on trail cameras, and witness their "attitudes" expressed in the size of rubbed trees.

Landscapes take on a certain aura when I superimpose you via a mental "hologram." Having learned to appreciate the stature, antler size, and cunning of a mature buck, it is only now that I can take you with me anywhere in my thoughts, spiced with a clear mental picture rather than a mere dream. Your image is much more precise than it was in the early days when you were not so well known to me. Also, through proper management you have proven that you are now something we heretofore never let you express, and this applies to your appearance as well as your behavior — how you interact with others of your kind and how you use your environment.

Sailors are guided by the stars in their pelagic travels; migrating birds navigate by invisible, yet necessary, magnetic fields; some sea-dwelling fish species, labeled anadromous by ichthyologists, utilize their sense of smell to locate the exact freshwater breeding grounds where their lives began and fulfill their role in perpetuating their species. Then there's my species, humans. How do we find our way through life? Parents and family provide the initial guidance, but it is those we encounter later, acquaintances and friends, who influence our decisions to go this way, not that way, turn here, not there. The caliber of my human guideposts is unequaled — each has come to me through a common connection — you, Mr. Whitetail. There were some I never had the occasion or pleasure to meet, Aldo Leopold for instance, yet they forged my thought processes through their writings.

I am only one of many, *e pluribus unum*, influenced by individuals such as the late Aldo Leopold, Dr. Larry Marchinton, Al Brothers, Marion Burnside, and the late Arthur Bentley. They have led by example — how they think, speak, act, and, perhaps more importantly, how they react. Exposure to these luminaries has directed my course through a life of natural-resource conservation, and you, my friend, have reaped the benefits of the very relationship you spawned.

I received a letter dated May 16, 1998 from a high school classmate and long-time hunting companion, Murphy Corbett. Murphy passed away in 2009, but his friendship and heartfelt words will remain treasures for my lifetime. A quote from his letter serves as an appropriate valediction for this dedication.

"Joe, he has been with you and in your heart and soul all your life. He has been standing there in the depths of the river swamp with his nose raised in the early November morn, his breath condensing in the morning chill, and he has given you that fleeting glance. You have seen his gray muzzle, his broad shoulders, the wide beam, the tall brow tines, and the swollen neck. In a flash of brown and white he moves and as you rise to catch one last glimpse — he is gone and he has managed to put every tree in the river swamp between you and him. But he was there and he knew that you were there and he graced your presence with his. May it last forever!"

Thank you Mr. Whitetail for showing the way!

ACKNOWLEDGMENTS

Obviously, *Firepot Stories*, which covers a broad category of entries over a time span of nearly 45 years, was accomplished through my association with fellow biologists, hunters and fishermen.

The frontispiece is a copy of an original oil painting by the late Mrs. Grace McDuffie, a long-time friend and resident of Elizabethtown, N.C., my hometown. Additional art work was provided by Dr. David Dalton, Dr. Mickey Hellickson, Gini Knight, Cynthia Watkins, Kenny White, Kitty Fisher Cole, and the late Arthur Bentley. Co-authors of four articles include Dr. Larry Marchinton, Gerald Moore, Al Brothers, and young Michael Blackburn. Several photographs were supplied by John Moran, Russell Tyler, Brian Murphy, Chip Salak, Peter Stuart, Donna Hamilton, Ian Gill, Dr. Grant Woods, Moya Pierce, Jimmy Clark, Michael Perry, Aldo Leopold Foundation, Australian Deer Association, Walter McDuffie, Phil Morlock, Mark Spinks, David Henderson, Dr. Jack Payne, Brian Proctor, David Soliday, Lindsay Thomas, Robert Clark, Phillip Jones, Bob Campbell, Margaret French, Tommy Rhodes, Kyle Harding, Dr. Mickey Hellickson, Dr. Jeffrey Kramer, Tes Randle Jolly, and Steve Guyton. Some photographers remain anonymous. I provided all other photos and artwork.

Editorial comments on selected articles/stories were provided by Dr. Larry Marchinton, Dr. Karl Miller, Dr. Craig Harper, the late Dr. Eugene P. Odum, Al Brothers, Brian Murphy, Lindsay Thomas, Kip Adams, Matt Ross, Steve Guyton, Gerald Moore, Peter Stuart, Scott Osborne, Ashley Demosthenes, David Henderson, Ray Beasley, and John Davis.

My wife, Donna, has served graciously as my critic throughout. In addition to suggesting a better word, a different direction, or correcting punctuation, she accurately reflected the intent of my writing. If a story was meant to be humorous and she laughed, or a more somber tone brought tears, I knew I had hit the mark. Our children, Moya and Hunter, frequently asked if there would ever be a time that we would not be working on an article. Now that they're grown and the book has finally reached completion, I can respond in the affirmative.

I am indebted to Margaret French, my late mother, for her support of my academic and professional activities, and especially my writing. My sister Julie and her family have been unfaltering in their support as well.

There are others, too numerous to mention, who will surface as the stories of this book unfold.

The final responsibility of pulling everything together was granted to John M. Burbage, editor, and Gill Guerry, designer, who turned my collected writings into *Firepot Stories*. I am most grateful for their professionalism and style.

INTRODUCTION

In everyone there is a book. Some simply live the book while others venture to put their opinions, feelings, experiences and philosophies into written form. Many young writers compelled to compose a book are burdened by a lack of experience. They must take the path of producing something historical, biographical, or fictional.

This book, *Firepot Stories*, is an autobiography of a sort; it's the collected writings of a naturalist, conservationist, wildlife biologist, sportsman, and raconteur. Stories run the gamut from humorous to satirical, happy to sad, factual to philosophical, instructional to educational — all entertaining, I hope, and told with a strong element of truth. To sum it up, this book is unabridged, unabated, unabashed, uninhibited, and at times bordering on unbelievable. Seasoned raconteurs must take liberties in conveying the intent of a story while protecting the temper of their honesty. Readers must maintain their guard while traversing uncharted waters, so to speak. So, read, relax, enjoy, learn, and dream!

Some books tell a story. In this book, however, each entry tells a story. Also, there is no connectivity or flow among this collection of writings. They are not arranged in chronological order; rather, they are grouped with some semblance of kin. With one exception, no story has a sequel, although there is a trilogy of stories centered on a single character. If published, the source (magazine, newspaper, journal, or speech) and date are provided at the end of the article. And, several entries were written long enough ago that they required a Paul Harvey approach like his characteristic closing "...the rest of the story." In six such cases the story's continuation is labeled: "Follow-up." A writer cannot be expected to maintain impeccable prophesy. When a statement stands the test of time there is reason for celebration, and when you are incorrect, set the record straight and move on.

A common thread that weaves its way through this book is the choice of appropriate quotes from Aldo Leopold, the Father of Wildlife Biology, and author of the epic book: *A Sand County Almanac*. There is redundancy, of course, since writings were crafted as independent entities. I refer to Leopold's Almanac as my outdoor bible and I read from it frequently and religiously. Therefore, I have no apologies for using some quotes on multiple occasions. Perhaps through this process the reader will "take a cotton to" particular quotes and use them in appropriate situations. Although he passed away when I was only one year old, his influence and mentorship throughout my professional career commanded a prominence in my book. Aldo Leopold was the compleat conservationist.

Campfires have always provided a focal point for outdoorsmen. Our distant forefathers relied on fires for warmth and to prepare food. To them, fire was the essence of survival. Through the ages, fire has remained as a bond among mankind. Regardless of age, creed, religion, or race, we are drawn to a fire for spiritual sustenance and guidance.

Many of the decisions that have shaped our lives originated from gatherings around a fire. Native Americans and European settlers were known to pass a peace pipe around a campfire. President Franklin D. Roosevelt is remembered for his "fireside chats" from the White House. He knew the importance of "setting the stage" in maintaining his rapport with America.

Sigurd Olson, a naturalist and writer from the Minnesota-Wisconsin northwoods, began penning his philosophy in his later years. He, like Aldo Leopold, had a reverence for the outdoors and a unique ability to convince his readers of the necessity of serving as players rather than controllers in environmental concerns. Olson's philosophy was the product of his lifestyle. Only months before his death in 1982, he reminisced that his life was "a series of campfires." He philosophized that, "Without intangible values, life has no meaning."

Gazing into the flames and rising sparks is mesmerizing. The sights, sounds, and smells of a campfire allow us to explore and ponder our deepest feelings. At fireside, we discover ourselves and develop lasting friendships with fellow fire gazers.

Campfires are synonymous with gatherings of hunters around the world. Methods of presenting the fire are as diverse as those who join to soak in the warmth. Many have moved the campfire inside their cabins, where the fire is presented via a fireplace or pot-bellied stove. The ambiance of a natural setting is replaced by memoirs hanging on the walls: sets of deer antlers connected by cobwebs, faded pictures of hunting scenes, a hornet nest found years ago and brought to the cabin for all to see, and a collection of other things. The décor of all hunting camps appears rather generic at a distance, but upon close observation each camp or cabin has its own personality, a reflection of its seasonal inhabitants. The same is true of conversations born of such surroundings. The focal point always seems to be the campfire, fireplace, or pot-bellied stove — all sources of warmth.

A degree of peer pressure exists among hunters to describe hunts in detail. "How did it happen?" one hunter questioned his successful companion. The response: "Well, he just walked into an opening and I shot." This hunter missed a crucial element of the hunt. Fellow hunters are hungry for details. How long were you in the stand? Was the deer alone? Did it approach from upwind or downwind? Did you use any sort of cover scent? Was your stand chosen because it was near rubs and scrapes or did it overlook a game trail? Did you see other deer before shooting this one? The questions could be endless, and usually are.

A seasoned hunter knows that campfires inspire detailed descriptions that provide chapters in many unwritten books on hunting each season. When told in detail, the story of a hunt answers all questions. Fellow hunters can learn from each encounter, as the storyteller extols his prowess or bemoans his misfortune. Sharing the details of a hunt bestows a mystique upon the quarry and pays tribute to the animal.

> *Ten thousand years ago that hunter would have stood by a fire and*
> *recounted the great deed to his clan brothers…It hasn't changed*
> *much…the ethical killer of the great stag or the great bear still*
> *commands attention by the fire as he recites his deeds. His peers*
> *still salute him, the old men still nod and remember, and young boys*
> *still dream of tomorrow's hunts.*
>
> – John Madson

Origin of the Firepot

Iron manufacturing had a profound environmental impact on the Southern Appalachian landscape in the 19th century. Mountainous areas possessed the vast quantities of natural resources necessary for the manufacture of iron including: deposits of hematite, limonite, magnetite, limestone, an abundant water supply, and expansive stands of hardwood tree species. Oak, hickory, beech, and maple were used to produce charcoal, which was the only fuel that produced enough heat to melt iron ore.

In the early 1800s foundries were established in upper east Tennessee, western North Carolina, and northern Georgia. By 1830 westward expansion of the iron industry had spread to the Cumberland Plateau, and Kentucky quickly became the third largest producer of iron products in the country. Peaking in the 1840s and '50s, the industry was supported by approximately 70 foundries throughout the Southern Appalachian region. Notably, the average 19th century foundry used about 300 acres of mature hardwoods each year. The combined effect of iron manufacturing rendered tens of thousands of acres treeless by 1860.

Expansion of this industry continued southward as well. The Palmetto Iron Works was established in Columbia, South Carolina in 1850 to produce ornamental iron works. Columbus Iron Works was established in Columbus, Georgia in 1853. Six years later, Schofield Iron Works began operation in Macon, Georgia. Kehoe's Iron Works was established in Savannah, Georgia in 1874, and the Chattanooga Plow Company in Chattanooga, Tennessee began in 1877.

A postcard, dated February 6, 1893, shows the Kehoe's Iron Works building in Savannah, Georgia. Black smoke billowing from six smoke stacks bears evidence of the magnitude of charcoal used to fuel furnaces and

Postcard of Kehoe's Iron Works in Savannah, Ga., dated February 6, 1893.

the vast acreage of hardwoods to produce the charcoal. Although various wrought iron implements such as bars for nails, wagon rims, mill gears, and plow points were produced, the appearance of a syrup kettle and two cane grinding mills on the postcard marked the significance of these products to rural families of the South.

The tradition of making, or "cooking", sugar cane syrup dates back to the mid-1800s and is still practiced by some today, even though syrups of all kinds line the shelves of modern-day grocery stores.

A holdover from days-gone-by was the Rev. Willie Manigault from McBeth, South Carolina. Born at the turn of the 20th century, he inherited the art of making cane syrup from his elders. I had the fortune of knowing this gentleman and would toot my truck horn each time I passed his small farm, which was only five miles from where I worked in the early 1980s. If he was out and about he returned the greeting with a bold wave. A mutual friend, Russell Tyler, stopped by one autumn day in 1985 and photographed Rev. Manigault as he fed sugar cane into the grinding mill turned by his faithful mule, Old Katie. The grinding mill was an Improved Columbus No. 11, produced by the Columbus Iron Works in Columbus, Georgia during the mid-1800s.

Improved Columbus No. 11 grinding mill.

The sugar cane juice was transferred to a kettle for cooking. Usually encased in an elevated brick column and covered by a shed, the kettle was heated by a wood fire from

Rev. Willie Manigault feeding sugar cane into the grinding mill as Old Katie turns the gears of the mill.

below. The process of cooking the sugar cane juice takes hours and care must be given to control the heat to prevent scorching the juice as it cooks slowly. Throughout the process the yellowish froth that collects on the sur-

Rare, double-kettle sugar cane syrup operation

face must be skimmed off. Eventually, the sweet, amber-colored cane syrup is produced.

Gerald Moore, UGA classmate and fellow wildlife biologist, visited me in 1985 at my new residence on an historic, lowcountry plantation. I had decided to create an outdoor gathering place for hunters in my front yard. Pieces of weather-tolerant furniture of all descriptions found their way to the place and were arranged in a circle. This would not be complete without the appropriate presentation of the fire. Gerald accompanied me to the river's edge where I had found the perfect container for an outdoor fire. It was a discarded, cast-iron cauldron — a syrup kettle — measuring 5 feet across and 20 inches

Original firepot setting on a lowcountry plantation in South Carolina.

Country stores once served as social centers for rural communities.

deep. A long crack had rendered it useless for cooking syrup or watering livestock until we came along with an alternate use. Getting it up the hill and into my El Camino was no easy feat as it weighed several hundred pounds and had no handles. Once it was positioned atop four sections of cross-ties, the stage was set for hunters' stories. This novel centerpiece was aptly named the firepot.

My front yard firepot setting became the spawning ground for many a hunting story and provided the impetus for this book. The popularity of our outdoor gathering place spread quickly throughout the neighborhood and antique syrup kettles became highly sought after. This marked the beginning of a trend that now reaches throughout the South and beyond. Firepots are suitable for roasting oysters and grilling wild game. Also, photographing flames yields interesting characters like a dancing Native American, a running buck, and the head of a buck with massive antlers. This is akin to cloud watching and seeing figures that are temporarily formed, and then whisked away.

This book, *Firepot Stories*, has several intended purposes. Foremost is the author's need to check this project off the list of things to do because there are grandchildren now. The art of storytelling is destined to become a footnote to history if the heritage of our young sportsmen and sportswomen isn't fostered. Hopefully, firepot settings and their associated stories will become so common across the land that childhoods without the social influence of a country store will develop normally despite the increasing "spell" of our modern-day communication styles. Country stores and telegraph machines kept our citizenry informed on matters of importance, but they've become obsolete. And finally, I wish to impart my love, respect, and knowledge of the outdoors to those who "travel" through *Firepot Stories* so more stewards of our precious natural resources are created and their stories are shared at fireside.

CHAPTER 1

THE BEGINNING

This N.C. Wyeth painting was on the cover of one of a 12-set volume of My Book House, 1950, published by The Book House for Children, Chicago. As a youngster I was so influenced by this image of a pioneer trapper that it became a goal to emulate his lifestyle. It marked my "beginning" as an outdoorsman.

Farewell to Black Lake? An Ecologist's Lament

"**M**an always kills the thing he loves, and we the pioneers have killed our wilderness. Some say we had to. Be that as it may, I am glad I shall never be young without wild country to be young in. Of what avail are forty freedoms without a blank spot on the map? …to those devoid of imagination, a blank place on the map is a useless waste; to others, the most valuable part." These painful words are those of a great man, Aldo Leopold, the Father of Wildlife Biology.

This quote can serve appropriately as a lament for the late Black Lake — a showplace among nature's remote holdings, which had existed from the period of glaciation through eons of time until the mid-1960s. Then man stepped from his role as part of the environmental community to the position of exploiter and despoiler in name of short-term profits for a vested interest. Black Lake and the wild land that skirted her shorelines were raped by draglines, bulldozers, and large earthmoving machines. Death was slow, but nonetheless inevitable. This is yet another example of a

My first published article!

spreading civilization that does not respect nature's life support systems on which we ultimately depend.

Some men justify such slaughter by selling an innocent public on misleading statements concerning the poor value of undeveloped land. The developers deemed Black Lake, "…no value to anything or anyone." It is evident that the value of Black Lake was viewed in terms of what it would be worth when altered and destroyed rather than what is was really worth in its original state. Furthermore, the developers had the audacity to imply that the lake was dying and is being liberated from nature, her supposed "killer," and given new life. This is a gross distortion of the process of ecological change that is natural to lakes. Some aspects of natural change can be reversed for the benefit of man, but destroying a whole system is certainly not the answer. This is an example of the strange and short-sighted philosophy that is applied generally to lakes, oceans, rivers, and forests in their natural state.

For those of us who were fortunate enough to explore Black Lake in her natural state and appreciate her aesthetic worth, these memories will last forever. Never was an attempt made to measure the economic value of seeing flights of ducks and geese come to the lake for safety and rest just ahead of the evening's darkness. Never was a price tag attached to the feeling of realizing that the lake was used by bear, deer, turkeys, otters, raccoons, etc., as witnessed by the presence of their tracks along the shoreline. This is the philosophical way of appreciating the value of wild country. Is it the fate of all the things we love and enjoy to exist only in memory? Certainly, progress must take place, but must it necessarily be a blundering probe, regardless of the concomitant results? Pollution, environmental destruction, and downgraded aesthetic worth can all result from progress; however, the magnitude is governed by the amount of conscientious planning. When the almighty dollar is of primary concern, as is most often the case, Mother Nature usually gets the rough end of the deal.

Black Lake was a unique lake. It had an interesting geologic history, and was one of a few of the bay lakes in the southeastern area of North Carolina. Now, a lake which once belonged to all North Carolinians is gone, along with all its natural inhabitants.

My purpose in writing this article is not to reprimand the developers of Black Lake, but to present a naturalist's view of what can happen to our environment as we complacently observe the workings of "progress." I will leave you with the words of Dr. Thor Heyerdahl, a world renowned adventurer-scientist and author of *Kon-Tiki*. "For hundreds of thousands of years, man has been a child of nature and part of its cycle. But he has spent approximately the last 5,000 years fighting nature. Until the last decade or two, nature has always been strong enough to resist, but now I fear man is starting to win. The worst catastrophe that could happen to man would be to win the battle against nature."

What can be done in the future to stop this indiscriminate destruction of our remaining wild country? Write to your Congressman, and to your Senators, Sam Ervin and B. Everett Jordan, and express your views about the conservation of our wild country in Bladen County and North Carolina. Find out what they feel can be done to enact a land-use proposal. Official guidelines should be initiated to help distinguish between those areas suited for development and those areas to be set aside for ecological or historical reasons.

Author's Note: *This article marked my debut into the world of publishing. Concerned about the plight of Black Lake, I penned my comments and mailed them to The News and Observer newspaper in Raleigh, North Carolina. At the time, I was conducting my coursework for a Master of Science Degree in wildlife biology at The University of Georgia, and was working part-time for Dr. Eugene P. Odum, renowned ecologist. Dr. Odum assisted with editing my article before it was sent to the newspaper. Much to my surprise, the article appeared as a feature in the Sunday newspaper, July 2, 1972. A check for $25 was mailed to me for submitting the article. Elated about the check, I made a Xerox copy and mailed it to my Mom in North Carolina. Several days later we were visiting by telephone and she informed me that she had endorsed the "check" and deposited it in my hometown bank. Having already cashed the real check I had to call the folks at the newspaper in Raleigh and apologize for what appeared to be double-dipping. I also had to send them a check for $25 to even the score. Small town banks certainly were trusting in those days!*

Bladen's Black Bear Population – Out on a Limb

In 1981 I wrote a newspaper article expressing my concern for the continued well-being of black bears in North Carolina, particularly those in Bladen County. The one statement in that article which best described the state of affairs at that time was: "Swamp drainage, housing developments, industrialization and new highways are all marks of progress, but the black bear is getting caught in the undercurrent."

The following excerpts were taken from my master's thesis which resulted from 26 months of research on bears in Bladen County during the mid-1970s. These selections are intended to familiarize the readers with historical and biological facts before any attempt is made to explain the current situation or to predict future trends.

"In 1975, black bear populations in North Carolina were given the status of 'special concern' during a symposium on endangered and threatened plants and animals. The decline in bear numbers was attributed primarily to accelerating habitat destruction resulting from human encroachment, especially since the 1950s. The desired management regime entails preservation and manipulation of habitat, continued regulation of harvests, and public enlightenment of the bears' place in the ecosystem.

"Black bears in the coastal region of North Carolina require a complex of habitat types to meet food needs at different seasons and provide alternate foods during years when major food producing species have low yields. Large inaccessible hardwood swamps containing dense vegetation and expanses of water are also essential for escape cover. Another important habitat function is to provide protection during winter, a particularly critical period when females are rearing cubs. Isolated or protected areas of Carolina bays serve this purpose; however, bears use tree cavities if available. Most of the large trees on my study area (Colly Swamp) had been removed by extensive logging in the past.

"Vast acreages of bay habitat are being converted to farmland, and slash pine plantations are replacing longleaf pine-scrub oak habitat on sand ridges. Such alterations reduce mast potential (ability to produce acorns and berries) and probably increase bear dependence on swamps, which produce food irregularly. This loss of mast-producing habitats coupled with periodic mast failures will result in poor condition of bears for denning, reduced reproductive rates, emigration, and increased human-bear encounters (for example, depredation of crops and bee hives). Factors relating mast abundance to population dynamics are numerous and complex. Several biologists have reported that puberty, litter size, and frequency of litters were closely related to food quality and quantity. Therefore, I believe that large Carolina bays, sand ridges, and major swamps must be protected if the Coastal Plain bear population is to be maintained.

"The bear sanctuary program, established in the early 1970s was intended to provide 'protected' areas which could serve as nuclei for reproduction and dispersal. Evaluation of each Coastal Plain sanctuary, and thus the sanctuary program, is now possible using information from the present study on black bear habitat requirements, range size, and population dynamics.

"Maintaining the black bear as a game animal is the best approach to ensuring its existence in the Coastal Plain of North Carolina. It is desirable to have a constituency with a vested interest in the bear who will work to counterbalance the conditions that

Black bear cub rescued in a forest fire during my research project in the 1970s.

have fostered its decrease. Bladen County harvest data indicated a constant exploitation rate of approximately 20 percent (15 bears), which apparently was not excessive. The population appears to be capable of sustaining this rate if properly managed.

"Regulations can be used to improve the sex and age structure of the harvest. Analysis of statewide data revealed that a preponderance of the adult females harvested were killed in the early part of the hunting season with bears (mostly males) in younger age classes constituting a major portion of the late season harvest. Information gathered during my study indicated a trend toward decreased activity, especially among adult females, during autumn. Based on these findings the North Carolina Wildlife Resources Commission delayed the 1976-77 hunting season's opening date and obtained the desired result — fewer adult females in the harvest. The population response should be monitored closely to determine the long-term effects on population dynamics.

"An approach to reducing harvests might be to eliminate the use of dogs for taking bears. A change from this traditional hunting technique, however, would greatly reduce the quality of the hunting experience as perceived by most bear hunters. Game managers must strive to preserve quality as well as quantity experiences for the hunter by maintaining hunting traditions when possible.

"Effective management of any game animal depends ultimately on the degree of compatibility with other public interests. In eastern North Carolina the primary conflicts with bear management involve agriculture (mainly corn farming) and apiculture (bee keeping). Also, many conflicts arise with uninformed individuals who feel bears are a threat to their personal safety, or that bear management involves stockpiling animals for the enjoyment of hunters. Consequently, black bears have an undeserved public reputation for fierceness, and many people fail to understand that hunting regulations are designed to limit animal populations to a size compatible with their 'natural' environment; therefore reducing their intrusion into adjacent areas. There also exists an opinion among the well-meaning public that bears could be best 'protected' if removed from the list of game animals. Actually, bears would be degraded to the status of vermin and thus be subjected to unregulated persecution by shooting, trapping, and poisoning. Obviously, a well-founded public education program is an integral part of game management.

"The future of the black bear population in eastern North Carolina depends on the degree to which this valuable resource can be used wisely and, most importantly, on the amount of suitable habitat preserved."

The known annual harvest of black bears in Bladen County during each of the last two hunting seasons has been more than double the number for most years during the 1970s. Similar increases also have been reported from our neighboring Pender County (to the north). Furthermore, according to reports from many people who travel throughout Bladen County, bears are being seen regularly in areas not frequented during our lifetime. What has happened to cause this seemingly overnight change in hunter success and bear sightings? Is the bear population experiencing a boom in response to the drastic change in habitat conditions? If this article ended here you would be led to believe that bear numbers are increasing by leaps and bounds. This certainly is NOT the case! I will attempt to explain these events with a "cause and effect" approach.

The area in which I conducted my black bear research project from 1974-76 spanned from Bladen Lakes State Forest eastward to Kelly and encompassed 210 square miles. Approximately 77 percent (162 square miles) of the study area was considered bear habitat in 1976. Since that time nearly half of this prime habitat has been permanently lost primarily to agriculture and to a lesser degree to the forestry industry and housing developments. This reduction in suitable living quarters has prompted a variety of responses by both bears and hunters. Bear numbers are decreasing but their density per unit area of habitat is increasing. Concentrations of bears in small areas and the proficiency of hunters at predicting escape routes have enhanced hunter success. Dispersal of bears into unfamiliar habitat has rendered them more vulnerable to hunters. Also, due to a decrease in the availability of naturally occurring foods, bears have become more dependent on bait piles (mainly corn) placed in the woods by deer hunters. This accounts for the sharp increase of bears taken by deer hunters during the past two years. However, legislation has been passed recently to prohibit the shooting of bears over bait in Bladen County by any hunter.

Now, you probably have the opinion that closing the bear season would solve the problem. Remember what was emphasized in the previously mentioned excerpts from my master's thesis. Regulated hunting is the most sound and humane method of keeping an animal population in balance with its "natural" environment. Actually, the recent annual harvest rates are simply a reflection of this "balance" at work. Unfortunately though, we must realize that our perception of the black bear as a game animal in Bladen County inevitably will be lost in the undercurrent of progress. Such a point cannot be argued when the common reply is, "We must accelerate the agricultural, forest and housing industries to accommodate the demands of a growing civilization."

Periodically the President of the United States delivers a state of the union address. It is during such an address that the Commander and Chief shares with the common people his views of the good, bad and ugly actions of government. We hear the idealistic plans to perpetuate the good, correct the bad and abolish the ugly.

Having been closely associated with black bears for over a decade, I felt an obligation to share my personal assessment of this noble animal's status in my native Bladen County. Contrary to the normal objectives of a "state of the union address," I simply wanted to impress upon the people of Bladen County that they are fortunate to have coexisted with an animal that symbolizes a marked change in our life style. My feelings are most appropriately expressed in a quote by the late Aldo Leopold, father of game management (wildlife biology), from his book entitled, *A Sand County Almanac.* The quote reads as follows: "Man always kills the thing he loves, and so we the pioneers have killed our wilderness. Some say we had to. Be that as it may, I am glad I shall never be young without wild country to be young in. Of what avail are forty freedoms without a blank spot on the map?"

Note: *This article was printed in The Southeastern Times newspaper (Clarkton, NC), Wednesday, October 7, 1981.*

Follow Up: In the aftermath of my research and preparation of my master's thesis most of the critical components of a sound black bear management program were in place. The first year of mandatory reporting of harvested bears occurred in 1976. There were 28 black bear sanctuaries throughout the state, and many were in the eastern portion (Coastal Plain). The sanctuary program began in 1970 and totaled approximately one million acres. A change in the timing of the hunting season to later in the fall was implemented to reduce the number of females in the harvest. However, the advent of large-acreage agribusinesses beginning in the early 1970s had converted tens of thousands of acres of bear habitat to agricultural areas in the Coastal Plain. This loss of habitat combined with a corresponding loss of hunter access presented a road block to the recovery of the black bear resource. Nearly a decade of the agribusiness industry came to an abrupt end as bankruptcy forced most of the large farms out of existence. As a result, the remaining farms provided food sources for black bears while thousands of acres reverted to optimum bear habitat. Finally, a primary missing component of a successful black bear management program, habitat, was on the mend. Hunter access to private lands increased in relation to the increase in bear habitat.

The season limit of one bear remained in effect as the bear population rebounded. Annual harvests of approximately 150 bears in the Coastal Plain during the early 1970s climbed to over 1,000 by the new millennium. The black bear sanctuary program initiated by the N.C. Wildlife Resources Commission in 1970 now consists of about 350,000 acres, but there are probably 1.5 million acres of de facto sanctuaries — properties where bear hunting is not allowed by the landowners. Interestingly, the combination of a one bear limit and the availability of larger-than-average animals due to an increase in age structure resulted in greater selectivity among bear hunters. Almost by default, bear hunters were practicing quality bear management. During the years from 1976 to 2013, bear hunters harvested 1,045 bears over 500 pounds, 222 over 600 pounds, 17 in excess of 700 pounds, and one weighing 880 pounds, a North American record. This selectivity of large animals has increased the survivability of females, which usually weigh less than 300 pounds. In fact, the percent of females in the harvests has ranged from 38-42 during the past 10 years. Population growth in the Coastal Plain is reflected in the record harvests of 1,701 bears in 2010; 1,605 bears in 2011; 1,844 bears in 2012; and 1,780 bears in 2013. By comparison, the black bear harvest in the mountain unit increased from 485 in 1999 to 1,207 in 2013. Two-thirds of the occupied black bear range exists in the eastern portion of the state, and North Carolina has the largest coastal population of black bears in the eastern United States. Also, bears in eastern North Carolina are larger than their counterparts in the mountains due to a longer growing season of preferred natural foods and access to extensive agricultural areas producing corn, wheat, and soybeans.

The black bear management program in North Carolina has been a resounding success. As the black bear population density increases in traditional mountain and coastal regions and populations spread into areas previously unoccupied within recent history, the cultural carrying capacity is approaching. Now, wildlife biologists are faced with the dilemma of managing a high density bear population while maintaining the status of the black bear as a noble game animal without infringing on the demands of an increasing human population.

The concluding comments in my master's thesis and newspaper articles from the late 1970s and early '80s were rather bleak, but based on the increasing degree of habitat destruction or conversion primarily in my home county and the site of my two-year study of black bears. Fortunately, this trend reversed in the 1980s throughout the Coastal Plain and there has been a corresponding increase in the black bear population.

According to Mark D. Jones, black bear biologist with the North Carolina Wildlife Resources Commission, the future of the black bear will be determined by the following factors: changing public attitudes, better regulations and law enforcement, new research, continued cooperation from hunters, and better bear management. If these factors remain in play the future appears bright for this symbol of wildness in North Carolina.

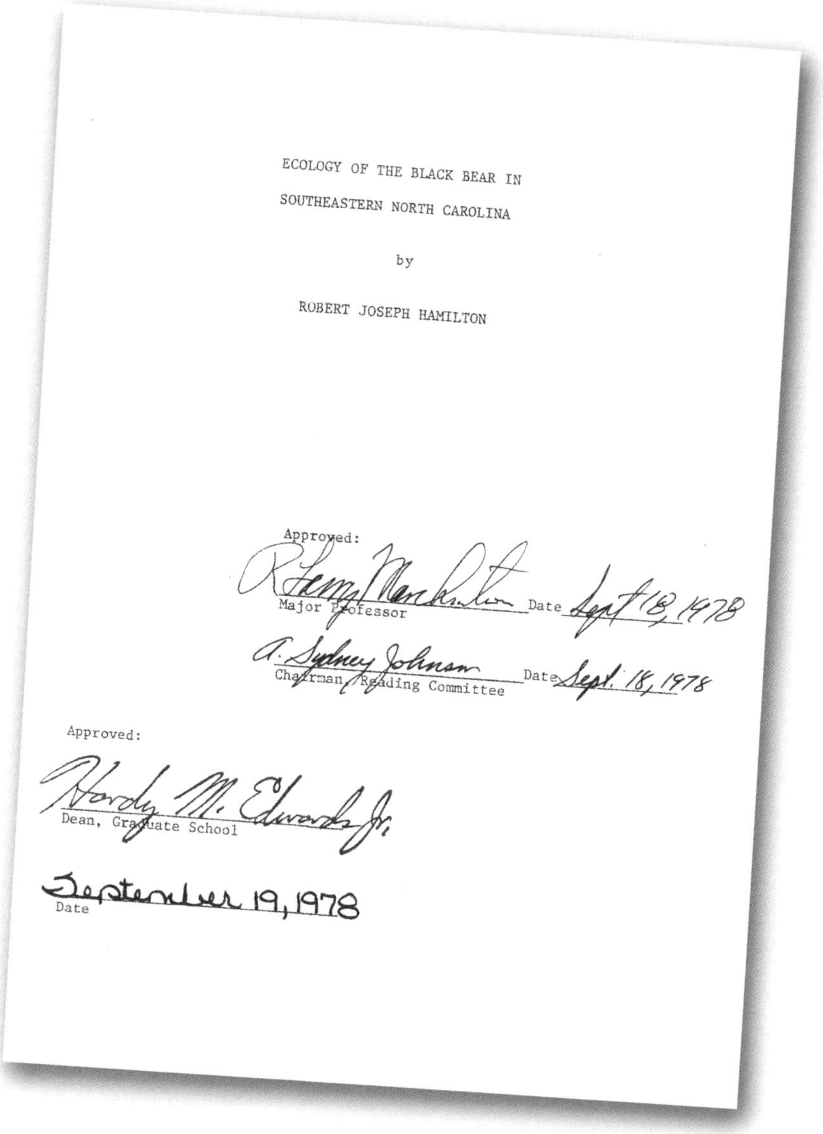

ECOLOGY OF THE BLACK BEAR IN
SOUTHEASTERN NORTH CAROLINA

by

ROBERT JOSEPH HAMILTON

Approved:

Major Professor Date Sept 18, 1978

Chairman, Reading Committee Date Sept. 18, 1978

Approved:

Dean, Graduate School

September 19, 1978
Date

Signature page of my master's thesis from The University of Georgia.

CHAPTER 2

SC WILDLIFE MAGAZINE ARTICLES

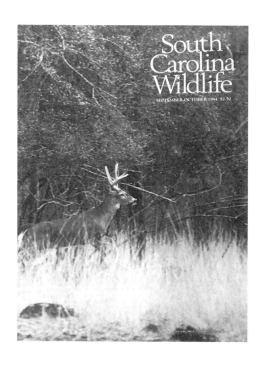

My first two officially published magazine articles appeared in South Carolina Wildlife. These were the first of many published articles on the novel topic of quality deer management (QDM).

Bob Campbell

After only 3½ years, the deer pens at Dennis Wildlife Center in Bonneau are filled with trophy bucks. Research confirms there are no glamour-laced secret formulas for producing top quality whitetails.

Quality Bucks – Exploding the Myths

The superior antler development and body size of bucks awes visitors to the deer research facility at the Rembert C. Dennis Wildlife Center in Bonneau, South Carolina. Occasionally, a seasoned hunter would come and gaze at one of the large-antlered bucks and guess his age to be 6 or 8. In fact, the animals were just 3½ years old. Perhaps the buck's gray face gave him the appearance of an old timer. Possibly it was the large-frame body or that unbelievable set of antlers.

Such antler development is not a result of some complicated effort in genetic engineering. There is nothing magical involved. These bucks were obtained as fawns from the wilds of South Carolina, and several came from areas characterized by small-antlered bucks. They are maintained on a well-balanced, high protein diet and, due to the long-term aspect of our studies, the animals are allowed to mature.

Two factors of paramount importance in antler development are nutrition and age. During the early stage of a buck's life, nutritional intake primarily sustains the demands of rapid body growth. Only the left-over nutrients are directed to antler production. As a buck matures, the portion of extra nutrients becomes greater. Peak antler development usually occurs between the ages of 5½ to 7½, followed by a downward trend in symmetry and size. Because intense hunting pressure results in most bucks being harvested as yearlings (1½ years old), few bucks ever reach the older age classes or exhibit exceptional antler development. Therefore, many hunters rarely have the opportunity to observe a well-nourished, mature buck.

Storytelling sessions in the country store or barber shop have spawned their share of myths about whitetail antler development. One theory holds that bucks having spikes as their first antlers will always have spikes. Another prominent misconception is that a buck's age can be determined by the number of antler points. Others find it difficult to believe that bucks typically shed their antlers each year.

Understanding genetics' role in antler development can dispel several myths. During the 1970s, Texas Parks and Wildlife Department biologists demonstrated with penned deer that the antler growth potential of spike-antlered yearlings is inferior to that of branched-antlered yearlings. Their studies indicated that bucks that were spikes as yearlings sired a high percentage of offspring that were also spikes as yearlings. Furthermore, genetically superior bucks having branched antlers as yearlings tended to produce offspring with comparable antler characteristics.

It is common knowledge among wildlife biologists that the occurrence of spike-antlered yearling bucks in a population can also be directly related to nutrition or the degree of competition for quality food, regardless of genetic background. Generally, as population density increases so does the percentage of spike-antlered yearlings. Conversely, optimum habitat and herd conditions can produce yearling bucks with eight, 10, or even 12 points. We have demonstrated at Bonneau that antler size and number of points will normally increase with age if nutritional intake remains constant; diseases, severe parasite infestations and poor diet, however, can reverse this trend.

Mother Nature controls the annual cycle of antler growth through seasonal changes in day length (photoperiod). Antlers begin growing in late winter and progress rapidly until late summer. During this period, the antlers are sheathed in a hair-covered, leathery membrane that transports materials essential for growth. This is the "velvet" stage of development. The antlers are soft and warm to the touch and are blunt-tipped. Damage to the antlers while in velvet often results in broken points, deformities, or the production of abnormal points.

As day length shortens, in late August through September, antlers begin to harden. Bucks rub them vigorously on bushes or small trees to remove the velvet. Older bucks usually are the first to indulge in this activity. The time required for complete removal

Velvet shedding dates range from the last week in August to mid-September. Older bucks usually are the first to indulge in this activity. The time required for complete removal of velvet varies from a few minutes to a couple of days. Each morsel of the shredded velvet is eaten by the buck and all traces of blood are licked from the small trees or bushes.

of velvet varies from a few minutes to a couple of days. Each morsel of shredded velvet is eaten by the buck and all traces of blood are licked from the small trees or bushes.

Hormonal changes brought about by the photoperiod ready a buck for the "rut" or breeding season. Subsequently, the gradual increase in day length in January and February suppressed hormone levels, breeding activity diminishes, and the antlers are dropped or "cast." The cycle has been completed only to commence again within a matter of weeks.

Nutrition comes into play here, too. Bucks on good range will retain their antlers up to two months longer than those on a low plane of nutrition. Therefore, a rather broad range of antler casting dates can occur in a region with varied habitat quality and deer densities. This brief interval between cycles combined with a range of antler casting dates probably accounts for the fact that "antlered" bucks can be seen during any month.

Two Texas wildlife biologists, Al Brothers and Murphy E. Ray Jr., authored a book in 1975 titled *Producing Quality Whitetails*. Their pioneer work during the late-1960s involved the practical application of basic deer herd management techniques to produce genetically superior bucks with well-developed antlers.

The book's acclaim spread quickly throughout Texas and into the Southeast. Popular sporting magazines followed suit with a rash of articles on the topic. Unfortunately, perhaps, for those who glean much of their biological savvy from popular magazine articles, the techniques employed in producing trophy class bucks often are oversimplified and laced with glamour. As a result, a wave of excitement about "instant" trophy bucks hit the deer hunting fraternity.

After witnessing the impressive antler development of native, run-of-the-mill bucks in our research facility, a number of lowcountry hunters asked, "Do you think it's possible to have bucks like that on our hunt club property?" The adage, "seeing is believing" provides the answer.

Interest in managing for better quality bucks could not have been more timely. The South Carolina Wildlife and Marine Resources Department was to host the fifth annual meeting of the Southeast Deer Study Group in Charleston in 1982. Al Brothers was asked to present the keynote address and discuss quality deer management. He accepted on the condition that local deer hunters were encouraged to attend the meeting. Attendance usually consists of 100-150 wildlife professionals, but the number of participants in the Charleston meeting exceeded 300.

Brothers' address was provocative and stimulating. His opening comments were directed to wildlife professionals. "Fellows, we are spending too much time talking about management practices among ourselves." Wildlife professionals were encouraged to promote proper game management through demonstration, information and education programs, and technical assistance. To the group of landowners, managers, and sportsmen, Brothers made a plea for active involvement in game management rather than fulfilling the role of mere consumers.

Several quotes from his keynote address follow as an introduction to the future of quality deer management in South Carolina.

"With respect to deer herds in the southeastern states, I would like to make a few personal observations — not based on facts, but based on feelings, talking with other people and a little bit of experience.

"Most southeastern states are experiencing deer population increases in areas that formerly had low populations. These areas usually have healthy deer on good nutritional levels; they have good reproductive rates, good buck/doe ratios and some of the best bucks in the state are usually taken from these areas each year.

"Conversely, the traditionally good deer areas are exhibiting or beginning to exhibit symptoms of deer herd and habitat deterioration. Some of these symptoms are lowered reproductive rates, widening buck/doe ratios, poor nutritional levels, and in far too many instances a buck harvest composed of mostly yearling age-class bucks.

"Currently, there is a tremendous increase in persons interested in 'trophy' buck management. First, let me give you my definition of a trophy buck — I had much rather refer to them as quality bucks. A quality buck is one that is mature, has not been nutritionally deprived, and has representative antlers for his age class. Additionally, I look upon quality bucks as a by-product of the successful manipulation of food, water, cover, protection and harvest. Unfortunately, too many individuals are under the erroneous assumption that to have quality deer one only needs to regulate the harvest.

"Through the years I have found that most individuals will not initiate any management effort until deer herd conditions have deteriorated to alarming levels. Then these same individuals expect to be able to reverse in one or two years what took many years to destroy. It is far easier to maintain a good herd than to take a poor herd and bring it back to a good level."

Texas-style trophy management maintains deer population levels below the carrying capacity of the habitat. Maintaining the buck/doe ratio at 1 to 1 or 1 to 2 requires a considerable effort but it is imperative. When harvesting antlerless deer, hunters are cautioned to take only adult does to avoid including button bucks (six months old) in the harvest. The quality and distribution of bucks among age classes are important aspects of herd composition. Under a trophy management regime, the three categories of bucks harvested are spikes, trophies, and culls. Intermediate bucks, animals with small, branched antlers, are allowed to move into the older age classes and mature. Recognizing an inferior mature buck requires an eye for detail and a genuine knowledge of deer, therefore, "culling" should be left to the scrutiny of the most experienced hunter.

Deer hunting conditions in South Carolina are vastly different than those encountered in the Texas brush country, where trophy or "quality" management is so widely practiced. Two major differences are land ownership and traditional hunting methods. Trophy deer management in Texas is an integral part of the large ranch system where high-fencing is equally important to domestic livestock operations.

Before discussing the application of trophy management practices in South Carolina, it is worthwhile to mention some of the existing conditions that pose a dilemma for wildlife biologists and managers. Intensive management for quality deer is currently not practical for the majority of hunt clubs in South Carolina. Also, such a management plan is not well-suited for public hunting. Therefore, this discussion will not apply to public lands in the Game Management Area program.

Supply and demand have become a problem for deer hunters on public and private lands alike. Each year, hunting activity on public lands has increased. In the private sector, there has been a trend toward the formation of new clubs and an increase in the average membership, changes due in part to rising costs of land leases. In many cases, the carrying capacity for hunters is being exceeded. Large expanses of land have a network of roads to facilitate forestry operations, but this form of progress has increased the efficiency of hunters using four-wheel-drive vehicles, CB radios and dogs in pursuit of deer. The cumulative effects of all these modern-day changes have put emphasis on "quantity" harvests rather than "quality" harvests.

A doe quota program for private lands has been in effect for 17 years and generally, the number of tags issued has increased annually. During the 1984 hunting season 14,155 tags were issued to 1,284 doe-quota cooperators in 27 counties. However, a number of hunt clubs adhere to the buck-only harvest system. Harvest records of the typical buck-only club reflect a classic herd composition — a high deer density and an imbalanced sex ratio resulting from the protection of does, and a young age structure in the buck segment of the population caused by years of extreme hunting pressure.

Our department's game biologists are becoming more involved each year with clubs that are opting for quality deer management. We have learned through working with a select few hunt clubs during the past five years that a transition from traditional hunting methods to intensive management for trophy bucks is too great a step to take. The initial objective of an improved management plan should be to enhance the quality of the animals harvested. Thus, the term quality deer management appeared appropriate for the situation. Basic guidelines for Texas-style trophy management are followed in

Antlers from the No. 1 buck (on left, seen also in photo on page 34) and his twin sons at ages 1½ and 2½ show similar size and shape. The father, from Berkeley County, had a prolonged illness during the summer when he was 3½, which resulted in stunted antler development. Recovery was evident by the next year when he sported a nine-point rack with a 17½-inch spread.

quality management, with the only difference being the harvest of 2½- and 3½-year-old bucks with well-developed antlers instead of 5½ or older trophy class bucks.

When considering a change to quality deer management, hunt club members must first define their criteria for the quality of animals to be harvested, which in turn will determine the intensity of management efforts. Other factors to be considered are acreage of the hunt club property, existing agricultural and forestry practices, deer herd sex ratio and age structure, habitat quality, habitat management to be employed such as food plots and prescribed burning, management practices on adjoining property, degree of isolation and access, possible poaching problems, number of club members, frequency and type of hunting and, if the property is leased, the terms of the lease agreement.

What are the general harvest recommendations during the first couple of years for a club with the classic herd composition problems of overpopulation, an imbalanced sex ratio and a young age structure in the buck segment of the population? A heavy harvest of adult does only will be the most expedient way to lower population density and balance the sex ratio. This approach requires a great deal of commitment and is not readily accepted by most hunt clubs. A combined harvest of adult does and a quota of quality bucks with eight or more antler points is the next best method, followed by a combined harvest of adult does and a quota on spikes and quality bucks. The least intense management plan would be the harvest of adult does, spikes and quality bucks with a quota on does only.

Bucks with small, branched antlers are excluded from the harvest at all levels of quality deer management. The recommendation for not harvesting spike bucks initially is designed to maximize the number of bucks passing into the older age classes at the expense of perpetuating undesirable genes in the population. Only after population density is being maintained below the carrying capacity can genetically inferior yearling bucks be identified.

Maintaining complete harvest records is as essential to deer management as it is to a successful business. By closely monitoring the annual trends in his data, the manager has a foundation on which to plan his harvest for the following season. Accurate records will serve also as a measure of management efforts over a period of time.

Harvest records should include weights and ages of all deer. Since most hunters are unable to age deer accurately, a jawbone should be collected from each deer and appro-

The No. 5 buck from Hampton County exhibited exceptional antlers each year. At age 4½ his massive nine-point rack had an outside spread of 19½ inches. As a yearling the father weighed 139 pounds and had a 12¼-inch, seven-point rack. His yearling son weighed 108 pounds and had spike antlers. The genes in this case could have come from the mother, a factor that must be considered in studying the effects of heredity on antler development, body size, and behavior.

Robert Clark

priately labeled. Aging is usually done by an experienced biologist or manager. Lactation and/or pregnancy should be noted in the does. Recording antler measurements is an absolute necessity. Antler measurements should consist of number of points, greatest spread measured inside or outside the beams (be consistent), length of each beam and antler diameter one inch above the burr. Additional information may include date and time of kill, location of kill, condition of the animal, type weapon used, number of shots, and the hunter's name and address. Crippling loss also should be recorded and counted toward the season's quota. It is helpful to plot the kills on a map throughout the season so the harvest can be evenly distributed over the property.

Again, the intensity of management will determine how soon a deer population is brought to within the limits of the habitat's carrying capacity, when the sex ratio is one buck to three does or better, and when there is an ample supply of bucks in the 2½- and 3½-year-old age classes. Once these criteria have been accomplished, the annual harvest will be below that of strictly recreational hunting, but the population and the harvest will definitely be of better quality.

There are, of course, some words of caution for hunt clubs or managers to consider with regard to quality deer management. Hunt clubs with short-term lease agreements could manage themselves out of a place to hunt. The reputation of a well-managed deer herd could entice a more affluent club to compete for the hunting rights at a higher price.

There is an increased probability of poaching on lands managed for numerous, better-than-average bucks.

Quality deer management is not recommended on properties less than 1,000 acres. However, the effectiveness of such a program can be enhanced when a number of adjacent clubs are practicing the same management guidelines.

Following quality deer management guidelines is not easy and can cause discord within a club when a member's guest harvests the wrong deer. Guests usually are inept at aging and sexing deer under adverse conditions. It is unrealistic to expect a guest to comply with such restrictive harvest techniques.

Quality deer management is not well suited for dog hunting clubs because of the increased chances of mistaking small-racked bucks as spikes or button bucks as does.

Terrain, vegetation density, and hunter activity can affect the ability to harvest an

Robert Clark

The No. 6 buck from Colleton County obviously had great potential for antler development but got off to a slow start. He progressed from a three-point rack at age 1½ to an impressive 12-point rack with a 20-inch spread at age 4½.

adequate number of deer, and more specifically, to harvest older, more elusive animals.

Since deer-proof fences are not used in South Carolina and few areas are surrounded by geographic barriers, those involved in quality deer management can expect to lose a portion of their deer population to hunters on adjacent lands. The significance of this occurrence is minimized as acreage increases.

Under the very best of conditions, quality deer management requires complete compliance of all participants. They must exhibit patience with a program that will not begin to produce the desired results for two, three, or even four years.

Several years ago Al Brothers' words served as a warning. "Isn't it time we attempted to practice total deer herd management with respect to harvest by giving the antlered segment of the herd the same consideration we have given the antlerless segment? If changes in management practices are needed or contemplated for any program that goes against tradition, and if public support and action must be gained in 'selling' the program to the public, then the usual lag time between initiating change, educating the public, and obtaining results on a broad scale is usually 10 or more years. With regard to some deer herds and deer ranges, 10 years could prove to be disastrous."

Fortunately, in South Carolina, those with a vested interest in wildlife management have successfully kept pace with the demands of an increasing human population. The degree to which this challenge is met in the future will determine the quality of our wildlife heritage.

My intentions certainly have not been to criticize methods of hunting deer in the Southeast, but to present an alternative management approach allowing today's hunters to harvest the kind of bucks taken by their grandfathers in the "good old days."

In the most liberal sense of the definition, quality deer management is the application of selectivity in harvesting deer with a goal of maintaining a healthy deer population capable of producing better-than-average animals on a sustained basis. Involvement in such a program is the ultimate expression of one's respect for his quarry. Stewardship of the land and its resources is viewed by the enlightened sportsman as an obligation rather than a luxury.

Author's Note: *Reprinted by permission from SOUTH CAROLINA WILDLIFE magazine, September-October 1984; copyright 1984.*

Phillip Jones

Wary and watchful, a mature whitetail buck enters the rutting season in prime physical condition, well-fed and ready for the rigors of courtship.

A Quest for Quality

Producing quality deer populations depends on continued research, monitoring deer herd dynamics, the sportsman's basic knowledge of whitetail biology and support of needed changes in management practices.

In late summer, both the sportsman and the whitetail buck begin seasonal preparations that eventually may bring them together under the auspices of the hunt. Both, in fact, will be hunting. The buck will seek does receptive to breeding; the hunter will seek the bucks, generally "trophy" bucks.

The buck's preparation for mating is a seasonal matter controlled by the environment and evolution. The hunter's preparation is a traditional search for promising terrain where bucks range. Two of the fateful signposts that may unite hunter and buck result directly from the rut. Though the rub and the scrape are telltale signs that betray a buck's presence, understanding the complex behavior that produces scrapes and rubs eludes too many hunters.

The serious hunter with a lifelong interest in conservation and wildlife management needs to understand how deer population characteristics such as age structure, sex ratio and density relate to and affect the quality of hunting.

During summer, fraternal groups of adult bucks, often five or more, gorge themselves. Tremendous nutritional intake is normal at this time. Much of the nourishment goes into building fat reserves and the velvety antlers of mature bucks.

Subtle decreases in day length accompanied by decreasing temperatures stimulate alterations in bucks' behavior. Changes in photoperiod and other environmental conditions are monitored by the senses of sight, smell and hearing.

The pituitary gland, the brain's light-sensitive portion, receives messages transmitted through the nervous system. Reaction to changing photoperiod triggers hormone production that programs patterns of physiological and behavioral activity for the life-perpetuating mating season.

Antler development is completed by early September as hormone levels rise. Bucks thrash small trees and bushes to strip the velvet from their antlers. In less than a day and often within minutes, hard antlers glisten in the sun.

The tolerance that allowed bucks to browse together earlier disappears with the advent of hardened antlers, and fraternal groups disband. Bucks affirm their position in the social hierarchy through aggressive, threatening body postures with the young bucks engaging in light-hearted sparring matches. Actual knock-down drag-out fights are rare but occur later in association with the breeding season and involve dominant bucks of comparable size and age.

The weeks of gorging that stored fat and nourished a strong rack serve their purpose during courtship. While in the "rut" bucks must endure the rigors of a disrupted feeding schedule, and their weight can plummet 25 percent. Rather than serve as weapons of combat, antlers more often provide bucks a method of leaving telltale signs of their intent to mate.

The rut is the buck's quest for a mate. In making rubs, bucks deposit scent from seasonally active forehead glands located between the antlers and the eyes. A patch of

The rubs on saplings and trees that the hunter discovers are more than remnants of this shadow boxing; they are signposts to other deer, deposits of scent from the bucks' forehead and preorbital glands.

coarse, dark hair that can be spotted on adult bucks at a distance identifies this region of pheromone production.

The frequency of rubbing peaks soon after velvet removal, and decreases throughout the rut, although bucks will continue to make rubs until antlers are shed in early winter. Rubbed bushes, saplings and sometimes trees eight to ten inches in diameter provide visual and olfactory tips to other deer that a rutting buck is nearby.

Rubbing is one form of signpost behavior, a means of communication among white-tailed deer. Hunters often speculate that the diameter of a rubbed tree is some indication of a buck's size. To some extent a correlation exists between the two, but it is more a reflection of the deer's aggressiveness or social rank, not necessarily his antler or body size.

Studies conducted by Drs. Larry Marchinton and Karl Miller of The University of Georgia revealed that a buck makes from 69 to 538 rubs in a year with an overall average of 300 rubs per buck. Forcing antlers against trees and shrubs is strenuous, and repeated rubbing possibly explains why a buck's neck enlarges during the rut. Repeated rubbing exercises neck muscles, producing the same result as a body builder's weight lifting.

Another signpost is the scrape, a pawed area usually under an overhanging tree branch. When scraping, bucks mouth branches at antler level, often twisting and breaking small twigs. Simultaneously, they paw through ground litter to bare soil and then step into the circular depression, stand with back arched and urinate onto their tarsal or hock glands. Urine laced with pheromones drips onto the scrape.

The scrape is the buck's calling card for an amorous doe and a warning to competing bucks. The frequency of scraping is closely correlated with breeding and increases dramatically about the same time rubbing activity declines.

People commonly use the terms "rutting season" and "breeding season" interchangeably as if they share the same meaning, but there is a difference. Rutting season is the period when adult bucks 1½ years old and older are capable of breeding. Activities of rutting bucks include rubbing, scraping, and changing movement patterns, body posture and vocalizations associated with their seasonal breeding condition.

Breeding season is defined as the span of time between the first and last conception dates of does in a particular population. Adult does experience elevated hormone levels during early fall in response to decreasing day length just as bucks do. Although, not displaying any differences in physical appearance, does become much more active, particularly at night, when they are in prime breeding condition.

As the season of courtship approaches, scrapes become the center of attraction, functioning as a meeting place. A doe will urinate in a scrape, leaving behind a message that her trail is worth following. Pheromones in the urine signal her reproductive condition. This scenario, combined with increased activity of both sexes, develops into buck-doe chases characteristic of the breeding season.

Although a doe in heat or estrous may be sexually attractive to a buck, her actual period of receptivity usually lasts 24 hours or less. Thus, a courting buck may tend an estrous doe for several days before breeding is allowed. Most adult does in a given region can be expected to come into estrous about the same time since they receive equal exposure to environmental conditions, especially photoperiod.

If the adult sex ratio in a deer population is unbalanced (more than three does per buck), the short duration of receptivity while in estrous combined with the elements of tending time and possible hunter disturbance may force many does to conceive later. Such a sequence of events lengthens the breeding season, resulting in a less-pronounced peak in breeding activity.

The adult sex ratio during breeding season appears to be an important factor in the biology of deer populations. Mississippi State University (MSU) wildlife researchers used a computer model to simulate the effects of harvest strategy on white-tailed deer reproduction. Delaying buck hunting season a month in the fall increased the proportion of does bred on their initial estrous from 75 to 90 percent. Harvesting antlerless deer prior to peak breeding activity and decreasing buck harvest rates from 80 to 60 percent also increased the proportion of does serviced during their first fall season estrous.

A cooperative deer research project involving Clemson University and the South Carolina Wildlife and Marine Resources Department (SCWMRD) was conducted on

This buck is displaying the flehmen behavior, or lip curl, during courtship. Once thought to be a method by the buck to determine the doe's reproductive status, further research suggests that this behavior ensures that males and females are simultaneously in peak reproductive condition, according to Dr. Karl Miller of The University of Georgia.

the Alumax property in Berkeley County to evaluate the effects of adult sex ratio on the time and length of breeding seasons. During this five-year study, the annual harvest of female deer exceeded that of bucks. This native deer population exhibited the results predicted by the MSU computer model. Mean conception dates shifted from November 11 in 1981 to October 22 in 1985. The range of conceptions decreased from 96 days in '81 to 53 in '85. Body weights improved annually in response to a decrease in deer herd density because there was less competition for preferred food items.

Of significant interest to the deer hunter is the fact that antler development improved markedly because bucks were allowed to move into older age classes. Furthermore, a shift in mean conception dates resulted in an earlier fawning season. Fawns born by midsummer have a definite advantage over those coming later, and tend to exhibit better antler development and body weights as yearlings.

The knowledge garnered through researching reproductive patterns in white-tailed deer provides wildlife biologists a better understanding of past and present deer herd conditions. Perhaps more importantly, such information enhances our ability to predict future trends and to formulate management guidelines for the continued well-being of our state's number one big game animal.

The white-tailed deer is a prolific producer under optimum habitat conditions. Populations expanding into unoccupied range soon reach density levels that approach the land's carrying capacity or ability to support a particular number of healthy individuals. When the carrying capacity is exceeded, preferred food supplies are quickly depleted, forcing deer to subsist on foods with lower nutritional value. Chronic symptoms of overpopulation then surface: lower average body weights per age class, poorer antler development, decreased fawn production and increased occurrence of diseases and parasites.

Many deer populations in the Southeast exhibit some or all of these symptoms. How can this happen if annual harvest rates have shown steady increases?

The answer comes from analyzing components of the harvest. The harvest sex ratio displays a definite hunter preference for bucks. During the past five hunting seasons in South Carolina, 70 to 72 percent of reported harvests consisted of bucks. Another statistic revealing hunter preference and efficiency is the fact that 80 percent of bucks are 1½ years old or younger. Among other reasons, a stigma appears to persist with respect to harvesting antlerless deer. Perhaps this is a holdover from the past when there were fewer deer and hunters held the conviction that "if you kill does there won't be anything left to produce bucks."

Growing deer populations and increased hunting pressure have had an effect on whitetail reproductive patterns. SCWMRD biologists and technicians collected reproductive tracts during the 1970s from does brought to selected check stations in the Central and Western Piedmont hunt units. Fetuses were removed from the reproductive tracts and measured for age determination. Backdating the age of a fetus indicated a doe's conception date, and compiling conception dates from numerous does delineated range and peak of breeding.

The adult breeding season in South Carolina's piedmont region during the early 1970s ranged from late September through December, and possibly into January. Peak breeding occurred during the last week of October.

Since then, deer numbers increased but so did hunting pressure, particularly on the buck segment of the population. A gradual trend toward a distorted sex ratio and a

A balanced sex ratio is vital if the result of management is to be healthy animals. Rack-heavy bucks and slender, graceful does are the ideal end products of careful research, monitoring, and a willingness on the part of sportsmen to support the efforts of wildlife professionals.

younger age structure in bucks occurred by the late 1970s. The peak of breeding was less pronounced but appeared to have shifted to mid-November. Adding several "doe days" to hunting seasons during the early 1980s accomplished desired results. In 1986, the piedmont's breeding peak occurred during late October and early November. Future changes in harvest strategy may be necessary.

Our deer populations probably will not be able to maintain the status quo even if existing harvest rates of bucks and does continue because of the accelerating habitat loss we experience each year. Eventually, all available habitat will be occupied by deer. What then? Will symptoms of overpopulation become widespread? It's difficult to say, but prevention of such a dilemma depends on continued research, professional monitoring of deer herd dynamics, and, most importantly, the sportsman's ability to understand and support needed changes in management practices.

While some may be pessimistic about a situation that presently is only hypothetical, several factors can ensure that our progeny will experience the thrill of pursuing the wily whitetail.

Land acquisition for wildlife management is a primary goal of the state wildlife department. Moreover, wildlife habitat improvements on existing lands can enhance productivity.

The education of the sportsman certainly helps. Within this decade, books, magazine and newspaper articles, video tapes, and seminars by wildlife biologists have made significant contributions to hunter education. Today's hunters are better informed about the biology and management of their quarry than ever before, and an essential by-product of such education is awareness. A progression from awareness to appreciation and respect should help attain the desired goals of proper deer management. We have already seen how hunter information helps deer management practices.

Producing Quality Whitetails, a book co-authored by Texas wildlife biologists Al Brothers and Murphy E. Ray Jr., has had a profound impact on the traditional idea of "shoot any antlered buck and treat all does like the sacred cows of India." Brothers and Ray pioneered efforts to enhance deer quality through habitat management and manipulation of deer herd density, age structure and sex ratio.

To see how Texas-style management has been adapted to S.C. deer populations, read "Quality Bucks: Exploding The Myths," South Carolina Wildlife, September-October 1984 (pages 32-39 in this book). The article pointed out, "In the most liberal sense of the definition, quality deer management is the application of selectivity in harvesting deer with a goal of maintaining a healthy deer population capable of producing better-than-average animals on a sustained basis." State wildlife biologists believe "... involvement in such a program is the ultimate expression of one's respect for his quarry."

Unfortunately, misinformation is a factor the hunter must also contend with. Glamorous but often misleading articles in sporting magazines filled hunters with false hopes during the early 1980s. "Trophy buck" stories sent a flurry of excitement through the deer hunting fraternity. A number of clubs expecting overnight success attempted quality deer management programs but quickly encountered frustration. As if taking an adequate number of antlerless deer weren't difficult enough, having to pass up certain categories of bucks was simply too much for some hunters to endure. Dissension among club members undermined the commitment to quality deer management, and quite often traditional hunting methods were reinstated. Only the most dedicated clubs persevered to enjoy the fruits of their labor.

Despite the difficulty of breaking tradition, hunter education is making its impact felt, and more clubs are practicing quality deer management each year. The sportsmen who believe in the wise use of our natural resources are joining an influential faction with a dedication toward quality deer herd management.

Author's Note: *Reprinted by permission from SOUTH CAROLINA WILDLIFE magazine, September-October 1987; copyright 1987.*

CHAPTER 3

COUNTRY STORE CHATTER

*During my formidable years it was the country store that provided the
launch pad for many memorable stories of outdoor activities, particularly
hunting and fishing. Changing times have taken this venue from the scene,
therefore the art of storytelling must be kept alive at fireside gatherings.*

The Original Firepot Story

Way back in the 1950s, my preparation for deer hunting involved filling the pockets of my American Field coat with bubble gum, several flavors of Kits, Mary Janes, apples, oranges, and a handful of No. 1 buckshot shells. There were few deer in those days. In retrospect, my load could have been lightened considerably by leaving my 12 gauge double barrel and the buckshot at home. Anyway, I was usually preoccupied with snacking while deer hunting the Cape Fear River lowlands of southeastern North Carolina.

We used hounds in those days — blue-ticks, redbones, black and tans, walkers, plotts, beagles, and an assortment of pot lickers that always appeared to have the best personalities.

Occasionally I had to interrupt the dissection of an apple to ready myself for the approaching pack of hounds in full cry. More often than not, they managed to pass just out of sight. Several times, though, I put all my distractions aside as the baying got louder and louder. My heart began to race. They're heading straight toward me this time. All of a sudden, they appeared — a sweeping phalanx of deer hounds, but no deer! Perhaps they were on a practice run, I thought.

My education as a deer hunter was beginning to bud. One of the first bits of hunting lore I had to sort out on my own was that deer were usually well ahead of their canine pursuers. I shudder to think of the times when the hounds' voices were barely audible, that a deer passed my stand and saw me attempting to peel an orange in one continuous curl or carefully folding the paper wrapper from a peppermint stick. I had the preconceived and ill-perceived notion that deer hounds would be on the heels of their quarry.

That first deer, a nice cowhorn (spike), fell prey to my inherited side-by-side shotgun on January 1, 1961 during a torrential downpour on the last day of deer season. I have been an ardent student and admirer of the whitetail ever since.

Glenn Parker was the only man in my home county that still hunted. Furthermore, he was the first person I knew that used a scoped rifle — a .243 bolt action. Most of us who hunted with hounds thought Glenn was wasting his time waiting for a deer to happen by. But, he was very lucky with his new hunting method and folks began to change their opinion.

I traded a .22 semi-automatic rifle to Mr. Sam Culbreth, the first game warden I ever met, for a Model 94 Winchester 30-30 and a handful of cartridges. I filled several quart-size cardboard milk cartons with water and used five of the six shells to test not only the accuracy of my still-hunting rifle, but the "punch." Shots were fired at a range of less than 50 yards — offhand at that. Water and bits of cardboard exploded into the air and I was ready to put my deer rifle to the ultimate test. Confident and ignorant, I hunted an entire deer season with that remaining 30-30 cartridge. Wish I had saved it. Might as well have, 'cause it was never shot. That first deer rifle was traded for a Winchester automatic .243 and that, several years later, for a Ruger 44 magnum. The 44 was traded eventually for a bow and several miss-matched arrows.

Thirty years later, my favorite deer rifle is a Marlin 30-30, plain, without a scope. It's extremely accurate and efficient. Last season I took a long shot, but got the deer anyway.

Firepot gatherings are conducive to storytelling.

After trailing the doe about 100 yards and pulling her to the field's edge, I stepped off the distance between where the deer and I stood. Thirty-two paces! Most of my shots these days are less than 20 yards.

One hunting season, probably 1963 or '64, I kept a journal of deer sightings. Entries would sound something like this: "Saw the flash of a tail today while hunting the Waddell Place. The tail looked rather long — could have been a buck, but more than likely was just another doe." My deer sightings for the two-and-a-half month season totaled 26, including numerous tail flashes.

Perhaps my fondest and most vivid memories of hunting as a youngster in the late-1950s and early '60s were of prehunt and posthunt gatherings around a fire of sticks and twigs. We didn't have (or take) enough time to build a full-fledged log fire. Nevertheless, the fire served its age-old purpose. It was a focal point that forced hunters into a circle to hear the stories of everyone's activities since our last hunt. This circular arrangement appeared to erase barriers, namely age, so I felt as big as the rest and was more at ease when telling my stories. I was a teammate, an equal, and that was important to a young man.

My college years came, lasted an eternity, and finally passed. Suffice it to say that I entered the academic world as a deer enthusiast and emerged as a deer enthusiast with degrees in forestry and wildlife biology. A research project, focusing on reproduction in the whitetail, occupied my life for seven years — it was my first real job. An important lesson learned was that deer operate on a schedule without any regard for weekends, holidays, nights, or eight-hour work days.

Since 1985 my life has been filled with deer people (hunters) rather than directly with deer. In a four-county area of southeastern South Carolina's deer-rich lowcountry, there are more than 700 deer hunting clubs commanding my attention as a wildlife biologist. These clubs produce about 8,000 deer jawbones to be aged each year and require several hundred annual deer harvest reports. I am dealing with deer densities beyond my wildest dreams of the 1960s, and have reached the conclusion that as a commodity increases in number and/or availability, there is a corresponding decrease in the respect toward individuals. Thus, the whitetail's ability to procreate has reduced its status from a highly prized denizen of the deep forest to a common target of suburban woodlots. I am one who prefers to continue a relationship with the whitetail as a noble game animal. Growing participation in quality deer management bears testimony of the hope for deer hunting and management into the next century.

Several years ago, with the help of a friend, a cast iron cauldron was positioned in my front yard. Heretofore, when club members gathered in the autumn afternoons to plan the evening's deer hunt and reconvened later to exchange stories, there was no focal point — no fire.

This cauldron, measuring 60 inches across and 20 inches deep in the middle, once was used for cooking cane syrup. Later, it functioned as a stock-watering container until a lengthy crack resulted in what appeared to be a one-way trip to the trash heap; actually it was tossed over a steep bank along the river.

Now, surrounded by seasoned outdoor furniture, the syrup cauldron has another purpose and a new name. The firepot draws hunters and others for warmth and conversation, as did the "gathering" fires of my earliest deer hunting days.

Initially intended to serve the community, this forum now has universal influence. The Firepot Stories will be a regular feature in *Quality Whitetails*: Journal of the Quality Deer Management Association. I pledge to combine my professional background, the love of the whitetail, and my access to a wealth of firepot storytellers to provide a unique commentary on deer-related matters.

My goal is to bring romance back into the admirable sport of deer hunting through these Firepot Stories. We should revere the individual deer while maintaining a watchful eye on the entire population.

Firepot Stories will be a blend of William Faulkner's storytelling style, Henry David Thoreau's reverence for nature, Aldo Leopold's strength as an environmental prophet, and the infectious humor of Patrick McManus — perpetual youngster.

Note: *This story appeared in Quality Whitetails (V 1, I 1 – 1993/'94).*

Early Entries in My Deer Scrapbook

Author's Note: *Some uncommon words used as colloquialisms in this true story are followed by the correct spelling in parenthesis. Others are close enough that a little guesswork should pull you through.*

"The dawgs was squallin' as they come down along Brown's Creek. Instidyof (instead of) crossing the river or swimmin' down a ways and returnin' to the same bank to throw the dawgs off his path, the deer follered that ridge 'tween the river and the slough. They 'uz headin' straight as an arrow toward Skeeter Neck Landing where

Simp Singletary (left) and Ira Long with the legendary Beaverdam Buck, 1958.

Mr. Ira was on his usual stand at the log deck. Judging by the sound of them dawgs, my ole redbone bitch Lulu was out front and it 'uz a yellin'-size deer (actually a fawn) they 'uz runnin'. When they got nearly 'bout to Mr. Ira they turned and headed to where I was — at that little stream that comes out of Beaverdam Swamp. They hadn't hardly turned when a buck the size of a young bull busted out of a thicket less than 20 steps away. I barely had time to put the gun to my shoulder before shootin', and I don't rightly remember doing it, but I must of done it more or less like a flinch. Several buckshot pellets struck him in the forehead and he slid past me within a couple of steps — dead as a hammer!

"What happened was that ole buck would run a ways and stop, run a ways and stop. They'll do that to figure out where the standers are. He had gotten far enough ahead of them dawgs when he neared Skeeter Neck Landing that he winded Mr. Ira and turned my way. You've probably already witnessed it firsthand, but ole bucks especially are real juberous (dubious) once they've smelled you.

"We didn't have no scales handy, but we reckoned that ole buck weighed pert nigh onto 200 pounds. It took half a dozen of us, taking turns pullin', almost three hours just to get him out of the lowlands to the nearest truck. By that time he felt like a young bull, sure enough."

This event occurred in November 1958, on the Waddell Place along the Cape Fear

Simp Singletary (right) was on hand to celebrate my 1968 Halloween Buck.

River in southeastern North Carolina. I began hunting with this club in the early 1960s and our annual dues were $10 — for dog food. Simp Singletary, a charter member of the Waddell Place Club, and his wife lived in my hometown and I visited them regularly throughout my high school and college years. Simp told this story of the ole Beaverdam Buck over and over. One thing I learned was never to weigh a big buck 'cause each time the story was recounted the buck's weight edged upward. There were two gestures that always signaled to me that Simp was settlin' in for a tall tale. He would shift gears in his recliner, extend his legs horizontally, lean back and gaze at the ceiling. Also, he "wore" a toothpick or a wooden match, and when he was thinking about how to phrase a statement, he would roll the toothpick or match from one corner of his mouth to the other. During one of my last visits with Simp before he passed away in the '70s he adjusted the recliner, repositioned that ever present toothpick, and proclaimed, "Yep, that ole Beaverdam Buck tipped the scales at 252 pounds! He'll probably go down as the biggest buck ever shot in these whereabouts!" I offered no rebuttal and reacted as though the story had just been told for the first time.

Simp always assured me that if I stuck with it, someday I would happen upon a buck like his Beaverdam Buck, but not likely quite that big. Well, that chance came 10 years after Simp had made his mark in local deer hunting history. On Halloween Day, October 31, 1968, I crossed paths with a large buck while hunting on a tract of land across the Cape Fear River from my hometown, and less than a mile from the Bladen County Courthouse. That eight-point buck had a 21-inch antler spread and weighed, officially, 195 pounds. Incidentally, I still have the buck's jawbone — he was 3½ years old.

Simp was the first person I called to announce my accomplishment. He promptly locked the door to his shop and joined us in the backyard of a hunting companion. The buck was hung from the support of a basketball goal, photographed, and then dressed. We didn't have a proper skinning shed in those early years.

When the club was successful, and that was infrequent, we would take the buck (does were not legal then) to a nearby "backer" (tobacco) barn shelter for butchering. The carcass was divided into equal-size piles depending on the number of people on the hunt, plus one for the landowner. Hindquarters were scored to the bone with a knife and then chopped into portions with a hatchet. Tootie Butler, the huntmaster, would place a hand on a particular pile of venison while the successful hunter, with his back turned, would call out a hunter's name and so on until each portion was matched with a hunter. More often than not, the venison was wrapped in newspaper for the trip home where it was then to be soaked in vinegar, supposedly to rid the meat of that "wild" taste. Boy, we've come a long way with the convenience of walk-in coolers and appropriate wrapping materials: freezer paper and plastic zip-lock bags.

The mounted head of my Halloween '68 buck commands a prominent space in my office and my life. It serves as a constant reminder of my beginnings as a deer hunter and of those mentors — Simp, Tootie, Mr. Ira, and others — who, with their vivid recounts of past hunts, stoked the fire in my heart — the heart of a deer hunter.

Father Time has claimed my mentors and I have the responsibility of filling their shoes. I view this right of passage more as a privilege than an obligation. Now, with many years of experience as a deer hunter and manager and a desire to share my stories, I find this an easy task. A high school classmate, who hasn't hunted since then, recently asked me when I was going to grow out of this "hunting thing." My response, NEVER, I hope!
Note: *This article appeared in Quality Whitetails (V 7, I 4 – 2000)*

A Reunion and Revival

There can be no better way to begin a new year than spending quality time at fireside with your mentors. In early January 1996, Al Brothers and Horace Gore drove over from Texas for a week-long visit. Al needs no introduction to most deer enthusiasts. Back in 1975 he coauthored the pioneer book, *Producing Quality Whitetails*, with fellow wildlife biologist Murphy E. Ray Jr. Al recently retired after 30 years as wildlife/ranch manager for several privately owned ranches in the south Texas brush country. He has been actively involved in the QDMA as a Charter Life Member and has served on the QDMA's Board of Advisors.

Horace Gore, a college classmate of Al Brothers, is a recent retiree from the Texas Parks and Wildlife Department. During his stint as a wildlife biologist he worked with quail, turkeys, desert bighorn sheep, and deer. His last 12 years were spent as the upland game project leader and deer project leader. Horace now serves as editor of the *Texas Trophy Hunters* magazine.

John Moran

This photo of a cold January firepot gathering will have a special place in my office. From left to right are: Me, Bobby Harrell (Life Member of QDMA), Henry Fair (a local plantation owner and Charter Life Member of QDMA), Al Brothers (co-author of the book *Producing Quality Whitetails* and Charter Life Member of the QDMA), and Horace Gore (retired wildlife biologist with the Texas Parks and Wildlife Department).

The two Texans were on a mission: to visit with fellow professionals and hunting companions to learn first-hand about deer management in Georgia and South Carolina, and to share their vast experiences as deer managers. The occasion could best be labeled a reunion and revival.

During daylight hours we toured deer habitat on hunting leases and talked with landowners, managers, and club members. We even enjoyed the pleasures of hunting rabbits with Larry and Betty Marchinton's pack of well-trained beagles in the red clay hills along Georgia's Flint River. Somehow, hunting always seems to be an integral part of our visits. Although hunting techniques, terrain, and the size of our quarry were different this time, Al commented that the camaraderie was the all-important factor.

Each evening, usually following a meal of beautifully prepared venison, we gathered around a fireplace or firepot to talk "deer." Two things we seem to have in common is we never tire from observing deer (in the wild or on home videos) and the topic of deer always dominates our conversations. We're not close-minded though because several accounts of turkey hunting and fishing crept into our discussions. Admittedly, some of these stories had to be taken with a grain of salt.

Six nights of fireside chats brought us together with deer hunters from middle Georgia through South Carolina. The grand finale occurred at Millaree Hunt Club near Columbia, South Carolina. Our host was Mr. Marion Burnside, QDMA Life Member, club president, and a member of the board of directors of the South Carolina Department of Natural Resources. Marion has always maintained an open invitation for deer meetings. In fact, the Midlands Branch of QDMA holds regular meetings at Millaree. As a token of appreciation for his generosity, hospitality, leadership, and friendship, Mr.

Burnside was presented with a firepot to be enjoyed by members and guests of Millaree Hunt Club. Al Brothers completed the ceremony by lighting the first fire — symbolic of our efforts to bridge the gaps among deer people universally.

None of our nightly gatherings with deer hunters had a formal agenda. Naturally, all of us locals were keenly interested in learning more about deer management strategies in Texas. Al and Horace obliged by telling all they knew about deer from the hill country west of San Antonio, deer in the piney woods of east Texas, and especially those famous big bucks — *muy grandes* — from the south Texas brush country along the Rio Grande. The conversation eventually turned homeward and the questions began to flow.

What impact can we expect from coyotes? Both Texans agreed that we have fewer coyotes and generally higher deer densities. It is the very low deer population levels that can be affected by coyote predation. Furthermore, our average annual rainfall is three or four times greater than in south Texas and that accounts for our lush habitat by comparison. Such habitat and the common forestry practice of clear-cutting trees produce ample small animal populations, a primary food source for coyotes. These crafty predators are known to feed upon deer, especially early-born fawns and adult animals with physical problems, but their overall impact on deer populations should not be considered a threat. Two possibly erroneous assumptions could result from seeing a couple of coyotes feeding on the remains of an adult whitetail. One is that they caught and killed a healthy animal, and the other is that coyotes have a steady diet of venison. The late Paul Errington wrote in his book, *Of Predation and Life*, "Don't confuse the 'fact' of predation on the individual with the 'effect' on the population." His statement should calm any fears that coyotes will wreck havoc with our deer and wild turkey populations. I guess most of our concerns are born from dealing with a relatively new predator on the scene. A final note is that coyotes are here now, they're spreading throughout the Southeast (the Northeast and Midwest as well), they're here to stay and we may as well learn to accept them and get on with more serious management matters.

How much acreage do we need for quality deer management to be successful? Al Brothers countered this question with another. "How many bucks and does do you expect to harvest each year from your lease?" Al emphasized that in many instances the buck segment is comprised primarily of young animals, that buck-to-doe ratios are skewed toward does, and that the density is too high for existing habitat conditions. You must determine your management objectives on the basis of harvest history, hunter numbers and their expectations, the lease's acreage, and a strong consideration of what your neighbors are doing. Some clubs have been successful with quality deer management on tracts smaller than 500 acres because their neighbors were following the same or similar guidelines. The issue of minimum acreage is dependent also on the shape of the property, the degree of protection (gated access and no public roads bisecting the property), and habitat diversity and quality. The bottom line is that you can make a difference with total commitment of all club members and cooperation of your neighbors, even if you have a relatively small tract of land. Larger parcels allow more latitude in making management decisions, but you must have reasonable expectations for removal rates. Maintaining good harvest records will provide the necessary clues as to whether or not you are on track.

How soon can we expect results after beginning a quality deer management program? Al stated, "A question must be asked of you, first. Do you plan to run or walk toward your destination? If your club chooses to run, you will launch head-long into antlerless-ONLY harvests and habitat enhancement. Within a couple of hunting seasons a number of bucks will have reached the 2½ and 3½ age classes and the results should be obvious. Conversely, if your hunting companions decide on a less restrictive approach, then the desired results may not appear until the fourth or fifth year, if at all. There are so many variables to be identified and 'weighed' for each hunting area that only generalizations can be made. Seek professional guidance and get acquainted with your neighbors."

Where are all of those older bucks we've produced with five years of quality deer management? Well, some hunting groups have noticed a marked difference in the age and quality of their bucks. Others have had results ranging from mediocre to poor. The reasons for frustrations are numerous. Probably the single most important factor is that although more bucks are reaching the older (and wiser) age classes, most hunters have not changed their hunting techniques. As a whole, we are accustomed to harvesting young, inexperienced bucks. Except during the rut when mature bucks are most visible, hunters must be more innovative in crossing paths with the smart ones. This means seeking out the haunts of mature bucks — usually in areas with dense vegetation (limited visibility) and fewer deer. Don't expect to encounter mature bucks where does and young bucks are observed frequently. We have produced a different sort of animal by allowing them to get older. This is the ultimate challenge in hunting. Be persistent and realize that frustration can be a stepping stone to success.

One of the concerns expressed by those attending our fireside gatherings was the impact of in-holdings within hunting leases. Al Brothers and Horace Gore were sympathetic because they had similar problems in Texas. Obviously, extreme harvest pressure on small-acreage tracts within or adjacent to your property can put a drain on deer numbers. Liberal bag limits, long seasons, and baiting magnify the problem. Al's suggestions (in order of desperation) were to: "(1) Try to develop a cooperative by inviting the neighboring hunters to share management guidelines. Give the huntmaster and the landowner a gift membership in the QDMA so they will appreciate the universal nature of quality deer management. (2) Try to lease the hunting rights on small, problem-causing tracts. (3) Make an offer to buy the property. (4) Saturate the property boundary with wildlife food plots and deer stands, but keep them just out of sight for security reasons. Whatever you do, don't fall prey to having your management program dictated by a handful of neighboring hunters."

A similar situation involves the actions of poachers. For some the idea of letting a young buck walk is perceived as simply passing it on to poachers. Worse yet is avoiding managing for older bucks for fear of drawing the attention of poachers. These concerns are substantiated each hunting season as accounts of poachers' conquests hit the streets. Furthermore, the universal success of wildlife enforcement officers using "dummy" deer to apprehend poachers provides a more accurate measure of this deplorable activity.

There are several ways to thwart the activities of poachers. Provide each of your hunting companions with your state wildlife department's toll-free telephone number for reporting illegal hunting. If an infraction is observed, respond promptly and give details of the incident.

Contact the magistrates and judges in your area and inform them of your support in prosecuting game law violations. Encourage the local newspaper to publish the names of violators, their specific violation, and the fines imposed.

If violations like trespassing to hunt big game or shooting big game from a public highway carry light penalties in your county or state, perhaps you should express your concerns to the state's department of natural resources and to your local state legislators. The management of our wildlife resources is a team effort and your membership in conservation organizations like the QDMA is invaluable.

As you have witnessed, our deer conversations during the span of a short week covered a variety of topics. Not all of the questions asked by hunters had an immediate answer. Some of the topics warrant further comment and study.

Al Brothers' parting words are worthy of being shared with all QDMA members. "Even though there will be setbacks in your management efforts, and some have already occurred, hang in there and never give up."

I must confess that the quality time spent with family, fellow sportsmen, and mentors at the Hamilton Firepot has been rewarding beyond any dreams. May your hunting experiences lead to such rewards.

Note: *This article appeared in Quality Whitetails (V 3, I 1 – 1996).*

The Upside-Down Goat

W ay back in the 1960s the group I deer hunted with changed from week to week — we were not an organized club. Our hunting areas were along the Cape Fear River east, west, and north of my North Carolina hometown. There were no deer south of town in those days. We had the luxury of deciding where to hunt based upon how many hunters gathered at our meeting place on Saturday mornings.

Mr. and Mrs. Clarence Cain, neighbors of my grandparents, owned a 700-acre farm only a stone's throw across the river from the city limits. It was an unusual arrangement in my opinion. How could anyone have the fortune of owning a farm and yet choose to live in town? Obviously, the decision of residence was reached by a grownup and not subjected to the whims of a young teenager who thought life revolved around hunting.

Although the farm was mentioned every time I visited the Cains during neighborhood bicycle tours, I had never seen the place. My mental image included barns, tractors, fields, livestock, etc. I would be a freshman in high school before learning that it was a different kind of farm.

There was always a flurry of excitement that swept through our hunting group when we were invited to hunt new territory. Such was the case when a frequent participant in our Saturday deer hunts announced that his brother, Mr. Clarence Cain, had seen a few deer on his farm and wanted us to hunt there. This was the same property where, in the late-1940s, Clarence's brother Bob shot an eight-point buck that reputedly weighed 227 pounds. The mounted head hung for years in a dry goods store in my hometown. It was probably the first mounted deer head I had ever seen, and naturally I remember is as a monster.

For a long week thoughts of healthy farm fed bucks dominated my daydreaming. As a fledgling deer hunter, I assumed that an unhunted deer herd not only would contain numerous mossy-horned bucks, but also would make for easy pickings. Making assumptions is a behavioral trait among humans that sets the stage for education through triumph or humiliation. On one count I would learn that protection of a deer herd doesn't necessarily ensure an increase in the number of bucks with massive antlers. Habitat quality would eventually enter into my vocabulary, but it wasn't even a consideration in those days.

And what about my easy pickings assumption? From the second a deer's hooves first meet mother earth the animal is geared for survival. These gears were designed through generations of trial and error or evolution driven by one common tenet — survival of the fittest.

Another term that would come to me later was "innate behavior." A white-tailed deer is a prey species programmed to flee adversity just as the bobcat is blessed with the stealth and armaments to create adversity. Having flourished for millennia, the predator and prey relationship is a fine-tuned machine with each part integral to its successful function. This is a roundabout way of saying that my assumption was erroneous. Even without human intervention through hunting, a deer herd still has that built-in need for survival that is challenged daily and nightly by four-legged predators. Deer are always on edge — that's their nature.

A week of school seemed to last two, but Saturday finally came around. We met at our usual place in town and proceeded (caravan-style) across the river toward Mr. Clarence's farm. The procession turned from the highway onto a two-rut dirt road that was blocked by a locked gate. Years ago, someone was driving around the gate, so Mr. Clarence placed a board, laced with nails, in the culprit's path. The next day his brother had four flat tires. Time heals most things, and the two brothers had made amends.

We traveled through a beautiful stand of longleaf pines with an understory of turkey oaks. There were no fields. The farm was simply a block of woods occupied by countless hogs, somewhat domesticated. We assembled in the yard of an abandoned house. With stick in hand, Mr. Clarence drew a map of his property in the sand. Then, each hunter was assigned a "stand" for the morning's hunt. Once the standers had ample time to find their positions, the dogs were released. Soon enough, the hunt was in progress. As we had anticipated, the dogs were in full cry on the hot scent of a wily whitetail within minutes. The race left the hillside quickly, swung down through the river swamp, and appeared to be completing a wide circle when the stander next to me shot twice. Silence of the hounds signaled a successful hunt.

In those days our hunting group accounted for only about a dozen deer each season. So, when someone got lucky the hunt was over, the deer was brought out for skinning, and the venison was divided into as many portions as there were hunters. Although the buck was a youngster with spike antlers, this was a time for celebration, recounting details of the hunt and sharing stories.

Still wet behind the ears as a deer hunter, I was particularly enthralled with the skinning process. While the older, more experienced hunters proceeded with the task, I stood nearby with my hands in my pockets and watched. WHUMP!!! Something hit

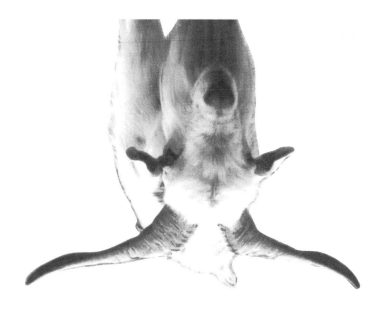

me from behind, lifted me off the ground, and put me flat on my back. Resting on my elbows, I leaned my head backward to get a look at my attacker. The view of an upside-down goat is etched indelibly in my memory. Needless to say, everyone else thought the incident was hilarious. I was humiliated beyond description. Mr. Clarence remarked, "Oh, I forgot to tell y'all about that sneaky billy goat. He'll get you if you aint lookin'."

Well, having that goat to contend with added spice to subsequent hunts on the Cain farm. He didn't have a name; rather, folks just referred to him as Mr. Clarence's goat. And, with his ploy of hiding until his victim was in the wide open before launching an attack, the ol' goat gained quite a reputation. Daily farm visits to scatter shelled corn along the road enabled Mr. Clarence to maintain the necessary rapport with his razor-backed, piney woods rooters. The property was fenced only for a short span on either side of the entrance gate, so the token offering of corn kept the free-ranging hogs on a routine and in touch. Several muffled honks from his '47 Pontiac's horn drew the swine like a magnet. When it was time to take a few hogs to market Mr. Clarence tossed a handful of corn into a holding pen and closed the door when he had a load.

I had learned about selling livestock during visits to my grandparents' farm in Tennessee. Farmers used weight as the measure of an animal being "topped out" for market. The best I could discern from watching Mr. Clarence over the years was that he used length instead of weight as a measure for market-bound hogs.

Anyway, the goat became quite a nuisance, especially when Mr. Clarence was concentrating on catching and loading hogs. When Mr. Clarence's back was turned the goat would appear out of the blue and butt him squarely in the rear. A few stings from a BB gun gave the goat a newfound respect for his owner, but put him in a foul mood for everyone else invading his domain.

One of my cousins came down from Fayetteville to spend the weekend with me. I had promised John a Saturday deer hunt as our entertainment. As luck would have it, we were invited back to the Cain farm. During the obligatory map drawing in the sand, everyone kept an eye out for the horned marauder. He was nowhere to be seen. One elderly gentleman speculated that my attack was rare since the goat avoided crowds and preferred lone quarry. Speculations like that just added mystique to the occasion.

John and I were directed to stands along the John G. Branch, very near the abandoned house — too near! An uneventful morning of hunting gave way to lunchtime. We had to walk through the yard of the old house to join the other hunters at the entrance gate. We would not admit to fear, but I'm sure each of us wore the look.

Walking sideways like two crabs enabled us to scan 360 degrees for the sly one. The technique seemed to be working pretty well until we reached the epicenter of the yard. John shouted, "There he is! His head is poking out from the back corner of the old house! HERE HE COMES!!!" We dropped our guns and made a beeline for the roof of the junked '49 Chevy panel truck. The gate was too far away. For a period just short of eternity, the goat circled just like the shark in the movie Jaws circled the boat.

We were worried about missing lunch and the rest of the weekend as we stood helplessly on the rooftop. I noticed that sheets of burlap material had been used as seat covers. If I could drape a section of burlap over the goat's horns and face, perhaps we could escape. John agreed that it was a good idea. With a wad of burlap in hand I moved cautiously onto the hood and placed my legs around one of the big cone-shaped headlights. The goat crashed into the fender below with a vengeance. When he attacked a second time, without hesitation I tossed the burlap in his direction. I'll admit it was a blind throw, my eyes were closed, but by golly it worked. The hooded goat raised on his hind legs and proceeded to pronk around the yard with the antics of a hooked Gulf Stream marlin. John and I were absolutely spellbound. We should have been fleeing, but who could leave such a spectacle?

All of a sudden the burlap fell to the ground. The goat bounded onto the hood and then to the rooftop between John and me. A stopwatch couldn't have timed our split-second decision to head for the gate. With 30 yards to go, I glanced behind and saw a wide set of horns getting wider — closing the gap. The gate was still too far away. I grabbed a low-hanging tree limb and swung up to safety. John missed the limb. He and the goat were going around the tree at amazing speed. All the while John was extending a hand and begging me to pull him up. Despite the excitement, I knew that gravity was not in my favor. It would be much easier for John to pull me out of the tree than for me to pull him up. At that point I figured it was every man and goat for himself. Besides, John was doing a fine job of keeping the tree between him and the goat. Eventually he got lucky, grabbed the limb, and climbed up to join me.

One by one our hunting partners gathered at the gate. Imagine their ringside seats to see two young fellows up a tree with a crazed goat patrolling in tight circles. I had been humiliated once again by Mr. Clarence's goat.

There wasn't a deer to skin that day, but everyone on the other side of the gate thought it had turned out to be a great hunt — one to remember!

Note: *This article appeared in Quality Whitetails (V 5, I 3 - 1998)*

Tes Randle Jolly

Foggy Morning Gobblers

The 1983 meeting of the Southeast Deer Study Group was hosted by the Georgia Department of Natural Resources in Athens, Georgia. Although the topic of deer hunting naturally spills over into casual conversations among biologists, the timing of this annual event (February) turns one's thoughts to spring turkey hunting. Yes, many deer biologists are turkey hunters, too.

Carroll Allen, a Georgia DNR wildlife biologist and former University of Georgia classmate, invited me to join him for a turkey hunt during the upcoming season. He had a hunting lease in Oglethorpe County about 25 miles southeast of Athens.

It was in that same county that I caught the chronic turkey-hunting bug while in graduate school during the 1970s. Carroll's invitation was accepted with anticipation of a memorable return to my old haunts.

On a brisk, foggy morning of the season's opening week in late March, we passed through the rural community of Philomath and arrived at his hunting lease well before daybreak. A map of the property was posted in their clubhouse, an abandoned farm residence. Carroll pointed out certain topographic features, including a pasture bordered by a creek that ran through the property. We decided to begin our hunt there, especially since Carroll had seen two mature gobblers in the pasture during the previous deer season.

The pasture was about 300 yards long, divided lengthwise by a fence, sloped toward the creek bottom and was dog-legged — it had a gentle bend in it. At the lower end of the pasture a gap in the fence marked the place to await the sound of a gobbler announcing daybreak.

We stood back to back, allowing audible coverage of 360 degrees. Silence among the barred owls and chuck-will's-widows signaled a change of the guard. Now, the only avian sounds were emitting from "Ray Charles" birds, the early risers. *Ray Charles, Charles, Charles; Ray Charles, Charles, Charles* was their song. Ornithologists call them cardinals.

The sky was battleship gray and a thick blanket of fog hugged the ground. My position provided a rather obscure view up the pasture. What's that black spot in the distance, I wondered? It looked like a lone fence post — too narrow to be a deer. Turkey? It couldn't be. No respectable turkey would leave the safety of its perch in such poor light. Furthermore, heavy fog usually keeps turkeys on their roost longer in the morning. My thoughts ran the gamut from practical to impractical. Whatever it is, it wasn't there minutes earlier when we walked through the pasture. It must be a turkey! I whispered over my shoulder, There's a gobbler in the pasture 'bout 200 yards away. Without even turning his head Carroll exclaimed, "Sure there is."

He didn't take me seriously until I began groping frantically through my essentials bag for a head net and my favorite diaphragm call. I motioned for Carroll to lie down at the base of the fencepost so he would have a view of the left pasture. I'll take the right side and call — you do the shooting. A slight ridge across the pasture prevented a view of the "subject" when we were lying on our bellies. Still not totally convinced, Carroll asked, "Are you sure it's a turkey — a gobbler?" Well, not exactly, but we're gonna soon find out.

I was a bit cotton-mouthed. A long-bearded gobbler can do that to you. After rolling the diaphragm around in my mouth to collect just that right amount of moisture (spit), I uttered three seductive yelps. Much to our surprise a resounding *gobble-obble-obble* erupted from the fog. Carroll inhaled deeply, and then began emitting short breaths in vibrating fashion. The tip of his gun barrel bobbed like a telegrapher's finger relaying a long message. With his attention focused completely on the phantom gobbler, he didn't see that I was equally rattled. Taking advantage of his excitement, I said, don't shoot too soon — don't you miss that bird. I really put the pressure on with that statement.

We were laying only a couple of feet apart, but due to the honeysuckle vines entwined in the fence, I could see nothing on Carroll's side. It was time for another call to see is he has moved. *Yelp...yelp...yelp. GOBBLE-OBBLE-OBBLE!* He's much closer and following the fence toward us. Carroll machine-gunned another series of breaths. Minutes seemed to pass, but it was more like 30 seconds. I couldn't wait — *Yelp...yelp. FUTOOONG!* That old gobbler was drumming less than 40 yards away, but still out of sight.

GOBBLE-OBBLE-OBBLE...GOBBLE-OBBLE-OBBLE. A double gobble! He's lonesome and he's comin'. "I knowww," Carroll sputtered. The swishing of turkey feet in the grass followed my next two yelps. All of a sudden a humiliating, gut-wrenching sound filled my ears. *Putt...putt...putt!* That wily rascal had smelled a rat (two rats), sounded his alarm and turned to run when I yelled, SHOOT!

BLEWSYOW! The turkey rolled, but quickly recovered and ran toward the fence. Carroll jumped to his feet, tripped and stuck his gun barrel six inches deep into the pasture. Somehow the turkey went under, through, or over the fence to my side. I issued the *coup de gras* before Carroll could swing and pull the trigger. What a stroke of luck. Carroll's gun barrel and his turkey had been saved.

We exchanged a handshake in celebration and sat on a nearby log to recount the hunt

Mark Spinks

A fine pair of Oglethorpe County gobblers.

and clean the dirt from Carroll's gun barrel. Based on a traditional rule among gentlemen hunters, Carroll was given credit for the gobbler. The story of this unusual and somewhat comical hunt would be told again and again. But, it wasn't over yet. Another gobbler sounded off several hundred yards up the creek. Without hesitation we gathered our gear and headed upstream. After closing the gap a bit we decided to stop and listen. The bird gobbled again, and simultaneously another one gobbled back at the pasture. Carroll said, "Try your luck with the pasture gobbler and I'll continue upstream since you're not familiar with that territory."

I turned to run, got tangled in a vine, tripped and sampled the creek bank with my gun barrel. Twice on the same hunt — that's one for the record. I used a stick to remove most of the dirt from my barrel, then dipped it into the creek for a final cleaning.

Arriving back at the pasture I realized the gobbler was still in the woods, so I sat at the base of a large oak about 30 yards from the pasture's edge. He responded immediately to my call, so I repeated. Every time he gobbled while approaching I returned a series of yelps. Instead of continuing along a straight path and the ultimate collision with me, he swung wide, beyond gun-shot range.

I had called too much to the wise old boy. A two-year-old gobbler is usually more accommodating, and a volley of calling can be enjoyed, at least by the hunter. In terms of a quality experience, I'll put my money on a two-year-old gobbler every time. Older, more experienced birds are cagey, therefore not the best of conversationalists. In fact, hunting old toms is akin to predator calling. The quarry approaches silently and usually from the side or back.

He entered the pasture and began strutting and gobbling 45 yards away. He may as well have been in China, 'cause 30 yards is my limit for shooting. He periscoped his head and neck each time I called, but 45 yards was his limit. He would come no closer. Stalemates are common when hunting older gobblers, especially if the caller is loquacious.

The calls of passing crows elicited a response of gobbling, but he ignored my beckoning. BLEWSYOW rang out in the distance upstream, followed by a "shock" gobble from my bird. Fifteen minutes later, Carroll stepped proudly into the pasture with another fine gobbler draped over his shoulder. *Putt...putt*, and my long-bearded gobbler vanished. Perhaps our paths would cross again later. If so, I would use a more subtle approach to calling, and he may teach me yet another facet of turkey wisdom.

Carroll had ended his season in one morning with a limit of two mature gobblers. Was it really over? As long as this experience remains in our memories, I think not. **Note:** *This article appeared in Quality Whitetails (V 6, I 1 - 1999).*

Ruffled Grouches and Copper Spaniards

Twenty years ago a wildlife biologist friend from western North Carolina was touring a mountain property with its new owner from Florida. As they walked along a winding logging road a feathered bomb exploded from the edge of an ivy slick, the colloquial name for a laurel thicket. The Floridian commented, "You know, I've seen a bunch of those ruffled grouches on my property. Next fall I'm gonna bring my Copper Spaniard up here and do some hunting."

Throughout my life as a hunter, I have had the fortune of encountering some genuine characters. What I remember most about these hunting companions are certain words or phrases that appeared fitting for the occasion, but were not quite on target. Technically, this slaying of the King's English is known as a malapropism. With that bit of trivia taken care of, let's proceed with storytelling.

Two brothers, both retired farmers, belonged to the deer hunting club that I was a member of during my high school years in the 1960s. Every Saturday morning it was ritual to build a small "campfire" and recount the week's happenings before going deer hunting. This was also an opportunity to tell stories from bygone hunting days. Our huntmaster's name was Tootie, but neither of the brothers could ever get his name right. One called him Nudie and the other always referred to him as Doodie.

One early morning at fireside the conversation turned to doe shooting. The storyteller, one of the brothers of course, spoke in a lower-than-normal tone 'cause in those days our deer hunting was bucks only — it was illegal to harvest does. Anyway, he went on to tell about a particular hunt in which the hounds were running a deer toward the dirt road where he had been assigned a "stand." Not one, but three deer crossed the road about 100 yards away. The first was a buck, the second a doe, and trailing was a "yelling-size" deer. Much later I discovered that a yelling-size deer was being called a yearling, but in reality it was a fawn. According to Mr. Tommy, "Them deer hit the woods across the road and come straight towarge me. I could hear 'em breaking limbs and stuff as they got closter. I raised my single-shot Ivory Johnson that had a 36-inch barrel and knowed

any second it was gonna be 'Katie barred the door' for that ole buck. When the first nose cleared the bushes, I let the hammer fall and the deer slid to a stop — it was the doe and she lay dead as a wedge. That darned buck turnt and run straight object me and that murkle bush. I never 'spected it, but them deer swapped places 'tween the time they crossed the road and got to me." One of the other old sages, with a nickname of Simp, piped up and said, "Tom, that's what we call a 'scuse-me deal.' Them thangs jest happen."

Back to the ruffled grouches. Years later, my hunting exploits took me beyond the reaches of my southeastern North Carolina homeland to the Appalachian Mountains in search of ruffed grouse. It was near Balsam Gap, North Carolina that the first grouse fell to my gun. Later, during graduate school in the 1970s, fellow wildlife classmates and I hunted the rugged terrain of North Georgia's mountains near Clayton. Access was poor and birds were scarce, as one would expect of any animal on the fringe of its geographical range. Therefore, my interest in grouse hunting waned until I began turkey hunting in the mountains of South Carolina a decade later.

My secret turkey hunting spot was Norton Bottoms along Tamassee Creek in Oconee County. The spot was secret because it was 1½ miles behind a locked gate in the Sumter National Forest, and few hunters are adventuresome enough to hunt such places when others are much more accessible.

One spring morning at gray daylight I was awaiting the usual calls of owls and crows to elicit the wake-up call of a gobbler. Off in the distance I heard a *thump… thump…thump, bump, bump, bump, ump, ump, ump.* A ruffed grouse was drumming! Immediately, a turkey gobbled and the hunt was on. I didn't see the gobbler or the grouse, but decided right then to renew my acquaintance with the renowned "thunder chicken" in the fall.

That next October a week of vacation was dedicated solely to the pursuit of Palmetto State ruffed grouse. Knowing the location of one grouse, I spent the first two days hunting other places recommended by a local informant. Those two days were grouseless. The morning of the third day I entered a small town restaurant to have a solid pre-hunt breakfast. Two gentlemen, obviously hometown folks, nodded as I slid onto a stool at the bar. My accent gave me away as being from somewhere else, but the camouflage shirt revealed my intentions. "You up here a'huntin'?," one of the men asked. "Yep," I responded. "It aint deer season yet, what you a'huntin'?" "Pheasants," I exclaimed — an attempt to impart my limited knowledge of Appalachian slang. I knew that ruffed grouse were called mountain pheasants by the locals. My hope was that the conversation would continue and possibly result in some good leads on "pheasant" haunts.

"Had any luck?" Nope, I've only been at it for two days. Both men chuckled somewhat apologetically and turned simultaneously to their coffee cups. When the conversation appeared to have halted abruptly, I asked, "Have y'all seen any pheasants lately?" After a long pause, one man squinched his eyes and asked his partner, "Who's that feller that lives south of town jest past the dumpsters?" "You mean Gus Amos?" "Yep, that's him alright! I heard someone say that he seen one cross the highway near his house 'bout three year ago." I thanked them for the tip, quickly finished my breakfast, and headed straight for Norton Bottoms.

Within an hour I was sneaking along the bank of Tamassee Creek trying to ward off the feeling that I may as well be hunting a saber-toothed tiger or a woods bison. Nevertheless, my quest for the elusive grouse took me upstream. Each ivy slick along the main creek was grouseless. Near the headwaters, there was one remaining feeder stream that held my last chance. I walked along the trickle of water, stepping cautiously from stone to stone. Just ahead, a mountain laurel was protruding horizontally from the bank at about waist level. Upon approaching the barrier I thought this was the perfect vantage point for a wily old grouse. Do I stoop to pass under this laurel or do I climb over? Either way I would render myself momentarily useless as a gunner. Go under was the decision. When my hands and gun were nearly touching the ground, fate struck. The Norton Bottoms grouse exploded into flight. A load of number six shot brought down a shower of leaves, but no feathers. That grouse would not be seen or heard again, at least not by me, until the next turkey season.

My remaining vacation days were spent in the lowcountry deer woods. Now that's something you can sink your teeth into. There's nothing quite like deer hunting.

Note: *This article appeared in Quality Whitetails (V 6, I 2 - 1999).*

Railroad Hunts – Then and Now

Old Silver surveyed the assemblage of Saturday morning deer hunters in the parking lot of Wam Squam country store. His responsibility as huntmaster was to select the appropriate territory for each hunt. Unlike today, our hunting club had access to more spots than we could get around to. Forty years ago there were fewer deer, so acreage was the equalizer. The decision on where to hunt was based on several factors including the rotation plan, the number of hunters, the number of hounds, and primarily the whims of the huntmaster.

There was always that moment of anticipation, and sometimes anxiety, as we awaited the day's plans. Our favorite spot was the Sugar Loaf area along the northern banks of the Cape Fear River in southeastern North Carolina. Sophie's Island, Wolf Pit, Big Savanna, Wright Cemetery, Twisted Hickory, Double Curve, Saw Dust Pile, and the High Hill were all names of traditional deer stands (crossings) associated with Sugar Loaf. Longleaf pine flats, Carolina bays, sand ridges, hardwood swamps, and cypress

Bill Corbett, huntmaster — AKA: Old Silver.

ponds comprised the habitats of our favorite hunting spot. However, Sugar Loaf was reserved for special occasions — holidays, large groups of hunters, and the like.

On this particular morning in the 1960s the decree was issued that we would travel to the neighboring county and hunt the Railroad. If Sugar Loaf was on one end of the scale, then the Railroad was on the other. Response to the announcement was predictable. Faces lengthened and nervous feet shuffled in the sand. The exception was Old Silver. His homeplace was near the Railroad, one of his beloved boyhood haunts.

Hunters rushed into the country store to stock up on a day's worth of necessities: drinks, beanie-weenies, sardines, crackers and cheese, Mary Janes, oranges, apples, and whatever else it took to fill the large pockets of hunting coats. We knew it was going to be a marathon hunt, with lunch on-your-own and ALONE.

When everyone had loaded into pick-up trucks Old Silver held his left arm out of the truck window and motioned to depart, much like a Civil War general would have signaled "charge" to his faithful troops. We followed as if in a funeral procession rather than on a hunting trip. The Railroad hunt was a dreaded occasion.

The Railroad split the middle of nowhere. Longleaf pines, turkey oaks, and scattered patches of gallberry bushes held the world together. The only sign of human presence was the Railroad, piercing the horizon in each direction. Hunters were positioned at strategic stands along the endless stretch, the hounds were cast, and the hunt was on, and on, and on, until the setting sun brought a long-awaited end to a grueling day.

I can honestly say that during numerous Railroad hunts I never saw a deer or a train. My conclusion after many hours of pondering was that trains and deer must pass through under the cover of darkness.

The monotony of the Railroad hunt spawned many a hunter's tale. Remoteness and time set the stage for minds to wander and your eyes to play tricks on you. If you stared down the tracks long enough, strange creatures would appear at the woods' edge. It was the perfect placed to see a long-tailed cat, although Jonathan Jenkins was the only hunter to admit seeing such a critter.

One of our club members, nicknamed Moto because he resembled a Sumo wrestler, emerged from a Railroad hunt with a story that occurred during his lunch. He was eating saltine crackers and cheese. The crumbs that accumulated on his pants drew a flock of tiny, black and white birds. According to Moto, they hopped up and down his legs eating cracker crumbs. Several birds landed on his hands and pecked inquisitively at his fingernails. "I don't think they had ever seen a human before," was Moto's explanation. Our read was that Moto had suffered from Railroad hallucinations prompted by prolonged solitude.

Veterans of this hunt learned the secret of spending long hours alone with infrequent interruptions from the hunt itself. Inventory your food cache and dole out items on a timed basis. Ray Beasley looked at his watch — 3:00 p.m., and nothing left but a honey bun. Savoring small bites would lessen the agony of waiting for the hunt's end. At 3:05 when Ray had finished his last morsel, his attention focused on movement way down the tracks. Afternoon heat waves prevented identification at long range, but the figure appeared to be approaching. Ray tossed his bun wrapper to the ground, licked the sweetness from his fingers, and readied for the arrival of a big buck running along the tracks to elude the hounds. Eternity set in and anticipation heightened. The approaching figure began to take a more definite form, that of a hound and not the buck of Ray's dreams. The hound's gate was steady. He seemed to be on a mission. Without ever acknowledging the hunter, he approached, sniffed the bun wrapper, turned and backtracked into oblivion down the Railroad. Ray's hunt was successful because something happened to break the monotony.

We were standing around a hunter's fire one night awaiting the return of the hounds from who knows where and someone noticed Preston Eaton's shotgun — a single shot. "How darned long is that barrel, anyhow?" "Forty-two inches," was the proud reply. Knowing that the common "Long Tom" barrel is 36 inches long, we pulled out a ruler to verify Preston's claim. It was 42 inches long! Marshall Dawkins stepped forward and said, "Look at what I'm shootin'." His shotgun was a double-barreled 10 gauge that shot solid brass, three-inch shells.

The Railroad hunt affected folks in different ways. Some became so disillusioned that they quit deer hunting altogether. Old sages like Preston and Marshall beat the odds by equipping themselves with guns that allowed a longer reach down the tracks. And then, there was Old Silver. He hunted the Railroad because it was there — a tie to his boyhood days.

As fate would have it, a railroad forms one boundary of my present deer-hunting lease in South Carolina's beloved lowcountry. When the sun sets on the last day of this hunting season, the last of this millennium, I will have enjoyed the best season of my life. A successful season can be assessed in many ways. Bucks with eight or more points have been observed on nearly half of my visits to the deer woods. Weights of harvested does reflect a healthy deer herd and optimum habitat conditions. Everywhere I travel hunters are anxious to discuss their involvement in quality deer management.

The rumble of trains passing my hunting territory takes me back to those Railroad hunts ages ago and serves as a constant reminder of the strides we have made in deer management and the enjoyment of deer hunting. It seems appropriate that a railroad bisects our neighborhood, the birthplace of an organization now known internationally by its acronym — QDMA.

Note: *This article appeared in Quality Whitetails (V 6, I 4 - 1999).*

Voices from the Deer Woods

There was no better theater for the distant drone of barrel-voiced deer hounds than the Cape Fear River lowlands in southeastern North Carolina. Extensive stands of towering hardwoods provided perfect acoustics for the characteristic voices of walker, blue-tick, black-and-tan, and redbone hounds used by our hunting club in my boyhood days.

Changes through time brought us in contact with a wider variety of hunting dogs. When large tracts of bottomland hardwoods were harvested, the ensuing thickets drowned the deep voices of our traditional long-legged hounds. We found that "squealy-mouthed" dogs could be heard better under these new habitat conditions. The high-pitched dog voices also were more audible during windy weather.

One might think that our preference for dogs changed by design, but I must admit that availability was the determining factor more often than not. Therefore, our pack of hunting dogs could best be described as a Duke's mixture. They looked like a line-up of canines from the local pound. Their personalities, idiosyncrasies, quirks, and voices were as varied as those among as many folks. Aside from all of these differences, they had one thing in common — they enjoyed a "hot" deer race.

Charlie was a trash dog. He won the lottery the day our huntmaster, Mr. Bill Corbett (AKA: Old Silver), picked him up at a trash dump and tossed him into the station wagon with a dozen of his kind. "You gotta teach 'em to ride before you can make a huntin' dog out of 'um," were the words we heard more than once from Mr. Corbett. Charlie was a reddish-brown feist — the breed of dog you would expect to see on the cover of a squirrel hunting magazine. He was a quick learner, and he was fleet afoot as well. He didn't bark. He yipped…but, not very often. Combined with his speed, Charlie's frequency of yipping was such that if you heard him yip three times, the deer probably had already passed you. Charlie accounted for the demise of many an old buck, 'cause they were accustomed to approaching a road with caution, looking and sniffing for danger before crossing. Charlie's speed and cadence of voicing negated this survival trait of old bucks, making them more careless and us more successful.

Possum was a lying walker hound. He couldn't run without barking. Those versed in the ways of dogdom would label him a babbler. When we released a pack of hounds, Possum was held back until the other dogs had gone. Then, you would aim the truck's tailgate in the direction you wanted to send Possum. He opened as soon as he hit the ground and continued to bark until the hunt was over. That wasn't all bad. Possum made critters stir and he kept hunters from sleeping on their stands. One day while we were breaking for lunch someone asked a visiting hunter if he saw anything on the morning's hunt. He very enthusiastically commented, "I almost saw one deer twice!" When asked for the details, he proceeded to tell of hearing a lone dog, an old barrel-voiced dog, heading in his direction. He readied himself and waited, and waited, until the big white walker came running by barking every step of the way. "That was the first time," he exclaimed. About an hour later the same white dog returned, still barking every breath. "I must have had my head turned in the wrong direction both times the deer came by." We didn't bother to tell our visitor about Possum's lying nature, and he went home thinking he

A typical Blue-tick Hound.

had almost gotten a shot at a big buck — twice!

One of our hunting buddies had a bird dog/hound cross, named Ugly. She did so well her first year that her owner went to the vet's office and "officially" changed her name to Pretty Ugly. She was fast, too, he bragged. "Ninety percent of the times you heard her, you'd be looking at the deer." Pretty Ugly was a squealer as a youngster, then she had a litter of puppies and thereafter had a chop-mouthed voice. In houndsmen's terms, a chop-mouthed dog emits short, loud barks in rapid succession.

Nothing lasts. This once noble approach to hunting deer has been relegated to its twilight years through conflicts with the demands of our spreading civilization. I have joined the ranks of those who reflect on bygone hunts with a tear in my eye and a smile. The voices of deer hounds remain steadfast in the deer woods of my memory.

Many were the times when the older fellows of the hunt club would proclaim, "Hit don't matter whether we even see a deer or not, just as long as we hear a good race." An anonymous author shared his feelings and penned this quote:

"And sometimes I think that life
Holds the most for him who can thrill
Not at the spoils of the strife
But the sounds of the dogs on the hill."

Note: *This article appeared in Quality Whitetails (V 8, I 3 - 2001).*

Zorro was not a registered Plott Hound, but he looked and acted like one. That was all we cared about.

Three Zorros

A half century ago, youngsters were entertained by a host of Western characters on TV. The list included Roy Rogers and Dale Evans; the Lone Ranger and Tonto; Gene Autry, the singing cowboy; Lash LaRue, who used a rawhide whip instead of a sidearm; the Cisco Kid and Poncho; and Hop-A-Long Cassidy.

There was one who didn't fit the mold — Zorro. His episodes were staged in the days of Spanish rule in southern California and all of the characters spoke with an accent. He dressed in black, wore a black mask and cape, rode a black horse named Tornado, and defended justice with a sword, the slim-bladed type used in fencing. The sword was never used to inflict bodily injury. Once the bad guys were subdued with a flurry of swordsmanship, the hero would leap onto his black horse and disappear into the cover of darkness. Law enforcement officers always appeared moments later to find their bewildered subjects standing unarmed and bearing Zorro's signature mark — a "Z" cut with his sword into their clothing.

Zorro was my favorite because he was unique. I even attempted to emulate his antics with a homemade sword crafted from a "skint" dog fennel with a paper cup as a hand guard. The name Zorro was destined to be a part of my life, forever.

David Cross worked in his family's hardware store in my hometown. I hunted deer in those days, the early '60s, with David, his grandfather, several of his cousins and a few others. We had a mixed pack of hounds including beagles, blue-ticks, red bones, walkers, black-and-tans, Julys, and "sooners". While at work one day, David heard a dog barking in the parking lot behind the hardware store. The dog had "treed" a house cat on the wheel of a logging truck. After investigating, David found the owner and purchased the dog for $10. We were always looking for an addition to our pack to add some flavor. This dog fit the bill. He was basically jet black, but there was a hint of brindled tan marking around his head and underside. We decided that he was a Plott Hound, although he could have been classified as one of the "sooners." Whatever he was called by his previous owner, to us he was Zorro.

Zorro, like his TV namesake, was a unique character. He was a loner, so much so that we had to put him in a pen all to himself. He didn't want another dog close to him. He was so prone to fight that we had to construct a petition in the dog box to keep him separated from the other hounds while in transit. When cast, the pack would follow the driver (dog handler) with noses to the ground in an attempt to strike the cold trail of a feeding or traveling deer. Zorro would jump from the truck's tailgate, wait for the scene to quieten, and then head off in the opposite direction. He hunted like a pointer, crisscrossing through the woods until he encountered a bedded deer. Zorro relied heavily on eyesight and he traveled in a head-up fashion checking for scent rather than holding his nose to the ground as characteristic of trailing hounds. A high-pitched, squeally voice was the telltale signal that a deer was in the wind with Zorro close behind. On many occasions the other hounds would rally to Zorro's lead. But Zorro never abandoned his search for a whitetail to join a chase initiated by the pack.

Usually, not long into a chase an ol' buck would gain enough distance from the hounds to have the luxury of checking the wind, thus eluding the standers (hunters positioned at known crossings). Deer are reluctant to break cover when pursued by hounds, often running parallel to a field border or road. Given the opportunity, a deer will approach a road cautiously, use all of his senses to check for danger, and then proceed across. With Zorro in pursuit, deer literally had to throw caution to the wind. He was fleet of foot and he voiced sparingly. Many hunters, accustomed to the constant drone of an approaching pack of deer hounds, were surprised and embarrassed by Zorro's technique. By the time you heard that characteristic squeal twice. a hoofed blur already would have passed your stand with black lightening at his heels.

Deer, too, get accustomed to the constant voicing of hounds and take advantage of this behavior. When I began deer hunting I thought hounds kept the deer in sight at all times. Not so. Through the millennia deer have been chased by members of the canine family and they have developed a variety of evasive maneuvers. Contrary to the panic-stricken expressions on the faces of the subjects in the movie Bambi, deer actually take this "cat and mouse" scenario into stride quite well. I have observed deer waiting motionlessly until the hounds were within yards before using a burst of speed to create a margin of safety.

Mr. Biddy McCulloch, a stalwart member of our hunting club, was a very stout gentleman who always wore bibbed overalls. On a deer stand he sat patiently on a rein-forced folding stool with a side-by-side 12 gauge laid across his knees. When his gun was shouldered you may as well sharpen your skinning knife. One day after a hunt, Mr. Biddy had a story about his favorite dog he often referred to as ol' iron eater, 'cause the dog once demolished a metal food bowl. "I thought I heard Zarrow (as he pronounced the dog's name) way off." Mr. Biddy would squint one eye to accentuate the distance. "Then he squealed again real close and I knew for sure it was Zarrow. That ol' buck he was running appeared and disappeared so quickly, I don't think even Jessie James could have got a shot off at him!"

Zorro filled our lives with excitement for 10 hunting seasons. Nearly 40 years later, those of us who grew up hunting together still tell Zorro stories. Although a $10 bill changed hands and Zorro became a member of our deer hound pack, we didn't own him. No one owned him! He belonged only to himself. In addition to being a loner, he was known to display his cantankerous attitude toward one of us, especially when it was time to unload from the dog box into the kennel after a day of hunting. With lips curled and a throaty growl, Zorro indicated that he was content just where he was. So, he often overnighted in the dog box. A good dog could get away with that kind of behavior, you know.

Years later, in 1987, I traveled to the land down under as a guest of the Australian Deer Association. The plan was for me to spend a day or two with one person, and then be passed on to another. One of my hosts was Zorro Parmigiani, a conservation officer with the Fisheries and Wildlife Department of Victoria. Zorro turned out to be as talented as my other acquaintances with the same name. He is a poet, song writer, singer, deer hunter, and friend.

A group of us went into the Australian Alps, locally known as the "high country," to hunt deer with hounds and camp for a week. Six straight days of rain kept us in camp sitting around a struggling campfire, telling hunting stories, and sharing jokes from continents 12,000 miles apart...building life-long friendships. One night as the rain had subsided, Zorro retrieved his guitar from the truck and sang songs he had written about hunting, hunters, and hunting dogs. Those songs were captured on a tape recorder and I now have the pleasure of sharing one of my favorites with American deer hunters. The bond between hunting dogs and their human companions is strong the world over and worthy of celebration.

NOTHIN'

From the day he was born he was man's best friend
Fine huntin' beagle from end to end
Didn't look too much for what he was worth
Oh, they called that puppy Nothin' on earth
Nothin' was a hound dog through and through
Nothin' was a hound dog fast and true
Nothin' had a nose so seldom wrong
But the trails run cold and Nothin' is gone
Late at night while the campfire burns
We've waited long for that hound's return
To see him arrive sorry and lame
When it's a lonely spur in the pouring rain
Nothin' was a hound dog through and through
Nothin' was a hound dog fast and true
Nothin' had a nose so seldom wrong
But the trails run cold and Nothin' is gone
Way up on the Thompson you can hear his bay
Deep in the ferns down the Bunyip's way
And the echoing billy tells where he'll be
You'll always hear his voice on the wind
Nothin' was a hound dog through and through
Nothin' was a hound dog fast and true
Nothin' had a nose so seldom wrong
But the trails run cold and Nothin' is gone
Yes, the trails run cold, but his memory...lives on

My life has been enriched by those acquaintances bearing the name of Zorro.

Note: *This article appeared in Quality Whitetails (V 9, I 4 - 2002).*

Elusive Deer

S he roamed her home range for at least 12 years before being harvested in the very same field where she was eartagged at age 2½. We know that whitetails are capable of living into their teens in the wild as long as they have adequate nutrition. So, why is this incident worth mentioning? This doe's home was on the historic Webb Wildlife Center, a 5,800-acre property along the Savannah River and owned by the South Carolina Department of Natural Resources (SCDNR). Each fall, 20 groups of 30 deer hunters (two groups per week for 10 weeks) visit this traditional hunting area for an afternoon hunt, a southern-style dinner, an overnight stay in a 12-bedroom plantation house dating back to the late-1800s, and a morning hunt followed by a full course breakfast. Afternoon and morning hunting periods lasted approximately three hours each, so every year 600 hunters hunted a total of 3,600 hours. Multiplied by 12, the age of the doe when harvested, the hours of hunting that occurred during that doe's life was an astounding 43,200. Furthermore, the average deer harvest during that 12-year span was approximately 200 deer per year, or a total of 2,400 deer. Whether the doe remained on the Webb Center property for 12 years or occasionally ventured onto a neighboring tract is immaterial. Hunting pressure is high throughout the neighborhood. What is noteworthy is that she ran the gauntlet for over a decade, and that is the epitome of elusiveness.

During my years as a SCDNR wildlife biologist I encountered numerous sick and dead whitetails and served as a diagnostician for those that had obvious diseases. One case history is quite memorable. A sick doe was found in September by members of a hunting club north of Charleston. The doe was 3½ years old and lactating, an indication that she had been healthy and a mother. But her physical condition had deteriorated from a chronic stage of hemorrhagic disease, a common viral sickness among southeastern whitetails. Hunting with hounds was traditional on the club where this sick doe was found, and the season begins on August 15 and runs continuously to January 1. For 3½ years this doe eluded hunters and their hounds, predators, and even automobiles, but not the tiny black gnats, or "noseeums," that transmitted her debilitating disease. She also had a congenital defect, a condition technically referred to as micropthalmia. Her eyes had never developed and she had been blind since birth!

Such incidents, although noteworthy and intriguing, are inconsequential to deer herds. Occasionally though, certain phenomena affect an entire herd or regional population. Last year's weather conditions rendered deer particularly elusive throughout the coastal plains of North Carolina, South Carolina, and Georgia. We witnessed the most bountiful supply of mast — acorns and berries of all sorts — occurring within the last 10 years. Also, this was the first year of ample rains following a five-year drought, and natural browse flourished. Deer had access to a cornucopia, a virtual Thanksgiving table of choice foods. Their response to this region-wide time of plenty was nocturnal activity. Throughout the 2003 season, hunters expressed their frustration with the unaccustomed lack of activity during the prime hunting periods of early morning and late afternoon. Young bucks, yearlings, were seen on a regular basis, but few mature bucks or does. Yearling bucks, teenagers of the deer world, are destined to remain active, it's just their nature. Another compounding problem within this three-state region is that the seasons are long and hunting pressure is constant. This situation combined with an abundant food supply kept deer/hunter encounters to a minimum. The end result was that many clubs harvested 50 percent or less of their customary annual numbers.

During the previous five years the local deer processing business was burgeoning, due primarily to high annual harvests. Deer are more active and therefore more accessible to hunters when natural and planted foods are affected negatively by drought conditions. The 2003 deer season was a stark contrast regarding harvest figures and many deer processors, especially the recent arrivals without a dedicated clientele, were forced out of business. There was an account of one frustrated deer processor who locked the door to his business and drove through his neighborhood to see if a newly established processor was shortstopping his regular clients. Competition was not to be found.

Hunters gathered at their usual haunts throughout the season and discussed the reasons for such a poor harvest. Some felt they had taken too many deer the previous season and now were feeling the effects. Others thought disease during the offseason may have decreased deer numbers. A dieoff of the magnitude to cause such a reduction in the harvest would have the deer woods literally strewn with skeletons, and that certainly was not the case.

Baiting is legal in coastal North Carolina and South Carolina, but not in Georgia. Those who use feeders witnessed a sharp decline in deer activity in late September when acorns began falling. Corn was sprouting beneath the feeders. Not even the ring-tailed, masked marauders (raccoons) of corn were frequenting the feeders. They, too, obviously preferred acorns.

Motorists are perhaps the only ones who benefited from the deer activity shift in 2003. Based on personal observations last fall, nighttime sightings of deer along highways were rare and there were fewer incidents of collisions with automobiles. A nurse friend of ours with a one-hour commute to work recently asked me, "What has happened to the deer along the Interstate?" Her unbiased observations as a non-hunter were the same as mine.

Adult bucks harvested in this region reflected the past and present. Antler development among the 3½- to 5½-year-olds was not up to par for their respective age classes, but fat reserves, especially late in the season, were much better than average. Prolonged drought conditions and their effect on food quality and quantity predisposed the bucks to poor antler development, whereas the recent abundance of high energy natural foods in response to a normal rainy season allowed fat storage as autumn progressed.

What does the future hold? Well, since deer thrived on natural foods throughout hunting season, the planted food plots were spared and should carry the load of extra deer until spring greenup. Already a month into the new year and acorns are still available. Bucks were casting their antlers by late December of the 2002 season, but they likely will carry their hardware well into February or early March this year. Antler casting dates provide an accurate barometer of deer herd health. Barring another drought, antler development should be back to normal in 2004. Reproductive rates are expected to reflect these optimum habitat conditions. So be prepared for an exciting deer hunting season this fall. As a bonus for those of us who also are turkey hunters, there should be more 20-pound gobblers this spring than in a great while. They, too, respond to good food.

Conditions vary across the whitetail's range. If your hunting is not productive at home, hit the road. The venison in the Hamilton freezer came from an area in Georgia less affected by last fall's acorn supply. Remember this axiom: When it's good to be a deer, it's tough to be a hunter, biologist, or a manager.

Note: *This article appeared in Quality Whitetails (V 11, I 1 - 2004).*

A Proactive Approach Against Poaching

Webster's Dictionary defines poaching as: (1) To trespass on another's game preserve to hunt or fish, or (2) To take game or fish illegally.

Early accounts of poaching date back to the feudal system of Europe when serfs "took" from the estate by means of subsistence hunting. The practice then and now is a "cat and mouse" game, but the need to bring home the meat has been replaced by the thrill of evading the landowner or game warden. Some hunters poach because they are reluctant to join a club for financial reasons or simply because they are misfit individuals who refuse to follow rules. Greed is a trait of many poachers. They are driven to get what they think is their fair share by any means possible, and at the expense of others. So, in a way, this socially unacceptable endeavor of modern day remains a throwback to feudalistic times when stealing from the landed gentry was somehow justified.

The literature on deer hunting and management is laced with references to poaching. Jim Steinbaugh wrote a chapter entitled: Game Law Enforcement in the 1975 book *Producing Quality Whitetails*, by Al Brothers and Murphy E. Ray Jr. Colonel Steinbaugh stated, "Perhaps the most destructive of all illegal hunting methods is that of night hunting. A few 'outlaw' hunters with a spotlight can kill more trophy deer in a few hours of night hunting than would normally be killed during the whole season on a well-managed tract of land."

The Wildlife Management Institute published *White-tailed Deer Ecology and Management* in 1984 and referenced illegal hunting or poaching on eight occasions. "Considerable poaching is carried out simply for 'the heck of it'...a type of recreation done with full knowledge and perhaps in part because of its illegality. Such hunting usually is a group activity, spontaneous or planned, often involving consumption of alcohol."

In the 1995 book *Quality Whitetails*, edited by Drs. Karl V. Miller and R. Larry Marchinton, I co-authored with Al Brothers and Dr. Rob Wegner a chapter entitled: Ethics for the Future. Here is what we had to say about poaching. "Our society is too

Gated road entrances can be "baffled" with plywood and appropriate signage.

liberal to tackle the cancer of illegal hunting head on. It is difficult for true sportsmen to seek higher fines and penalties (such as restitution or replacement fees) for chronic or flagrant game law violations. The real problem is that it is difficult to severely penalize someone for illegally taking an animal that is being referred to by the news media as a hoofed rat. To some, the whitetail has become more of a liability than an asset to our society."

Some states have "taken the bull by the horns" by strengthening game laws. Colonel Jim Steinbaugh, director of Texas Parks and Wildlife Department's Law Enforcement Division, emphasized that increasing penalties had dramatically reduced poaching activities in Texas. Trespassing with a firearm is now a felony violation. The restitution fee for illegally harvested bucks is based on their Boone and Crockett score. Law enforcement officers have even confiscated several helicopters used in illegal hunting.

Mr. Butch Thompson, wildlife and security manager of the renowned 825,000-acre King Ranch in Texas, said that 500 cases of illegal hunting were filed annually in the 1970s. Now, about 30 cases are made each year. His observations are that casual poachers have all but disappeared and drop-off hunter activity decreased as fines increased. But what remains are those professional poachers who sell 160-inch and better antlers to collectors for $5,000 to $6,000 each.

Throughout the Southeast many large-acreage properties and plantations attract poachers. The reasons are obvious. Most are in remote areas, they are not patrolled on a regular basis, and they are usually well managed — known by poachers as game-rich targets.

The view into private property can be obscured with a green screen. In this case, eastern red cedars provide the screen.

For decades landowners have waged a quiet war against trespassers and poachers. Signs are posted along boundaries, fences also mark the boundaries, and locked gates are erected on all access roads. When possible, new access roads are constructed with a crook near the entrance to decrease visibility into the property. Plywood or metal barriers are placed at the entrance to straight access roads to prevent poachers from shooting at game from an adjoining public road. Earthen embankments have been constructed along the edge of small fields or where a power line or gas line right-of-way intersects a public road. Green barriers have been created by planting cedars or shrubs along agricultural fields adjacent to public roads. Some desperate landowners have clearcut the timber along their exposed borders to encourage visibly impenetrable vegetative screens. The manager of a large property in South Carolina filed a permanent restraining order against repeat offenders of trespass laws. Ironically, it is the landowner, the one who pays taxes on private property, who must make the effort to protect their property against unwanted "guests." Trespass laws should be crafted in a manner that places responsibility on a would-be perpetrator to know that private land is just that — off limits.

The Quality Deer Management Association has attacked poaching from a variety of angles. Several branches have purchased "dummy" deer and donated them to wildlife agencies for law enforcement. The topic of poaching has been included in a number of deer management short courses conducted by the organization. Several articles about poaching have been published in the *Quality Whitetails* journal. One article entitled, "Poaching Isn't Hunting: Terminology is Important," was written by Dr. R. Larry

Marchinton. According to the author, "It is primarily legal hunters that fund anti-poaching efforts. It is they who stand the strongest in opposition to poaching."

If you are repulsed by the ongoing actions of poachers and you have information that may lead to the conviction of such people please contact your wildlife agency's toll-free hotline. Almost all states have a program designated for law enforcement assistance. The program in some states is referred to as Operation Game Thief. Other states have a TIP program, which stands for Turn In Poachers. Their telephone number is usually printed on all educational materials, and especially on hunting and fishing licenses. Report details of people, vehicles, time, and exact location when you call. Don't take matters into your own hands. Let law enforcement officers use your information in a professional manner. Contact a local newspaper reporter and encourage them to expose poachers through the press. The intent is to inform the general public that sportsmen join the ranks of all concerned citizens in condemning such activities. Establish a rapport with the magistrates in your area and discourage their leniency toward poachers. Also, either individually or through an organized support group, contact your elected officials and express the need to strengthen laws relating to trespassing and poaching.

John Bruce, Tasmanian rancher and stalwart member of the Australian Deer Association and QDMA, stated that, "Poachers deserve only to be disregarded by the hunting community as they are criminally diminishing the hard-earned achievements of hunter groups."

Poaching will have an international scope until attitudes and laws are changed. Historically, poaching has been regarded lightheartedly by the general public as a Robin Hood saga. The dangers resulting from poaching are often underestimated by non-hunters and particularly the courts. When a bullet leaves the barrel of a poacher's gun a bold statement is made. They don't know where you, your family, or your guests are; therefore they are not concerned with your safety. Poachers are a bane of society and should be treated accordingly.

Note: *This article appeared in Quality Whitetails (V 12, I 4 -2005).*

CHAPTER 4

HUNTING & WOODS LORE

In my early years as a deer hunter it was art perhaps more than photos of deer that nurtured my interest in the white-tailed deer. Artists were able to capture our dreams on canvas whereas photographers were challenged by limited access to mature animals in the wild. This particular artwork, done by my aunt Kitty Fisher Cole, was a Christmas gift to me in 1962, only one year after I became a successful deer hunter.

A Hunter's Path

*"A seasoned hunter, one with the hunting spirit, pursues
his quarry on each occasion with the enthusiasm of his
first encounter and with the reverence
as though it were his last."*

Our forefathers hunted out of necessity to provide food and clothing for themselves
and their families. The surplus of their pursuits was used for trade. Those early
hunters and gatherers who flourished, I suspect, were driven by an inner force probably
unknown or unrecognized, but it was present — the hunting spirit. The pace at which
one experiences the steps of hunting is an individual process. Suffice it to say that time,
tempered by experience, is the measure. Passing from one plateau to the next as a hunter
is quite subtle. Often, only hindsight will reveal the path to the present, with the future
direction remaining vague.

It has been said that some people live and learn while others just live. So it is with
hunters, some eventually attain the hunting spirit while others simply continue to hunt.
The quest for knowledge of one's quarry appears to me to be a mark of potential to
progress to another plateau as a hunter.

In the late 1970s two professors from the LaCrosse campus of the University of Wisconsin, Drs. Robert Jackson and Robert Norton, interviewed more than 1,000 hunters to
determine their development through the hunting process. Five distinct stages or plateaus
were identified in the study. Dr. James Swan, a native of Michigan and graduate of the
University of Michigan, elaborated on these stages in his book, *In Defense of Hunting.*

The Shooter Stage. According to Dr. Swan, beginning hunters are most concerned
with having some success to demonstrate their competence. Aldo Leopold referred
to this as the trigger-itch stage in his chapter "Thinking Like a Mountain" in *A Sand
County Almanac.*

The Limiting Out Stage. Here the goal is to harvest as many animals as the law allows. It is a measure of how well a hunter is mastering the required skills.

The Trophy Stage. Hunters begin to exhibit selectivity in what they take. Having
enough information about your quarry to regulate the number and kinds harvested
is assurance that participating in this stage as a hunter will not weaken the deer herd.

The Method Stage. The hunter is much more concerned about how he/she hunts,
with an emphasis on making a quick, clean kill. Many hunters turn to archery equipment or muzzleloaders, which necessitates closer, more intimate encounters with their
quarry. Hunters in the method stage often take along a camera and derive more pleasure
in observing wildlife, thus maximizing the intensity of the hunting experience.

The Sportsman Stage. Hunters at this final stage may turn to art to express their
fondness for hunting and wildlife. They often devote considerable time and money to
managing habitat and encouraging and teaching younger people to hunt. In Dr. Swan's
opinion, this is the golden age of hunting.

Dr. Stephen Kellert, a human dimensions specialist from Yale University, had identified a growing number of what he calls Nature Hunters. These people usually are

younger, many have advanced degrees, many have studied native cultures, and all have a keen interest in nature that is maintained year-round. They enter hunting as an almost spiritual pursuit, a sort of personal calling, and often are not influenced or encouraged by parents or peers. These hunters emerge from our modern society and begin hunting in an advanced Sportsman Stage.

The development of a hunter involves passing through a series of stages or plateaus, ideally toward an ultimate destination. Somewhere along the way, with proper influence from mentors, a hunter will realize that he or she has acquired the hunting spirit. The degree to which this process can be spread universally among the masses of hunters will determine our future.

If this development process sounds familiar, it should. There is a definite parallel with the doctrines of the Quality Deer Management Association. One of our primary goals is to foster stewardship through education.

Where do you fit among the stages of hunter development? You should do some soul searching before answering this question. I encourage you to read or re-read *A Sand County Almanac* and *In Defense of Hunting*. Your interpretation of messages within these books will change with experience as a hunter. Leopold's book has been my outdoor bible for more than 35 years, and I find something "new" with each reading of the *Almanac*.

The winds of change are blowing. Mankind is extending its tentacles into the heart of vitally important wildlife habitat around the world. The hunter/gatherer societies of yesteryear that spawned the likes of us have been replaced by urban societies who view hunting with disdain. While human populations continue to increase, our hunter numbers are waning. Given these trends, an optimist, aware of the efforts of wildlife organizations and land conservationists, would offer hope for the future of hunting.

How do we ensure that this prediction has merit? We stay the course that has taken several generations to plot. We stand with pride before all for what we are — hunters. We must strive to educate all those affected by deer and foster the principles of stewardship. We must protect those natural habitat types crucial to the well-being of our quests, and ensure our continued access as hunters. There is no question whether this effort should have a united front. If one loses, we all lose. Furthermore, we must police our own ranks by providing guidance for those exhibiting unacceptable behavior. We should not be held accountable for the actions of incorrigible individuals, because they are a bane of society as well.

Hunting's future will rest firmly on the shoulders of stewards who will persevere regardless of social pressures or an uncertain future. The Quality Deer Management Association appears to be at the forefront of this movement. We must remain steadfast in our convictions. Above all else, the leaders and mentors of any such movement have a responsibility to adequately prepare their counterparts of the next generation to carry the torch.

In the words of Dr. Swan, "All the seasoned hunters I have ever known speak with quiet reverence of knowing which animal or bird to shoot. It is not something that may be felt right away. Like any practice, it takes time, but it is a sense that has been the consistent guide of master hunters since the Paleolithic (Stone Age)."

This is my creed. A seasoned hunter, one with the hunting spirit, pursues his quarry on each occasion with the enthusiasm of his first encounter and with the reverence as though it were his last. I, for one, do not want to know when I have had my last hunt.

How do I wish to be remembered? Simply this: In his chest beat the heart of a hunter — a seasoned hunter who embraced the spirit of the hunt as he lived and how he lived so that those who follow will have a secure and well-defined path.

How do you wish to be remembered?

Note: *I presented "A Hunter's Path" as an inspirational speech at the 2004 QDMA National Convention, and the article also appeared in Quality Whitetails in August 2004 (Volume 11, Issue 3).*

Stalk · Look · Listen

This is a story about stalking deer. In some parts of the country this hunting technique is called still hunting. Throughout the Southeast still hunting means just that. You sit still and leave all of the moving to the deer. Another term for still hunting is stand hunting, but confusion creeps into the conversation here because those who use hounds to pursue whitetails position their hunters on stands. This kind of stand is intangible. It is not constructed. Rather, it is a "place" — a known crossing for deer verified by fresh tracks, an obvious trail, or tradition.

Probably the most fitting description for stalking originated in southeastern North Carolina — slippin' an' tippin'. Others refer to this hunting tactic simply as slip hunting. I remember quite vividly a particular hunter's posture as he demonstrated his newly found secret. Leaning forward and sliding his feet as if he were wearing heavy snowshoes he told his story in a whisper. "That old buck was a little out of my range, so while he was busy eatin' acorns around one of my favorite huntin' oaks, I just 'Indianed' up on him."

Well, this story is going to require some digressing to set the stage. I have been accused, more than once, of introducing a topic and then talking backwards, in a chronological sense.

It should be clear to anyone schooled in quality deer management (QDM) that sex ratio and buck age structure are important deer herd characteristics. The initial stages of a QDM program focus on balancing the sex ratio and allowing more bucks to reach the older age classes. Obvious benefits include a deer density in tune with habitat conditions, healthy deer in general, and better-than-average bucks. Once buck and doe numbers are fairly even and there is an ample supply of mature bucks, the ensuing behavior has a noticeable and measurable affect on the breeding season.

Although does may be in heat, or estrous, for several days, they are receptive to bucks only during a 24-hour period. Therefore, when you observe a buck chasing a doe it means she is not quite ready to breed. Her pheromones are telling the buck not to lose interest, so he remains nearby, tending her. It is during the pursuit of a "hot" doe that a buck emits the tending grunt.

The Stalk • Look • Listen technique is tailor-made for hunting during the breeding season on a well-established QDM property. Because you are listening more than looking, you can proceed through the deer woods at a brisk pace. The objective here in contrast to stalking is to cover as much territory as possible. Remember that does have small home ranges and the window of opportunity for applying this hunting technique is narrow because does are experiencing heat rather synchronously. Thus, a quickened pace will increase your chances of encountering a chase.

Get familiar with your deer woods prior to the hunting season. Knowing that deer like cover but usually will follow the line of least resistance, which often occurs where two habitat types meet (these are called ecotones), establish a Stalk • Look • Listen course to intercept these traditional travel lanes. Take along a small pair of garden snippers to prune branches, vines, or briars that might impede your movement or create unnecessary noise. Zigzag slightly to avoid creating a vista through the woods similar to a surveyor's line. Like deer, you should follow the path of least resistance by avoiding any "stumbling blocks" like logs, large rocks, or ditches. Become familiar with your course from either end. When hunting, you will have to select your approach based on wind direction. Always walk into the wind.

Inform your hunting companions of your intentions. File a "flight plan" so everyone will know when and where you will be hunting. Dress conspicuously for other hunters. Sad as it sounds, blaze orange is worn primarily to protect you from poachers, trespassers and the like. Don't worry, recent research by University of Georgia and University of California (Berkeley) researchers confirmed that deer see orange poorly or not at all.

The Stalk • Look • Listen technique involves sneaking from shadow to shadow. Always stop next to a tree to break your image, to use as a gun rest, and to cast a protective shadow. Since you're at eye level to your quarry, wear a camouflage mask and gloves. Pay particular attention to horizontal lines: a deer's back or belly. Look for the twitch of an ear or tail. Most of all, listen for that hog-like sound of a tending buck. If the sound is getting louder, prepare yourself! You know that whatever is up front is worth taking, if does are legal at that time. Allow her to present the buck to you. If the buck is a "taker" but does not offer a good shot, just be patient and remember the small home range of does (approximately 200 acres). You'll likely have another chance if you stay put.

One rather loud grunt on a grunt tube often will stop a tending buck long enough for you to get a good look and perhaps a good shot if he is what you want. If the courting pair is moving through dense cover, scan the terrain in the direction they are traveling and pick out an adequate shooting hole. Just as the buck enters that small opening, GRUNT!

When moving through your course, take a few steps, pause, and repeat. If wild turkeys inhabit your hunting area, you might consider yelping with a diaphragm as you move. Deer are apt to be less wary of "turkeys" shuffling along in the leaves than a "predator" sneaking quietly along. Hurry through open woods and rely on your eyes. When approaching or skirting thickets slow your pace and listen. A tending chase often is rather noisy. Listen for splashing, rustling leaves, and snapping dead limbs as well as the tending grunt.

Remember that the Stalk • Look • Listen tactic is most effective during the peak of the rut. My favorite hunting time is early morning, but deer don't punch the clock while courting, so try it all day long. By contrast, stalking is most effective during the crepuscular period: early morning and late afternoon.

While writing the details of this hunting method I decided to visit my lease and literally walk through each paragraph to see if any hints had been omitted. You know, sometimes things are done subconsciously. Therefore, sitting at a desk and writing about outdoor activities has its shortcomings. Field trips are good for writers, too.

The occasion was recent, September 27, 1994. As I walked along a logging road bordering a 10-year-old pine plantation my thoughts "jumped time" to last December. A few days after Christmas I was stalking this same logging road, but from the other direction. A fickle wind betrayed me and a large buck snorted indignantly, whirled, and bounded across the road. The pine plantation engulfed him as if it were hungry for venison, too. Conditions were poor for a shot, but my trusty binoculars captured the antlers — long points and a wide spread. He was so impressive that I watched his trail mornings and afternoons the next four days until season's end. Such bucks command a permanent spot in one's memory. We were destined to cross paths again.

A particularly large deer track crossing the road shocked me back from December '93. Within the next 50 yards that track and a smaller, slender one crossed the road half a dozen times. These were the tracks of a chase! That narrow window of opportunity, the rut, had opened. I knelt for a close inspection of the tracks. Tiny clumps of dirt kicked from the tracks' rims were still wet. Knowing they air dry quickly, I realized that this chase was taking place right now. Immediately I clicked into the third phase of my Stalk • Look • Listen mode. The "crack" of a stick sent me to the nearest pine for support. The doe jumped from the pine thicket into the road and was gone in another leap. Massive antlers exploded from the same trail that he had used last December to elude me. I was prepared this time, and my new rifle, a wedding present, became duly christened.

This buck will be revered during future firepot gatherings as the best of my lifetime. Antler measurements rank him with the famous Magnolia Buck and other top-of-the-line bucks from our neighborhood.

Quality deer management produces animals we are not accustomed to hunting — mature bucks. The QDMA provides information through seminars, videos, and publications to help us hunt smarter. Knowing the what, why, and when of deer behavior encourages the development of tactics like the Stalk • Look • Listen method. Give it a try and perhaps you and that buck of a lifetime will cross paths.

Note: *This article appeared in Quality Whitetails (Fall 1994).*

Rainy Day Stalk

This is a story involving a veteran hunter, an unscoped Marlin 30-30, 10 x 40 binoculars, and ideal stalking conditions — a light drizzle and a constant gentle breeze. My relationship with the 30-30 spans four decades and it remains my weapon of choice for stalking thickets. While visiting the "Father" of quality deer management, Al Brothers, in Texas during the early 1980s, I learned the importance of using good optics for hunting and wildlife observation. Aside from personal restraints, a stalker's primary nemesis is a fickle wind.

The setting is a South Carolina lowcountry plantation with extensive rice fields, now managed primarily for waterfowl and deer. Heavy rains marked the beginning of this November morning. Deer season had been going strong since mid-August. Eleven weeks of hunting pressure combined with nasty weather would certainly keep deer in the most remote recesses of the property.

By noon the rain had diminished to a drizzle, so the time was right for a stalk. An aerial photograph solved the dilemma of where to hunt. The grid pattern of rice fields revealed miles of canals flanked by densely vegetated banks. Deer use these canal banks as travel lanes and bedding areas, especially during foul weather.

My quest began at the southern end of a north-south bank. The breeze, barely perceptible at times, was quartering steadily from the northeast. An hour passed and only a couple of hundred yards were traversed. Each step of the way was preceded by methodical study of both canal banks through my binoculars.

During my earlier days as a novice stalker, I hunted without the aid of binoculars. In those days the forays were deerless — yielding only glimpses of white flags and indignant snorts. Eagle eyes are useless on fleet feet! Stalking deer is a slow man's sport.

Thirty minutes later and another hundred yards — still nothing but a few startled gallinules scooting across the 15-foot-wide canal and into cattails along the opposite bank. Such distractions can break a predator's train of thought and alert his resting quarry. I knew deer were HERE and maintained my composure and a snail's pace.

The binoculars were trained on a small opening in the brush about 20 yards away and on the opposite bank. Gently adjusting the focus allowed me to penetrate the cover one twig at a time. An antler tip emerged from the blur. A little fine-tuning of the binoculars and a main beam with two points and a brow tine developed. Jubilation overwhelmed me. I had stalked within a stone's throw of a bedded buck — possibly an eight-point monarch. Davy Crockett, my childhood hero, would have been proud, I thought. Nevertheless, I was numbed by my accomplishment.

Taking a buck was out of the question. My hunting arrangement on this property was to take does only, so a mature doe was the order of the day, although the thrill of hunting mature bucks remains the same whether they're pursued with gun, camera, or binoculars.

Two carefully placed steps produced a better view. Seven points and a 17-inch spread. What a magnificent buck! I can't believe how tight he's holding. He doesn't even know that I'm HERE, too. Those raucous gallinules didn't give me away after all. A good set of binoculars is not capable of compensating for an excited hunter's blurred vision. Sud-

denly, reality sobered me. I could see nasal bones — that's a cotton-pickin' skull! All my stealth and pride of accomplishment had been wasted on a pile of bleached deer bones. If old bucks go to the happy hunting grounds, I'll bet this hunt made him smile.

Before taking another step, I peered through a keyhole size opening on my bank. Two does were standing under the spindly branches of a young live oak, just 12 yards away. Their preoccupation with mutual grooming allowed me the opportunity to recover. Otherwise, history would have repeated itself — I would have proceeded carelessly, creating a second deerless blunder. Perhaps experience was slowly elevating me from the status as novice stalker to a higher level attained by my predatory ancestors whose survival hinged on stealth.

Realizing my purpose for the stalk, the doe with the longest head, the oldest, became the next entry into our property's data-collection log book. Once the necessary biological information was recorded (98 pounds, 3½ years old, twin female fetuses, 45 days old) the object of my quest was field dressed and placed on a hook in the walk-in cooler for a 10-day aging period.

I returned to the rice field bank late that afternoon to collect my other trophy — the buck's skull. As I approached the scattered bones a small basket-racked eight-point buck sprang from his bed only 10 yards away. The oval bed was DRY! Each of us was a bit wiser when that day ended because we shared a ringside seat in the drama. He, too, will remember my rainy day stalk.

Note: *This article appeared in Quality Whitetails (V 6, I 3 - 1999).*

Scouting

Scouting is a catch-all term that describes most non-hunting activities in the deer woods. It is a good excuse to get away from mundane things and go exploring, always in preparation for the hunting season.

Years ago I followed a set of human tracks that took me in circles, backtracking, and zigzagging through the woods. Deer rubs, scrapes, droppings, beds, and trails were encountered during my search. Finally, the tracks led to a young fellow sitting on a log. He appeared to be staring at something far away. In fact, he was so intent that I caught myself glancing frequently toward whatever he was looking at as I approached.

Dry leaves covered the ground, so sneaking up on him was out of the question. I made no effort to disguise my footsteps. When I was nearly an arm's length away, he sprang to his feet, emitted a blood-curdling yell, and assumed a semi-crouched position — like the stance of an offensive tackle in a high school yearbook. Startled by his response, I struck the same position. There we were, face to face, frozen in time like two opponents ready for battle. The mood relaxed when I asked, "Are you scouting for deer?" A weak "Yep" came from the track maker. "Seen any promising sign?" was my attempt to strike up a conversation. "Nope," was his only reply. What did he mean? I had been up to my ears in fresh deer sign for the past hour — a hunter's dream.

I had some scouting of my own to do. Either this nimrod was trying to protect a remote treasure, assuming I didn't recognize deer sign, or he was plain lost. I took a seat on the log, fetched a pipe from my coat pocket, painstakingly filled it with tobacco, and searched from pocket to pocket for a pack of matches. At last, with lighted match in hand, my attention turned to a distant woodpecker wrecking a rotten limb in search of some unsuspecting arthropod larvae. My all-the-time-in-the-world attitude was in full swing. The track maker finally broke the silence. "You, uh, heading out of the woods anytime, you know, soon?" "Yep," I replied. "Well, uh, if you wouldn't mind the company, I'll just tag along." He wasn't lonesome, he was LOST!

My scouting session had been successful on two counts. Not only had a promising hunting spot been discovered, but I also knew the track maker would never cross my path again. His chances of ever finding this remote spot were zilch.

Scouting is not just a walk in the woods. An ardent scouter knows plants (for food and cover), soils, weather, and animal behavior. Hunters who are successful year after year usually are the ones who consider scouting an important part of their preparation for hunting. We've known since grammar grades that homework pays off.

Have you ever had a classmate who never appears to get in enough studying? Well, I know of a deer hunter who takes his scouting that seriously. When one of his companions asks another of this fellow's whereabouts, the standard response is: "He's probably scouting." In fact, he would be labeled a perpetual scouter. With him, studying deer sign is a chronic behavioral pattern, so much so that he rarely finds time to hunt.

While anything can be taken to the extreme, there is some credence to scouting during times of the year other than the preseason "rush." Postseason scouting, particularly between late winter and early spring, can produce a wealth of knowledge. Deer trails are more obvious than during any other season. This is also a prime time to scout for

shed antlers.

A shed antler bears testimony of survival and spawns hope for next hunting season. Finding one is an educational process as well. Survey the dimensions: main beam length, number and lengths of points, and basal circumference. These measurements will enable a seasoned scouter to determine the previous owner's age class.

Antlers collected through a methodical search of your hunting territory should be cataloged according to location and date. Where an antler is found reveals a buck's favorite haunts, whereas the date will indicate the animal's condition. Generally, bucks in optimum health will carry their

The annual collection of shed antlers should be labeled by location and date.

antlers later into winter before shedding. Thus, a scouter worth his salt can survey the fall mast crop and predict the peak of antler drop. Abundant acorns mean a late drop and so on. Abundant acorns also mean that more bucks will pass through the hunting season unscathed. Food availability and hunting success have an inverse relationship. When one is up the other is down.

Such are the gleanings of a perpetual scouter. I confess to having this chronic condition, as well. There's only one thing that can hold a candle to deer hunting, and that is scouting — preparing to hunt deer.

Scouting on an area that is being managed for quality deer is quite different from scouting on traditionally hunted lands. The difference is in determining where mature bucks are rather than bumping around, essentially in the dark, to discover IF there are any around.

Note: *This article appeared in Quality Whitetails (V 7, I 1 - 2000)*

The size of rubbed trees usually increases as bucks mature in a QDM program.

Readin' Sign

Rumor has it that several freshman wildlife students were on a stroll in the woods and happened upon a set of animal tracks. One, who considered himself an outdoorsman, studied the tracks for a moment and commented, "Those were made by a deer, weren't they?" "Obviously," was the reply from a surprised classmate. The outdoorsman continued his observation of the tracks, then looked to the left and to the right. "Which direction was the deer going when he made these tracks?"

While readin' sign is a challenge to some, it is second nature to others. In fact, I met a deer hunter years ago who took scouting for sign so seriously that it became a year-round activity, an obsession. His intrigue with finding and interpreting rubs, scrapes, and tracks of all sizes and shapes was such that deer seasons came and went without a hunting trip ever being taken. Scouting prevailed.

My profession has taken me to the brink of being a perpetual scout, as well. Aldo Leopold, the first professor of wildlife management (University of Wisconsin, 1939-1948), influenced my thought processes as he did those of his students. Biographer Curt Meine wrote of Leopold's ability to have his students view the environment as a collection of separate but interrelated parts. On field trips, Professor Leopold would ask, "Why is that plant growing over there and not here?" He wanted his students to see the subtle differences in topography and to understand that an elevation change in inches could result in a transition to another soil type and that soil types have differing abilities to retain moisture and nutrients. The presence of an individual plant or a community of plants reflects a particular soil type's supportive capacity. In essence, some plants thrive in well-drained soils while other species must have their feet (roots) wet to survive. Asking "why" was Professor Leopold's first step toward having his students make an observation and then ponder the ramifications of change. In current day terms, he was encouraging the burgeoning scientists to think outside of the box.

Last fall, after four years of drought conditions, my neighborhood oaks reflected their stress. A scant acorn production was the symptom. As deer season progressed, I noticed a decline in average body weights among buck and doe age classes compared with previous years. Late in the season a number of adult does were observed to have a single fetus. Between Christmas and the New Year there were reports of bucks being harvested as does — they had already shed their antlers. I began finding cast antlers early in January. To substantiate my observations I positioned a camera in a well-used food plot and kept it active until March. The occurrences of antlered bucks decreased appreciably through January and there were none after mid-February. By contrast, in years of abundant acorns, weights are higher, adult does usually have twin fetuses, and bucks carry their antlers much longer, even into March.

Spring has arrived and turkey season has been open for three weeks. I have been visiting local check stations recently and thumbing through the data sheets filled out by successful hunters. The trend in weights of adult gobblers could have been predicted accurately after following the turn of events during deer season. Throughout most of the region there has been a decline in the number of 20-pound gobblers harvested, compared with previous seasons. A failed acorn crop has far reaching implications.

Readin' sign is not always a straightforward process even among wildlife professionals. It appears that as the number of factors increases, so does the difficulty of determining the cause(s) and effect(s). The plight of the bobwhite quail across the Southeast is an appropriate case in point. There is absolutely no dissention regarding the effect — quail populations have plummeted within the past quarter of a century. The list of potential causes would stagger one's imagination.

A ban on DDT, the chemical that caused thinning of egg shells particularly among birds of prey, resulted in a tremendous increase in avian predators at a time when stronger penalties were initiated to protect hawks, owls, and eagles from being shot, trapped, or poisoned.

Supporters of the anti-trapping movement targeted animal fur clothing by putting a social stigma on public display of such garments. Their ploy was effective, the economic incentive for trappers was removed, and furbearers, including many that present obstacles in quail management, are now having their first "hay day" since the colonization of America. Countless species of birds that nest in tree cavities or on the ground are paying the ultimate price for the naive actions of anti-trappers and the liberation of raccoons. Although well intentioned, these folks were not adept at readin' sign. Assuming that reason would have prevailed over emotion, many anti-trappers would have lost the zeal for their cause if the ramifications of their actions were known. Maybe not! Perhaps they should experience the thunder of a covey rise, or that bundle of yellow feathers, the prothonotary warbler, flitting from one cypress knee to another along a blackwater swamp. Those who fish in blackwater swamps of the Southeast refer to prothonotary warblers as "swamp canaries." These neotropical migrants nest in natural cavities usually only arm's reach away from hungry raccoons. Without the financial incentive to control raccoon numbers through hunting and trapping, many cavity nesters pay the ultimate price — yet another prime example of cause and effect.

Fire ants, armadillos, and coyotes now occupy a significant portion of quail habitat throughout the Southeast. All three of these animals are known predators of quail and/or their nests. The fire ant also is a major competitor for food, especially with young quail which are dependent on an insect diet.

Small farms have become artifacts, replaced by farming conglomerates that operate in vast acreages of agricultural fields. These corporate operations are known for their "clean farming," a practice that eliminates any vestige of quail habitat. During a period from the mid-1940s to the mid-1950s, approximately 10 million acres of agricultural lands were converted to forests. That trend continued on the heels of declining soybean and corn production and was accelerated by governmentally subsidized programs to create pine plantations in agricultural areas. Collectively, these changes in land use resulted in a noticeable decline in the amount and quality of quail habitat.

Another factor that we are quite familiar with is the white-tailed deer, an animal whose numbers have doubled since the early 1980s. Today's 32 million whitetails occupy a significant portion of the bobwhite's range and browse on a variety of plant species known to produce seeds that are vitally important to quail.

Cultivating your savvy at readin' sign can provide hours of relaxation and entertainment in the field. Take it too far, way outside of the box, and you might just end up confused or frustrated. In that regard, my hat is off to present-day quail managers who must contend with an overwhelming array of uncontrollable factors. Their commitment is the epitome of optimism.

As for me, I'm going to throttle back, resume my quest for that broad, blunt track in my deer woods and ponder the possibility of crossing paths with its maker next fall.
Note: *This article appeared in Quality Whitetails (V 10, I 2 - 2003).*

Shooting Sticks

Several years ago a hunting companion and I began making walking sticks from the dead lower limbs of eastern red cedar trees. If you have never worked with this wood you will understand our preference for cedar. The fragrance, red color, and the wood's texture and light weight provide the perfect combination for such a stick.

Trips afield were not complete without a walking stick. We became so accustomed to using a stick on woods walks that when hunting season rolled around we had another "prop." Traversing rough terrain became much easier with the aid of this third leg. You actually can move through the woods much quieter by using the stick. When stepping over a rock or tree limb, place the stick firmly on the ground in front of you to help maintain balance and control foot placement.

The walking stick acquired an additional purpose when I was stalking deer. For some uncanny reason a tree is never quite close enough to be used as a gun prop when a deer is seen. Those few extra steps to the nearest tree can alert a deer of your presence. That problem has been solved. The walking stick became that necessary "tree" for steadying my gun. Continued use increased my competence and confidence. My walking stick is referred to affectionately now as my "shooting stick." It has become as important in my list of hunting gear as my binoculars and rifle. In fact, if I could choose only two items for a quality hunt they would be my binoculars and the shooting stick.

Shooting sticks can be used in a variety of hunting conditions and their length and shape can match the situation. When stalking, I prefer a stick that is eye level in height.

The top of the stick is grooved (for a rifle rest) and cut at an angle so that it resembles a deer track. The point of the "track" is held away from you. Hold the stick vertically at three-quarter arm's length. The rifle's elevation can be adjusted by extending your arm to lower it or bending your arm more to raise it.

Stalking (still hunting in some camps) is a combination of slipping along quietly with frequent stops at locations providing a good vantage point of some likely deer crossing. I seek a large tree for such stops and lean back against it for support and to break my silhouette. Always stop in a shady spot. Place the rifle's forearm on top of the shooting stick and put the butt firmly under your armpit. You can maintain this stance comfortably for 5-10 minutes, and then proceed quietly to another "leaning" tree. When the opportunity arises for a shot, leaning firmly against a tree and supporting your rifle on the shooting stick increases accuracy.

Try this stalking tip. If leaf fall has occurred and moving quietly is difficult because of dry leaves, take along a diaphragm turkey call and yelp between stops. This technique has proven very successful for me.

Ladder stands are popular throughout deer country. The simplest ones are comprised of a ladder and seat, while others are equipped with a rifle rest. For those without a rest, a forked shooting stick can be used. Attach a horizontal brace two to three feet below the seat from both sides of the ladder to the tree. When shooting to the left or right the forked end of the stick can rest vertically on the horizontal brace. The top rung of the ladder can provide support for the forked stick when shooting directly in front of the stand. Grip the shooting stick and point your index finger at the intended target. You'll be amazed at how this technique will enhance your accuracy. We owe it to our quarry to avoid off-hand shots if at all possible. A shorter shooting stick can be used on ladder stands than the one for stalking.

During my younger years of deer hunting I was as at home in trees as squirrels. Father time has strengthened my affinity for the ground. One of my favorite stands now is a strait-backed chair painted forest green. But this stand is not complete without my shooting stick. I use my stalking-length stick and the hand position described for ladder stands. Also, this stand arrangement necessitates some degree of camouflaging with natural vegetation. Position the chair to face a well-used deer crossing and concentrate your attention on that one spot, since your freedom of movement while sitting is limited.

The use of shooting sticks dates back to the days of buffalo hunting out west. Stalkers in the Scottish Highlands use shooting sticks in pursuit of the majestic red deer. And tripod shooting sticks are popular among plains game hunters in Africa.

When using a rifle rest of any design, NEVER NEVER NEVER place the rifle barrel on the rest for shooting. The bullet's point of impact is dramatically affected.

The time has come for the shooting stick to be added to the ardent whitetail hunter's list of necessities. It is yet another way to show respect for your quarry by enhancing accuracy.

Note: *This article appeared in Quality Whitetails (V 3, I 2 - 1996).*

A Visit to the Rifle Range

Summer afternoons provide a fine time to make sure your rifle, ammunition, and scope are performing well. Preseason shooting is absolutely necessary, and checks during the hunting season are advised. Once a suitable combination of bullet weight and type, powder, and casing is achieved, avoid changes during the season. This can have a noticeable effect on "point of impact."

Learning birds by sight and sound can enhance hunting experiences. Bird activity and particularly alarm calls can alert hunters of an approaching deer. This is a common yellowthroat.

Last hunting season, one of the club members returned to the firepot rather long-faced after the evening hunt. As it was, his hunt had ended nearly two hours before dark. Accompanied by his young son, Dargan, for his first time in the deer woods, Roger had packed too quickly for the hunting trip. His .270 shells were left at home. He could not find his usual brand, but a box of the same weight shells was purchased at a country store only a few miles from the hunting property. They arrived at the club, signed in for a particular stand, and were off to the woods. Why the hurry? October had arrived and the older bucks were in their seasonal courtship stupor. You've got to strike while the iron is hot.

In the elevated stand with the rifle propped in one corner, Roger and his sidekick were busy with their binoculars. No deer moving yet; only some masked warblers flitting among the pine limbs flanking the stand. "Hey Dad, what kind of birds are they?" "Don't know, but I'll soon find out," the mentor replied. As Roger leaned over to retrieve the *Peterson's Field Guide* from his day pack, he saw the dark form of a deer gliding quietly through the pines just 75 yards away. When the deer entered a clearing, Roger was propped against the side of the stand with rifle ready. There was no reason to glass this buck's antlers with binoculars. He had 12 points and main beams that extended well beyond his ear tips, probably a 21- or 22-inch spread. The crosshairs settled on the massive shoulder as naturally as a compass needle points northward. Take a deep breath, release most of it, squeeze…boom! The buck looked to the left, then to the right, lowered his head, and resumed feeding. "How could I have missed? I had a steady rest…oh, no! The ammunition! It must have been the reason. I'm not going to risk a crippling shot. That's what I get for not testing my rifle with this new ammunition before hunting today." As luck would have it, a nice 10-pointer joined the other buck for an afternoon snack of lush wheat. He was studied through binoculars but the rifle remained in its corner, as if it were placed there for punishment. It was!

Incidentally, those feathered visitors were common yellowthroats. A lesson had been learned the hard way, but Roger also taught a lesson as he shared his hunt with us around the firepot that evening. He gave both bucks the benefit of the doubt by refusing to fire a second "stray" bullet.

I sat there, gazing into the glowing coals and feeling proud to be a hunting companion, but wishing all the while that 10,000 deer hunters could have been at fireside to hear Roger's story. "I'll never switch ammunition again without going to the rifle range," he said, "…and I'll always recognize a common yellowthroat when we're face to face. It was a good hunt after all."

Note: *This article was edited from the book: Quality Whitetails – The Why and How of Quality Deer Management. (Published in 1995).*

Leopold benches and a rocking bench surround the author's firepot.

Build Your Own Leopold Bench

S oon after Aldo Leopold became the nation's first professor of wildlife biology (game management) in the 1930s he purchased a 120-acre farm just north of Madison, Wisconsin. He wanted a weekend retreat from what he referred to as "...too much modernity." Owning a farm also would provide the Leopold family with an opportunity to practice land husbandry.

An old chicken coop was converted into rustic living quarters and affectionately called "the shack." Leopold designed and built benches for lawn furniture. They were simple, yet comfortable.

A Leopold bench will add flavor to any outdoor setting, whether it is a patio, a favorite spot in the flower garden or beside a hunting camp.

Treated pine is the most accessible wood for this project. Cost for the wood and hardware will run approximately $35 per bench. However, ingenious "scroungers" can reduce the cost and add a personal touch by using other woods, including oak, cherry, cypress, western red cedar, eastern red cedar, or Atlantic white cedar (locally called juniper).

Authentic Leopold benches are made of two-inch-thick stock, so these plans are tailored accordingly. Remember, commercially prepared boards are narrower than stated. For example, a 2 x 10 is actually 1½ x 9¼ inches, and measurements vary slightly.

Here's what you'll need (measurements are in inches):

Two 2 x 8 x 42 front leg boards

Two 2 x 8 x 24 rear leg boards

One 2 x 10 x 46 bench seat board

One 2 x 10 x 49 backrest board (to reach outside edges of front legs)

Six 5/16 x 3 carriage bolts with nuts and washers

Twelve three-inch deck screws to secure backrest to front leg supports and to secure

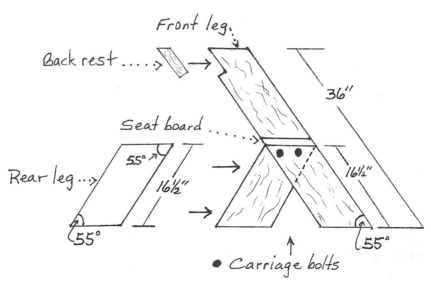

Assembly diagram by the author.

bench seat to tops of rear leg supports.

Cut the ends of the front legs at a 55-degree angle, with an overall length of 36 inches. Cut the ends of the rear legs at a 55-degree angle, with an overall length of 16½ inches. Cut the bench seat to your desired length, but a 46-inch seat is adequate for two people.

The backrest should be cut to reach outside of the tops of the front legs (49 inches). Adjust your saw to a 35-degree angle and cut the top edge of the backrest. This will allow the backrest to fit flush with the tops of the front legs.

Cut a notch for the backrest to fit into in the backside of the top portion of each front leg.

To assemble the bench, draw a line at a 55-degree angle on the inside of each front leg 16½ inches from the bottom of the leg. Align the rear leg with the pencil mark on the front leg, secure with a C-clamp and drill three 5/16-inch holes through both legs. Countersink the holes on the inside of the legs to allow for a washer and a nut. Insert the carriage bolts from the outside, place a washer and a nut on each bolt, and tighten.

Drill three holes the diameter of the deck screws through the bench seat one inch from the ends. Position the bench and secure it to the top of each rear leg using the three-inch deck screws.

Drill three holes in each end of the backrest. Attach the backrest to the "cut-out" section of the tops of the front legs using the three-inch deck screws.

When assembled, a bench can be painted, stained, treated with a waterproofing sealant or tung oil, or simply allowed to weather naturally.

Note: *This article appeared in Quality Whitetails (V 3, 1 2 – 1996).*

John Moran

Some bucks approach within close range when rattled in.

Calling All Bucks?

By Joe Hamilton and Al Brothers

Quality deer management can now go hand-in-hand with a type of deer hunting gaining popularity throughout the whitetail's range — rattling. For years hunters have been rattling antlers to "call" bucks in south Texas. This particular hunting technique is most effective in areas with an even adult sex ratio and numerous bucks in the 2½ and older age classes, thus the relationship to quality deer management.

Antler rattling and other calling techniques could have a negative impact on deer populations already exhibiting disproportionate sex ratios and high densities. For this reason, hunters must be informed about all aspects of calling deer, the shortcomings, dangers, and possible long-term consequences to the resource.

Rattling definitely is an exciting hunting technique. Areas that have been involved in QDM probably have enough older bucks to make rattling worthwhile. Because older bucks are sly, this hunting technique can become an effective means of harvesting when conventional methods fail to produce.

Before undertaking rattling, all hunters should be aware of the need for utmost caution and safety. Antler rattling and spring turkey hunting share many similarities. Bucks and gobblers exhibit similar responses to "calling." Some approach with reckless

When called by rattling or grunting, bucks usually surprise the hunter by simply materializing at close range. Don't rely on your sense of hearing — you will be embarrassed. Only the buck's antlers and ears are visible in this photo.

abandon while older and more experienced animals may use all available cover and sneak in cautiously. Others appear to disregard calls altogether.

The buddy system is a safe way to rattle. One person can rattle while the other observes from the ground, a nearby tree, or from an elevated stand. Take precaution that a distant hunter doesn't mistake you and your antler rattling for the real thing — fighting bucks. Wear international orange and refrain from using white antlers. Brown or black shoe polish will reduce bleached antlers' visibility and make for safer hunting.

Alert all fellow hunters of the precise location where you intend to rattle, and NEVER rattle on public wildlife management areas since you can't be sure of other hunters' proximity.

Skilled hunters know that rub locations occur in association with a buck's travel lanes between feeding and bedding areas, whereas scrapes more closely coincide with courtship and breeding. Timing is of the utmost importance in rattling. Since breeding seasons may vary from region to region, scout an area often to detect an increase in scraping frequency. Rattling is most effective just prior to and immediately after peak breeding activity.

When selecting your firearm, remember that most shots will be at close range. An unscoped rifle permits quick handling. If you prefer a scope, low magnification is recommended. Archers, as well, will find rattling an enjoyable method of hunting.

Antler rattling, like other hunting techniques, is a privilege that can be easily abused. Familiarize yourself with its limitations and portray the image of a true sportsman while enjoying the atmosphere of deer country. If all of the conditions for antler rattling prove favorable, you will see more bucks than ever before. You may want to take along a camera so you can share your experiences with others. Photographing a nice buck at close range makes an outstanding framed "trophy" for your wall. Also, when using a camera, there is no limit on the number of bucks than can be "shot".

Finding a suitable location to rattle should be no problem. Bucks prefer to travel habitat edges, old logging roads, and along streams. Fresh scrapes indicate good locations for rattling. Lean or sit against a tree large enough to conceal yourself with several smaller trees or bushes around it and face downwind. Bucks usually approach upwind. If you like, use a scent to mask human odor.

Antlers used for rattling need not be massive. A normal-sized eight-point set is sufficient. Remove the brow points to provide a better grip and avoid mashing fingers and thumbs during rattling. Wearing gloves provides a comfortable degree of protection. Just be sure the gloves don't interfere with your ability to handle your firearm. If you have trouble finding a set of real antlers, check the ads in sporting magazines for synthetic antlers or other rattling devices. Laws prohibit the buying or selling of deer antlers in some states.

Thrash a bush or small tree with the antlers. Pause a few moments, then gently put the antlers together and rattle for 15 to 30 seconds with a slow grinding motion. During the initial rattling phase only, thrash your feet in the leaves to simulate a scuffle, but conceal your movements to avoid being detected by an incoming buck.

Hold the antlers in your choice of a variety of positions: two-handed (with both antlers straight-away or with one antler toward you and the other straight-away), or one-handed (in a semi-kneeling position, stand on one antler base and rattle with another antler that is hand-held). The latter method is best for concealment and handling your gun or camera if you are alone.

Wait three to five minutes and rattle again more vigorously. If a rattling session fails to produce results in 15 to 20 minutes chances are that additional rattling there will prove fruitless, even though hunters with more experience at modifying the sequence may remain longer in a location. After a reasonable period of no results, quietly move to another location at least a quarter of a mile away and repeat the sequence.

Grunt calls can be used while rattling because fighting bucks often emit grunting and groaning sounds. When used alone, grunt calls may be more effective than rattling. Experience has proven that approaching bucks are less wary when lured by grunting. The two scenarios the caller is simulating are quite different.

Rattling is associated with two adult bucks in a dispute, usually over a doe in heat. Grunting is the sound that a tending buck emits while in pursuit of a doe in heat. An intruder in this case is approaching to displace a subordinate buck.

Calling bucks by grunting is a lot like calling turkey gobblers. There are personal preferences for calling sequence and the volume to be used. Terrain, vegetation density, and weather conditions also determine the technique of calling. Experience is the best teacher.

You should grunt with a two- or three-call sequence much like the basic three-yelp turkey call. Pause for a few minutes and grunt again. If a buck is approaching inquisitively, increase the frequency of grunts. Unlike turkeys, bucks are unable to pinpoint the source of your calls. Occasionally, a buck will stand 10 yards away so intent on seeing another buck chasing a doe that the caller is ignored.

Some bucks, especially subordinate animals, are repelled by calling. This usually happens when such a buck makes an unsolicited approach before the caller begins. The result is a flash of white tail. Calling "blind" (without having a deer in sight) is the most effective technique for beginning a calling sequence.

Grunt calls are useful in stopping a walking buck to provide a better look with binoculars or to get the crosshairs on him. Especially if the cover is thick, take a quick glance in the direction the buck is moving and choose a "window." Just as the buck is approaching the opening, make a single grunt and the buck will stop in his tracks — sometimes. It's worth trying though, because without giving a grunt, you wouldn't have a shot at all.

Attracting bucks by rattling or the use of grunt calls is exciting, yet can be frustrating. Some older fellows out there simply have their own agenda. Others approach and retreat with such stealth that you are left with the impression that nothing responded. Here are some tried and true "excuses" to keep in mind when your best efforts fail to put you in contact with a top-of-line buck on your hunting property.

- Even in the best managed deer herds, bucks of this caliber exist as a small percent of the total bucks. Some herds have none.
- During the rut these dominant, top-of-the line bucks are tending an estrous doe. It is extremely rare, if not impossible, to call such a buck away from is courtship.
- Bucks in this category are usually five years old and older and have honed their survival skills through experiences with hunters.
- Overcast skies with a slight breeze produce the most favorable calling conditions. Bucks are less responsive to calling during "bluebird" weather — clear and calm.

Don't become discouraged. Calling is effective at putting you in touch with those better-than-average bucks. Older, more crafty bucks must be patterned and pursued prior to the rut by still hunting or stalking (Indian-style) in their favorite haunts — the thickets. Manage your deer herd properly and the challenge will await your call. After all, isn't that one of our primary reasons for hunting?

Note: *This article appeared in Quality Whitetails (V 2, I 3 - 1995).*

Lessons of the Last Hunt

With the 2001 hunting season upon us, have you taken the time to reflect on the last hunt of the previous season? Where were you? Did you see or harvest a deer? Did you have mixed emotions of accomplishment, relief, and regret as sundown approached?

Deer hunters are more mobile today than ever before. Many of us have opportunities to hunt on numerous properties in our neighborhood and even in other states, provinces and foreign countries. Therefore, each hunting season results in an accumulation of last hunts. Something strange occurs with our psyches during the closing hours or minutes of a final hunt. Some fall prey to relaxed commitment to the management program and harvest an animal that would not have been taken earlier. There is often a feeling of desperation that ensues with the realization of this being a last hunt, especially on an area where the hunter is a guest, has no vested interest, and suffers no consequences. Conversely, seasoned hunters are keenly aware of such feelings and exemplify control even in trying conditions. This is a primary tenet of quality deer management: the

A typical Texas sunset marking the end of a day's hunting.

ethical pursuit of our quarry.

Last season I had the privilege of archery hunting on a Texas ranch in October. On the third and final day of the hunt our host stopped the pickup on a gas line right-of-way. He glassed several deer at a distance of 500 yards and said, "There's your buck, that big old eight-point with two smaller bucks. Good luck…we'll see you after dark."

The path of my stalk was scalloped, moving quietly through the brush and approaching the gas line perimeter every 50 yards or so and glassing to see if the bucks remained in position. My main concern while stalking was bumping into other deer along the way and having my presence announced.

Finally, I was within 100 yards of the feeding bucks when the massive eight-pointer walked across the opening and into the brush on the opposite side of the right-of-way. Without hesitation, I dropped to all fours and began crossing the gas line — like a javalina, which deer there encounter regularly. Several times I paused and glanced at the two smaller bucks. They appeared more interested in the oats and paid me no attention.

When I entered the brush a convenient cow path lead me in the direction of the massive eight-pointer. He had left the gas line at a 45-degree angle toward a line of mesquite trees. Once intersecting the mesquites, I glassed the thick underbrush. The buck was nowhere to be seen. Had I moved too quickly and spooked him? From the edge of a small clearing I took a stand and waited. Nothing! The long stalk had consumed valuable time and daylight was fading with each minute.

Instead of stalking blindly, I decided to stand my ground and attempt grunting the buck into range. Despite being cotton-mouthed with excitement, I managed to utter three short grunts. The buck responded immediately by thrashing a bush with his antlers. He was about 50 yards away, but still out of sight. With bow raised and knocked arrow vibrating to the pulse of my heartbeat, I waited. All was quiet. I grunted again and the buck attacked another bush much closer. As the veil of darkness engulfed us, we stood poised as predator and prey in the last hunt without ever making eye contact.

Oddly enough, while strolling along in the darkness to meet my host, I remembered a favorite Aldo Leopold quote about trout fishing. It seemed appropriate for the occasion. "I shall now confess to you that none of those three trout had to be beheaded, or folded double, to fit their casket. What was big was not the trout, but the chance. What was full was not my creel, but my memory."

That "big ol' eight-pointer" thrilled another hunter later during the gun season. His massive rack measured 21 inches wide and scored in the mid-140s. I will treasure the sundown shared with that Texas buck and hope that he was revered in his last hunt.

Yes, I remember where I was on the last hunt of the 2000 season. Just before dark on the closing afternoon I saw a young eight-point buck from my stand on the Leather Britches Hunt Club in the lowcountry of South Carolina. If all went well for him through winter, spring and summer, his presence will flavor this upcoming season.

A quality hunter pursues the noble whitetail on each trip afield with the enthusiasm of the first hunt, and the reverence as though it were the last hunt. I must confess proudly that within me beats the heart of a hunter, and I never want to know when I have had my last hunt!

Note: *This article appeared in Quality Whitetails (V 8, I 4 - 2001).*

The Making of a Deer Hunter

By Joe Hamilton and Michael Blackburn

Usually, when a hunt is over it's over. This is the story of a hunt that took nearly a year to unfold, but it was certainly worth the wait. When I returned to South Carolina from my October hunt on the King Ranch in 2000 there was a long list of "what ifs" to consider. My hunt came to a close as sundown dropped a veil of darkness between me and a superb eight-point buck that I had stalked all afternoon. We were only 30 yards apart in the end, but we eventually parted ways in the dark.

When considering distances, I looked at a map of the U.S. and located my home and the King Ranch — hundreds of miles apart. The afternoon of the hunt, we spotted the large eight-point approximately 500 yards away. Following a seemingly long stalk, the buck and I stood only a stone's throw apart. During the stalemate, I was influenced by my years of experience with deer in the lowcountry of South Carolina. It seemed appropriate to hold my position and call the buck to within range and an open shot. What if I had been more aggressive and stalked closer? From what I learned from Dr. Mickey Hellickson, my host, there would have been an opportunity to do just that, since the bucks on the expansive range are "huntable" in his terms. What if the buck had responded to my grunting and appeared in one of the two clearings I was watching? What if I had missed the shot after traveling hundreds of miles and stalking for several hours?

Mickey informed me later that someone had taken that buck during the gun season. My comment in the previous Firepot Story was, "I will treasure the sundown shared with that Texas buck and hope that he was revered in his last hunt." Months passed before I found out who the fortunate hunter was. Mickey sent a photo of the young hunter with his first buck. From that moment I have had no second thoughts of my last hunt for that buck. Although the buck would have topped my best with a bow by some 25 inches, I was relieved that none of the "what ifs" had resulted in a different outcome for my hunt. Rather, I am comfortable with my hunt after having read the story written by 10-year-old Michael Blackburn from Topeka, Kansas.

There is no doubt that the magnificent buck was revered in his last hunt. This momentous occasion was not only a first hunt; it was a milestone in the life of a boy and the making of a deer hunter. Knowing this buck, however briefly, has enriched my life and I look forward to crossing paths some day with young Michael, a symbol of promise for our future as deer hunters and deer managers.

Michael's Story

Last year, when I was 10 years old, my dad told me that I was going to go to Texas and hunt deer at the King Ranch. My dad said they donated the youth hunt that he bought. At the time, I didn't know exactly what kind of place the King Ranch was. This would be my first deer ever. I went hunting with my dad all the time in Kansas, but I wasn't old enough to get a deer permit to harvest a deer. At the time, I thought that I was going to harvest a small buck, maybe four or five points if I was lucky. Boy, was I wrong!

At first I was practicing with shotgun slugs, but my dad's friend Mark, who told me all about the King Ranch, thought I should use a rifle instead of a shotgun. He gave

10-year-old Michael Blackburn from Topeka, Kansas with his first deer.

me a Ruger .243, which is a great gun. After lots of practice, we flew down to Texas.

We got up at 4 a.m. and went to breakfast first, and that is where we met our guide (host), Mickey Hellickson. Mickey was nice and very smart. He is the deer expert at the King Ranch. When he asked if I wanted to eat, all I could think about was harvesting my first buck. When we got to the ranch, my dad, Mark, Mickey and I got into Mickey's truck and took off. About five minutes into the hunt, Mickey was telling us about this nice eight-point that he had been seeing and that we were going to try to find it. We were seeing all kinds of does and 10 minutes later Mickey said, "There he is." We all got excited at how big he was. This deer was huge.

The deer were in rut, and he was with a doe, and she must have been in heat. The buck looked at us, then chased the doe, and she ran off. I was thinking that he would get away. The doe came running toward us and went under the fence in front of us and crossed the road and ran off. The huge buck ran up to the fence and stopped and looked at us. I was so excited, I almost forgot what to do. The buck looked at the doe, looked at us again, and looked at the doe again. He went under the fence with his giant antlers and started to run across the trail. I was ready, and Mickey whistled and the big buck stopped and looked at us. I pulled the trigger and the buck jumped and ran away. My first thought was that I missed. Everybody looked at me and said nice shot. I started to get "buck fever" and was shaking. When we walked up the trail 40 or so yards, there it was! I really started shaking. The deer's antlers were wider than my shoulders. I think it scored 139 and that was with five inches of one of its hooked brow tines broken. Mickey, Mark, and my dad all congratulated me and shook my hand. All I could do was think about how huge the deer was, and I thanked Mickey over and over. That was the best experience I had in my life. My dad said I'll be "hooked for life," and he's right! **Note:** *This article appeared in Quality Whitetails (V 9, I 1 - 2002).*

Just Another Season... Or Was It?

Having fished his idyllic Alder Fork Creek for trout one morning, Aldo Leopold chronicled the experience this way in his epic book *A Sand County Almanac*: "I shall now confess to you that none of those three trout had to be beheaded, or folded double, to fit their casket. What was big was not the trout, but the chance. What was full was not my creel, but my memory."

January 1 is a bitter sweet day for me each year. It marks the final day of the deer season in South Carolina, and there is obviously a degree of sadness when anything of significance has come to an end. This is also a time of reflection, celebration, and thanksgiving for all of the events connected with a 4½-month deer hunting season. To paraphrase Leopold's quote, this is my account of the 2007 deer season. My freezer is filled to the brim with venison, all from adult does. My encounters with adult bucks were more numerous this year than any of my previous 50 seasons, and although none of those bucks from earlier dreams were taken, the chances were there. My memory is filled with quality experiences.

Rattling was particularly productive during late September through mid-October of the '07 season. I settled into my 10-foot tripod stand one afternoon for a rattling session. Before I could get started two bucks put on the real thing about 60 yards away. My response was to "fight" louder. When I ceased my simulated battle all was quiet in their direction. Within a minute or so I caught a glimpse of a buck retreating. He walked through a thick hardwood stand and appeared as a shadow passing behind a bar code. My binoculars pierced a small gap in the trees and revealed a nice buck just south of maturity. His antlers were nothing to take your breath, although I mounted a couple of bucks in the 1960s with smaller, eight-point racks. It takes two bucks to have a fight, so where was the other one? I rattled again, but got no response, at least initially. Then, he was approaching very cautiously from the southwest while my ancient enemy, only a gentle breeze but nonetheless an enemy, rendezvoused with him from the northeast. My location had been revealed and I sensed as though the wise old buck had "felt" my intention. With head lowered and tail tucked tightly he followed the first buck's path of departure. Again, the binoculars were used to assess the antlers when gaps in the trees allowed such. The first gap provided a view of a very long G-2, possibly 10 or maybe 12 inches in length. WOW! This one deserves another look. I nervously settled the

The author with Paul Warren, the man who took him hunting for the first time when he was nine years old.

binoculars in a gap ahead of the departing buck. As he passed through I was awed by the 20+ inch wide rack with numerous tall points. The binoculars were replaced quickly by my scoped rifle and I searched frantically for another gap through which to send a projectile. There was not one, and the buck vanished as whitetails are so adept at doing. In retrospect, I should have simulated a grunt-snort-wheeze call to sequester that wise old buck instead of dragging him to a fight with my rattling antlers. He may have approached more aggressively and more quickly, thus putting him in my crosshairs before the smell of Old Spice turned him toward safety. What a hunt! I couldn't wait to tell my wife, Donna, who was in a stand about 300 yards west of mine. Hang on, I thought, this hunt isn't over yet! The buck was heading in Donna's direction. Would he allow himself to be seen by two hunters the same season, much less the same day? My guess favored the elusiveness of a mature buck, but the chance was there. The remaining 45 minutes of daylight produced only the sounds of distant shots, nothing close. Donna's gun remained silent.

I don't remember the five-minute walk from the stand to my truck — that buck had derailed my thought process. As the truck was cranked those darned headlights illuminated automatically. When a driver can't remember to turn on his headlights he shouldn't be driving anyway. Oh well, enough about modern-day technology. I could see the dim form of someone approaching with a determined pace. It was Donna, and instead of going to the passenger's side of the truck she came to my window like curb service at an old-timey, drive-in restaurant. She had that deer-in-the-headlights look and I knew a story was about to unfold. "I've just seen the biggest buck of my life," she blurted. "He walked out on the trail 20 yards in front of my stand as I was putting my gloves and binoculars away. It was too late for a shot so I retrieved my binoculars from the pack. I was having difficulty getting him in my field of view when he lifted his head, and oh my gosh, those antlers were tremendous!" I asked her to describe the rack. She said, "All I can say is that it was very wide and very tall, and the deer's body completely filled the opening in front of my stand. You should have seen him!" My weak response was: "I did." "Why did you pass him up?" "I didn't, it was him who passed me up! " It has taken me a while, but I have learned that big, mature bucks and small chances to harvest them go together. Nevertheless, that buck's presence electrified hunting visits the remainder of the season.

He'll be around next season — probably larger, definitely smarter, and the chance of getting him — well, it'll be smaller. I can't wait to resume my role in the drama. Experiences like this will ensure that Donna will accompany me more on hunts in '08.

A long deer season affords the ardent hunter ample opportunities to log many memories of hunts, big bucks, and hunting companions. One of my fellow hunters deserves special recognition. Russell Mixson has spent countless hours mentoring his two young sons, Bret (8), and Shane (12), and another youngster, James Rumfelt (14). In the last two hunting seasons each youngster has taken his first deer after much target practice and time spent as an observer in the deer stand with Russell. They've earned that rite of passage onto another plateau toward adulthood. Russell followed in the footsteps of his father into the deer woods and now has passed along the heritage to a younger generation.

QDMA Life Member Russell Mixson with his sons Shane and Bret and a friend James Rumfelt.

Emails have become a sign of modern times. This deer season my email log was filled with news from fellow hunters near and far proclaiming that their youngsters, boys and girls, had gotten their first deer. Mentoring is working — let's hope it can eventually overcome the net annual loss of hunters. The QDMA's Mentored Hunter Program will be in full swing this fall. Countless unsung heroes like Russell Mixson have taught us to be hopeful that hunters have a future and that through proper management we'll continue to have better deer and better deer hunting.

I had the distinct honor and pleasure of hunting the afternoon of January 1, 2008 with Mr. Paul Warren, who took me deer hunting for the first time in 1956 when I was nine years old. Fortunate for me, there were many mentors during my early years as a deer hunter. My path so far has been strongly influenced by deer and deer hunters. Hopefully, my dedication to the noble whitetail and enthusiasm for the wildlife profession have at least partially paid my debt of gratitude to my mentors.

So, for me and an increasing number of deer hunters/managers the 2007 hunting season was the best ever. What can we expect from the 2008 season? The answer to that question is up to you, my fellow hunters.

Note: *This article appeared in Quality Whitetails (V 15, I 1 – 2008).*

Musings of a Naturalist

Each fall I'm drawn to the collection of short stories of Havilah Babcock in his 1947 publication entitled, *My Health is Better in November*. As head of the English Department of the University of South Carolina and an avid sportsman, he possessed that combination of academic acuity and outdoor prowess necessary to put an interesting story on paper. His fireside manner of writing has been an inspiration.

I share his belief that good health and hunting seasons go together. The only difference, though, is that Dr. Babcock's prime time outdoors was November, the beginning of quail season, and my prime time has become year-round. The quality of a week for me is determined by how many days boots are worn — some weeks, every day. My work with The Nature Conservancy as project director for an area in southeastern South Carolina encompassing nearly three million acres involves spending time afield with landowners, making annual monitoring visits to properties with conservation easements, and identifying forest or habitat types and their associated plant communities on properties that are in the process of having conservation easements placed on them.

When I announced my decision to leave the Department of Natural Resources for my current position, a co-worker asked if I was exchanging my rod and gun for a butterfly net. Knowing full well that the comment was made in jest, I was committed to directing my energy toward land conservation. Nevertheless, the idea of a butterfly net stuck with me.

Although I have a bachelor's degree in forestry, a master's degree in wildlife biology, and 30 years of experience I am surrounded by botany books and other plant and animal identification materials. My job requires that I be a jack-of-all-trades regarding knowledge of the environment, therefore I am constantly honing my skills as a naturalist. As a result of this continuing education process I find that my hunting and fishing experiences are enhanced by having a more complete understanding of the many intricate relationships in natural systems. It is humbling to recount one's personal experiences, but the intent is to challenge all deer hunters/managers to become more knowledgeable of their natural surroundings. In doing so we will be better stewards of our natural resources and our image in the eyes of the general public will be enhanced.

In October I was invited to deer hunt in a coastal island residential community where quality deer management is practiced. Unfortunately, many other developed islands along our coast have relegated their deer management to sharpshooters for safety reasons. The stand assigned to me was positioned in the southeast corner of a wildlife food plot. Once settled in the stand I realized that the wind was carrying my scent directly toward the plot, thus rendering my chances of seeing a deer very unlikely. To while away the time I began making a mental list of every plant in sight. Wildflowers were blooming in profusion. A strange, black and yellow butterfly interrupted my botany lesson. There I sat with a rifle across my lap when I really needed that butterfly net! A fellow naturalist, Bruce Lampright, told me after the hunt that I had encountered a zebra longwing, a common resident of Florida and a rare visitor to the cooler climes. That October hunt was special; I had learned a new critter. Several weeks later I saw another zebra longwing on a rose bush in my very own yard. I "netted" him with my

Zebra longwing butterfly.

digital camera and presented the framed photo to a former co-worker, in jest of course.

I sat in a "classroom" late one November afternoon following a day of field work, one of the necessary steps toward protecting a 1,700-acre property near the Savannah River with a conservation easement. My classroom was an opening in the woods planted with a mixture of wheat and oats. My desk was a deer stand overlooking the food plot. My role at the moment was to assist the new property owner by harvesting a doe or two, but that would not happen this day. Rather, my classroom filled with bucks – four of them! A spike and six-point entered the food plot first and began feeding. Their stovepipe-shaped bodies revealed their age as yearlings. When I began working with the manager of this property in the early 1980s the yearling bucks averaged only 67 pounds live weight and a majority of them were spikes. A six-point yearling would have been rare in those days.

Minutes later an eight-point buck emerged from the woods. He was the classic 2½-year-old with a sleek body and spindly antlers with a 12-inch spread. I once heard a plantation manager refer to such bucks as "happy" bucks. He said they made the hunters happy, but more often than not a successful hunter would comment, "Wonder what he would have looked like in two more years?" Progressive clubs usually raise the bar for antler standards once they remain on a plateau for several years. Clubs that settle on low standards often experience frustration among a certain faction of the members with higher ideals. In this case patience is a virtue.

Having watched my share of hunting episodes on the outdoor channels I expected to hear heart-throbbing music when the fourth buck entered the plot. He was regal. His rack would have scored in the mid-130s Boone and Crockett. Sure, bucks like this are common on some well-managed properties elsewhere, but not here historically. What changed? The soils were the same, and the genetics of the deer herd hadn't changed. It was through quality deer management that the habitat had been improved markedly, and the sex ratio and age structure, particularly buck ages, had improved. Now, weights and antler development reflect a lower deer density and an ample supply of quality food.

That night I called the property manager to share my observation. I sensed a note of pride in his voice when he reported that their management program produced several exceptional bucks in that category each season. The mere presence of mature bucks on a property intrigues me. It is difficult to describe the feeling of knowing that such bucks actually live on a particular property when you've witnessed the alternative. There was a time when visions of old, mossy-horned bucks appeared only in the dancing flames of a hunter's fire.

When I emerged from the darkness of the hinterlands on my way home, I felt a sense of encroachment from the increasing number of lights — signs of civilization in areas that once were deer woods.

That November afternoon hunt was one to remember. It took place where I had walked deer trails for over a quarter of a century. The conscientious landowner has ensured that generations of hunters like us will continue to pursue the noble whitetail by protecting this special piece of the world with a perpetual conservation easement.

This protective document encourages forest and wildlife management, hunting, fishing, wildlife observation — the traditional uses of the land — but, most important, the property will never be developed despite increasing human populations in the neighborhood.

Note: *This article appeared in Quality Whitetails (V 12, I 1 - 2005).*

Blackgum [*Nyssa sylvatica*]

Blackgums occur in a variety of soil types from boggy to sandy and can be found from southern Ontario, Canada to Minnesota, south to Texas and Florida and in all eastern states from Maine southward.

This tree is also known as sour-gum or pepperidge and was called tupelo by Native Americans. The elliptic leaves are dark green and glossy. Blackgum fruit, technically referred to as drupes, are half-inch long, appear in fall, and are bluish-black. The yellowish-white seeds are football-shaped and have grooves running their entire length.

Young trees have a narrow, triangular shape, and mature trees usually attain a dome shape and a height of 40 to 60 feet. The limbs, most visible during winter, have a characteristic horizontal appearance. Blackgums prefer full sunlight but will tolerate filtered shade, and prefer acid soils.

Blackgums provide an abundant and varied food source for wildlife. The fruits are eaten by ruffed grouse, bobwhite quail, wild turkeys, wood ducks, over 30 species of songbirds, several species of squirrels, small rodents, gray foxes, opossums, raccoons, coyotes, black bears, and white-tailed deer. Beavers eat the wood, especially from young trees. Flowers attract pollinators and they attract a variety of insect-eating birds. Deer browse on the lush sprouts of seedlings. This is particularly important considering the thousands of drupes produced by individual blackgums with their seeds dispersed by soft mast-eating wildlife species that ultimately result in lush sprouts for whitetails. Understanding such interrelations in nature is the "art" of wildlife management.

Blackgum tree in winter showing horizontal limb structure.

Dr. Craig Harper and his University of Tennessee graduate students measured browse preference by white-tailed deer on three different sites in Tennessee over a seven-year period. This research has been partially funded by the QDMA. One site is in the Ridge and Valley physiographic province in east Tennessee, one is on the Cumberland Plateau, and the other is in the Upper Coastal Plain in west Tennessee. Thus, the results are applicable across a wide area with considerable differences in deer densities and herd structure. Browse species occurrence varied at each of the three sites. However, there were only two species browsed more than would be expected, based on availability, at all three sites — blackgum and greenbrier. Interestingly, honeysuckle was present at two sites, but at both, honeysuckle was browsed less than would be expected based on availability. As a result, the researchers consider blackgum browse preferred by white-tailed deer over honeysuckle. This was visually apparent as well.

119

When conducting timber stand improvement (TSI), try to retain blackgums throughout the stand. Release those trees with good trunk and crown form, and if trees with poor stems or crowns are removed, don't chemically treat the stumps. This will allow them to sprout and provide additional browse. Nutritionally, blackgum leaves consistently provide approximately 12 to 14 percent crude protein with less than 20 percent acid detergent fiber (a measure of lignin content and di-

Blackgum drupes (berries) and football-shaped seeds.

gestibility) through the growing season until late summer/early fall, when digestibility decreases.

For those of us who must endure the sweltering heat and humidity and biting insects of July and August throughout the Southeast, blackgum trees offer a glimmer of hope that fall and its cooler weather are on the horizon. Blackgums are among the first plants to change color, with a flush of dark burgundy to red leaves by late September.

Note: *This article appeared in Quality Whitetails (V 14, I 6 -2007).*

Puttin' Up

The activity of puttin' up is tied to man's ability to adapt to a variety of environmental/habitat conditions. In that way we are much like our beloved whitetail. This deer species has populated a major portion of two continents by being adaptable — by having a versatile diet and having the ability to live in extreme climates from the subtropics of South America to the icebox conditions of southern Canada.

Early man, the Cave Man and Native American Indians, lived from hand to mouth, which necessitated moving with the food supply. A more settled lifestyle among our pioneers eventually followed. The ability to save food for lean times when game was scarce and during winter when vegetation was scarce was the key to survival.

Much has changed since those early times of man's arrival on the planet. The many conveniences of modern day have robbed us of the necessity of direct involvement in storing food and cutting firewood for cooking and warmth. There still remains a fiber of genetic influence from our forefathers to express our independence as hunters/gatherers.

Many of my summers as a youngster were spent on my grandparents' farm in east Tennessee. The structures there bore an air of independence. A cistern had been used to collect rainwater from the gutters of the home. The old smokehouse, used later for storage of gardening tools, still maintained that characteristic smell of smoke where meat was cured and stored in the "old" days. An outdoor privy dated back to the establishment of the farm and continued to be functional, although its use was more of a novelty for those of us who chose to go "Daniel Booneing" all the way instead of using the available modern-day indoor plumbing. My favorite place was the root cellar. There's something about the smell of cool, moist soil that ties us to our dependence on the land. The root cellar was under the house and had a wooden door that led to an excavated chamber via steps cut into the ground. Shelves had been cut into the earthen walls of the cellar and there was a collection of all sorts of "canned" vegetables, fruits, and jellies. And there were potatoes — lots of them.

The 4th of July was Independence Day for the potatoes, although their exposure to the outside world was brief. Potatoes were dug from the garden and hauled directly to the root cellar — thus the name. Each layer of potatoes was sprinkled with lime to prevent rotting. I was unaware at the time of the long-lasting effects of participating in granny's continuous involvement in puttin' up things for later.

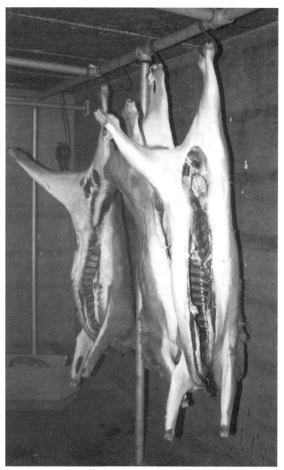

Field-dressed does in a walk-in cooler awaiting processing for the family's freezer.

I am a hunter/gatherer in a time that this behavior is no longer necessary. So why do I do it? Why do I put up several deer each season? Why do I stock my freezer with fish and shrimp during summer? Why do I toil on the back end of a chainsaw and axe to have plenty of firewood? The answer is simple. I feel driven to do these things. Perhaps this is innate behavior, but I think my grandmother instilled within me the need to stock up on supplies.

Grocery stores are common now throughout our communities and it is no longer necessary to can perishable foods at home and fill our freezers. However, hunters, and deer hunters in particular, exhibit characteristics of our forefathers with regard to puttin' up venison. Deer populations of today offer ample opportunities to fill our freezers in a single season. The thrill of the hunt is as strong in us today as it must have been several generations ago. What I think is missing in some of today's hunters is not the

Puttin' up firewood is an ongoing activity throughout the fall and winter for firepot gatherings.

thrill of encountering a deer while hunting, but the satisfaction, or even relief, that meat is being acquired. Our professed respect for the individual deer — buck or doe — is shown through hours of practice at a rifle or archery range, and ultimately with proper shot placement. An obligation that we should take as seriously is the utilization of the venison. Taking venison to the table completes the circle of involvement in deer hunting. This is the ultimate expression of our role as hunters/managers. If you don't care for venison or have more than you need, just contact organizations like Farmers and Hunters Feeding the Hungry and donate the meat to a worthy cause. On the other hand, if you simply can't find a suitable recipe, I suggest that you refer to Renee Miller's "A Taste of Quality" venison recipes in each issue of *Quality Whitetails*.

Hunters now account for only seven percent of our nation's population and those in the anti-hunting category represent an equal number. Our future as hunters will depend on how we influence the silent majority of the population. Recent polls have indicated that most non-hunters approve of hunting IF the game we acquire is property used. We are fortunate in our household to have many visitors — family and friends. There is never a doubt that a gathering at our firepot will be centered around a meal from the wild — usually venison. Of course, this also means that an ample supply of firewood must be available. So, puttin' up venison and cutting firewood are responsibilities that I "inherited" from my elders. Each firepot gathering is akin to the original Thanksgiving, except no one is wearing buckskin or feathers, although they are definitely there in

A 1960s photo of Granny French in front of the sloped entrance to her root cellar on the Tennessee family farm.

spirit. It's great being an old timey deer hunter in the second millennium. As mentors, we are obligated to share our traditional ways with the younger generation. In doing so, we revere our quarry, the noble whitetail, and ensure the future of deer hunting.

Note: *This article appeared in Quality Whitetails (V 13, I 6 - 2006).*

CHAPTER 5

MEMORABLE DEER

John Moran

*This collection of bucks resulted from the annual buck harvest on a
3,200-acre property in the South Carolina lowcountry only four years into
a quality deer management program. Each buck generated a memorable
story, and collectively they gave credence to a movement that was destined to
create more stories of memorable deer.*

The "Pacman" Buck

In 1985 I became involved with a hunting club that was ready for a change. The 3,200-acre property had long been home to a herd of several hundred cattle. Habitat conditions for deer were marginal at best. Tradition ran deep with deer hunting. Driving with hounds, the use of shotguns and buckshot, and buck-only hunting were the norm. This common scenario, repeated year after year, had produced very predictable results: A young age structure in bucks, an imbalanced sex ratio, poor antler development and body weights, high parasite levels, and too many deer for existing habitat conditions.

First, the cattle herd was drastically reduced and those that remained, for economic and aesthetic reasons, were moved to pastureland adjacent to the highway frontage. Improved loblolly pines were planted in portions of abandoned pastures. Pine plantations were designed to connect all isolated hardwood lots and to delineate wildlife openings ranging in size from two – five acres. In some areas, pine plantations and wildlife openings formed a checker-board pattern, some produced a zigzag effect, while others were aligned in a serpentine arrangement. A portion of each wildlife opening was planted in a spring-summer mix of browntop millet, grain sorghum, and Egyptian wheat; the other was reserved for a fall-winter combination of rye, wheat, and oats. Cattle removal and the establishment of wildlife food plots dramatically improved habitat conditions for deer and the pine plantations would soon provide much needed escape cover and bedding areas.

The initial recommendation for the 1985 deer harvest was a real icebreaker. Adult does ONLY were to be taken and 25 antlerless tags were prescribed. Why weren't the hunters allowed to take at least a few spikes? This approach was designed as a quick fix to a long-developed problem. There was a deficiency of bucks, and most yearlings were spike-antlered due to poor habitat and late summer fawning. Popular literature at the time did provide some stumbling blocks in convincing hunters to pass up those "inferior" spikes.

One particular buck, born in the summer of 1984 just prior to the big transition to quality deer management, provided a classic case history. It would take four years for the story to unravel, but it is worthy of being recorded.

Early one October morning in 1985, I was rambling through an island of hardwoods, just exploring, but with gun in hand. Scattered live oaks were pouring their bounty to the ground, for the first time in decades not for hungry bovines but for deer and a host of other wild creatures that relish acorns. Only one year in the absence of cattle a profusion of dog fennel patches provided instant cover for deer, and me, too. I drifted through one patch after another along a string of live oaks. When approaching the fringe of one patch I spotted a lone deer feeding beneath the draping limbs of a mighty live oak. What a Southern setting!

Back in those days I used a plain 30-30 (no scope) and hadn't yet been introduced to the luxury of binoculars. My best weapons were stealth and patience. To get a better look at this deer I had to "Indian" up on him. Dog fennels provided the necessary concealment. Each time he lowered his head to gather acorns I took a few cautious steps.

Cynthia Watkins

Needless to say, but I will anyway, the wind was in my favor. Any stalker worth his salt takes care of the wind problem when he puts his first foot into deer country. The deer stalker who disregards the wind, even for a split second, may as well be knocking a golf ball around instead.

Eventually, I found myself sharing the oak's canopy with the little spike buck, not needing a scope or binoculars for inspection. He had a biological tag! His snow white belly hair extended up in a circular fashion where the flank meets the hind quarter. This spot, about the size of your hand, was on both sides. He was marked for life, definitely an individual.

His preoccupation with feeding was interrupted by the sudden realization that I was an out-of-place lump. His response was true to generations of whitetails — a snort followed by long bounds with white flag aloft. But he stopped only 30 yards away and turned for another look. I remained a stationary, odorless (downwind) lump. He walked 10 yards closer and stood with the innocence of a yearling. I decided it was my turn to make a move and chose a stance that I'm certain whitetails hadn't been programmed to handle as a prey species. I leaned forward, and began shuffling toward the curious animal with my arms swinging from side to side — like a gorilla. Too much and too different. He bolted as expected, but stopped and again walked toward me. This episode was repeated three times before he developed a distrust of gorillas, even though the two species never shared the wilds of the same continent.

The bizarre encounter was shared that evening at fireside with a close friend, Coot Wooten, and his hunting companion from Michigan. Next morning the Blue and Gray put history on the shelf and went stalking together. Naturally, we made a bee line for the area of my previous morning's encounter. We were slippin'-an'-tippin' through the oak grove when the Michigander tapped me on the shoulder and whispered, "There he is running through the bottom!" Yesterday's lesson had paid off, and the spotted buck vanished as evolution would have had it. My hunting partner turned to me and said, "When that buck is running the white spot on his flank opens and closes like the computerized 'Pacman' symbol." The spike was an individual — now with a name, too, "Pacman."

A month later I saw Pacman within 100 yards of our first encounter. He wasn't seen again the remainder of that hunting season, but he had gained a reputation among our hunting group.

The 1986 hunting season brought changes in our management plan. We increased the antlerless tag issuance to 50 and added eight-point bucks with a minimum 16-inch antler spread to the harvest. The ice had been broken and tradition cast aside. We were up and running with quality deer management. Despite the excitement over all of the bucks that were being seen, I was concerned that Pacman may have dispersed, as many yearling bucks do, to an adjacent property. The season was well into October, the peak of the rut, when our paths crossed again only a quarter-mile from the oak grove. Those unmistakable white spots were as prominent as they were in 1985. He had a six-point rack with a 12-inch spread. He was safe on both counts, number of points and antler width. The word spread quickly that Pacman was still with us. He was seen by one of our members a month later and not again that season.

In November 1987, I was stalking along an old farm road early one morning. It was that magical time of steel gray light just before sunrise when big bucks appear out of nowhere. Is it the strength of one's faith that brings results, or are the eyes and ears of a seasoned hunter most keen at that time?

The pine plantation on my right was designed with deer hunting in mind. A 75-foot swath was left unplanted to provide for a wildlife opening and a stand location with good visibility. Depending on wind direction, either end of this swath was a good spot for a stalker to begin a morning's hunt.

A south wind was passing perpendicular to the swath so I positioned myself in cover at the east end and fixed my eyes along the straight pine border. The sharp crack of a tree limb interrupted the early morning silence, but there was no follow-up sound — it didn't hit the ground. Strong wingbeats drew my attention skyward as a bald eagle crossed the swath carrying, somewhat awkwardly, a six-foot tree limb. Only then did I realize why the cracking sound was not followed by a thump. That limb never hit the ground! Eagles and other raptors are among the earliest nesters and it was time to refurbish its nest with a layer of freshly broken, dead tree limbs.

Apparently the eagle's activity had aroused other interests as well. I glanced back to the line of pines to see half a deer protruding into the swath. The profile of a massive rack and that characteristic buffalo shape of a mature buck elicited a rush of excitement that drives our quest. He looked my direction, yielding a view of his 18-inch spread with eight long points. A couple of steps and the buck was in full view, complete with a white circle in the flank/hind quarter region. The Pacman buck had reached our "keeper" category. He was safe in my rifle sights, though. I was content to remain scouter and doe harvester. This location extended Pacman's home range a half-mile southward, encompassing nearly 300 acres over a three-year period. Did he travel more or had he become that adept at using the tangle of cover in his relatively small home? He was not seen again in 1987.

When the 1988 deer season rolled around our hunting group had reached the fine-tuning stage of quality deer management. Some mistakes had been made along the way as expected, but they were the exception rather than the rule among our regular hunters. When a visitor was invited to hunt, the members were apprehensive. Although the management plan was discussed in detail prior to each hunt, we soon learned that some didn't pay attention, some made hasty decisions and others exhibited undesirable hunting habits: shooting long distances under poor light or taking shots at running deer.

Such problems are inherent in any management plan that deviates from the norm — from tradition. There is never ample time to grill a visitor or new member on all phases of ethical behavior. Certain assumptions must be made by the host, but not always without a price — a compromise of the management objectives.

On one particular occasion a visiting hunter had unloaded his rifle and climbed down from his stand at the end of an afternoon's hunt. Darkness was closing in quickly as he stood waiting to be picked up by his hunting companions. Out of the shadows appeared a giant buck. The hunter fumbled around in his coat pocket for a cartridge, loaded his rifle, and took an off-hand shot at the walking buck. When he recovered from the muzzle blast there was no buck to be seen.

Moments later his companions arrived and he told them the buck had run off in "that" direction, pointing to the northwest. There was no initial indication that the buck had been hit, but they decided to return after supper and resume the search.

Following the northwest direction produced nothing. Then someone commented, "What if the buck ran to the right instead, heading southeast?" Sure enough, he had done just that and had fallen within a stone's throw of the hunter's vacated stand. Carelessness had nearly deprived us of the privilege to revere an exceptional animal.

His nine-point rack was massive, with an outside spread of 20½ inches. The buck with white spots on his sides would not be seen again. Pacman would not be forgotten either.

What can we learn from this story? Without his biological tag, this buck would have been the sole keeper of his life's history. We would not have known that an "inferior" yearling buck with three-inch spikes would have transformed into such a magnificent animal at age 4½, or that he was never seen outside his 300-acre home range. We should also understand that neither the host nor his guest is being criticized. Rather, the behavior described is a product of our society and traditions. It is the mission of the Quality Deer Management Association to curtail such behavior through education and example.

Note: *This article appeared in Quality Whitetails (V 3, I 4 - 1996).*

A fine buck robbed of his dignity by a poacher's bullet.

David Soliday

The Big 'un That Didn't Get Away

Scenes like this are all too common throughout deer country worldwide. The scavenged remains of this once magnificent buck were discovered early this hunting season in southeastern South Carolina.

Laying only 50 yards from the highway, the buck could have been, but wasn't, hit by an automobile, especially since 166 deer were killed by motorists in Colleton County during 1994.

The number of deer/vehicle collisions and crop damage caused by deer would be intolerable without the role of sportsmen in controlling deer density.

Colleton County's annual deer harvest has averaged nearly 7,000 over the last four years, and the male-to-female ratio has averaged 48:52. The sportsmen of Colleton's deer hunting clubs are to be commended for their efforts in deer management. In the not too distant past, petitions were circulating throughout the county to make it illegal to harvest does. Education set the stage for change.

Many Colleton clubs have been involved in quality deer management since the mid-1980s. They have reduced the harvest of young bucks, thus allowing them to reach older age classes represented by bucks with larger antlers and heavier body weights. Harvest pressure has shifted toward the female segment of the herds to control density and bring about a better balance between deer numbers and existing habitat conditions.

The desired result of such a management regime is to maintain a healthy deer population that is also compatible with other land uses including agriculture, forestry, and highway travel.

Involvement in quality deer management has spread to over 40 states — again, testimony of concerted efforts among sportsmen to become better educated about their favorite big game animal, the wily white-tailed deer. The educational path begins with awareness, which leads to understanding and culminates with respect. Proper management and ethical hunting are among the benefits of this educational process. Everyone, not just sportsmen, but the general public, should be proud of this accomplishment in wildlife management.

Early this deer season a local sportsman observed a particularly nice buck for 45 minutes. The wide antlers with numerous points glistened in the late-afternoon sun as the buck chased a doe into and out of thickets, round and round, back and forth. It was that time of the year — the rut was in full swing.

What a buck this would have been as the first one for a hunter. He was much better than average. Why wasn't a shot taken? Was the buck too far away? Nope! It wouldn't have been this hunter's first deer. He was saving it for his wife, who had taken several does that season and passed up many small bucks.

Well, that ol' buck showed up again as luck would have it. This time he lay stretched out on the ground, robbed of his dignity by a poacher's bullet. He had traveled only 20 yards to cover before collapsing, and obviously was not pursued by his assailant. Often, if a deer doesn't fall in its tracks the poacher will not look for the animal at the risk of getting caught in the act.

Each day and night our highways are traveled by unscrupulous vandals with guns in hopes of getting their deer the easy way. Such people are not worthy of being called sportsmen. Their actions are not only illegal, they are unethical and show disrespect for the deer and the sportsmen who pursue them.

Another rather common practice among poachers is to put their partners out along the highway to enter private property — posted land. When they discharge their firearms either in this situation or from a public highway, the safety of other people is NOT a consideration.

Unfortunately, this story was not fabricated. The 5½-year-old nine-point buck with a spread of 18½ inches and an approximate weight of 180 pounds didn't get away, but the one who shot him did. My intent is to inform the general public that sportsmen join the ranks of all concerned citizens in condemning such activities.

There are a lot of eyes and ears among the general public. If you are repulsed by the ongoing actions of poachers and you have information that may lead to the conviction of such people, please contact your wildlife agency's toll-free hotline (i.e., Operation Game Thief or Turn In Poachers). The more details you can provide (time of day, type of automobile, license number, etc.) the better the chance of conviction.

Most states have strict penalties for nighthunting, but trespassing to hunt big game and shooting deer and wild turkeys from a public highway during daylight hours often carry ridiculously light fines. Regarding human safety, nighthunting is far less dangerous.

In the not-too-distant past, poachers were put on a pedestal in some communities for their "hunting" savvy and ability to elude game wardens. Times have changed! Sentiment is now that convicted poachers and their violations should be exposed in local newspapers as would any other criminal activity.

Members of conservation organizations like the QDMA and The National Wild Turkey Federation must support state wildlife agencies in developing strong enough game laws to deter the intolerable behavior of poachers. Until these problems are addressed our back door will remain open to game thieves.

Note: *This article appeared in Quality Whitetails (V 2, I 4 - 1995).*

A hypogonadal buck, or cactus buck, taken by the author in the Texas brush country.

The Cactus Buck

Experienced deer managers have developed an eye for undesirable antler characteristics. Unfortunately, many bucks are taken each year by hunters who thought they were removing "bad" genes from the herd. In most cases, these bucks are young and have an uneven number of points or have deformed or broken antlers due to an injury. Time is the solution to most of these problems because they are not necessarily genetically related. The ability to recognize permanent antler deformities comes only through experience and education.

Labeling bucks that have undesirable antler characteristics as culls is a problem, too. This designation denotes some degree of inferiority and therefore is demeaning. The term "management deer" is more descriptive, desirable, and fair. With few exceptions, only mature bucks that have been allowed to exhibit their potential should be taken as management deer. Remember, adult bucks have reached an age when elusiveness is their creed, regardless of their antler development.

The Cactus Buck had been seen by Al Brothers for several years in a particular portion of a Texas ranch. Called the Horse Trap pasture, this area was vegetated by mesquite and prickly-pear cactus, so typical of south Texas brush country.

Dr. Larry Marchinton and I alternated our pursuit of this odd critter over a three-day period. The buck was odd because his antlers were still in velvet in late-December. He had been seen for at least three years, and his antlers were always in velvet.

Morning and afternoon hunts the first day allowed me to reacquaint with the specific sights, sounds, and smells of this strange land I had visited many times. The buck remained a phantom — testimony of that craftiness that comes so naturally to adult whitetails.

Following a three-hour stint in a tripod stand on the second day, Larry decided to stalk through deer country quite different from those familiar haunts of his native Florida flatwoods and the Georgia Piedmont of his present home. He was destined to cross paths with the Cactus Buck. Their encounter was normal by stalking standards. Having seen the hunter first, the buck stood statue-still as he was silhouetted by a bright sun.

Larry's glasses were covered in dust, yielding a poor view of what he thought was the velvet-antlered buck. Rather than stand eye-to-eye with the buck, Larry decided to walk away while cleaning his glasses. The ploy was to no avail. Although his age-old predator was retreating, the buck's compelling response to having been seen was to join the wind. The hunter's only options were to take a risky running shot or just watch. A fundamental rule was heeded: When in doubt, always give the quarry the benefit of that doubt.

During lunch when everyone was accounting for their morning's outing, Larry was asked if he had seen the Cactus Buck. "Yep, I passed him up," was the response.

The buck was allowed to settle. He was not pursued that afternoon or the next morning. We knew that constant pressure would send him underground to keep company with the moles. Where else do big bucks seek refuge?

The weatherman allied with the buck on our third and final day of hunting. Strong winds filled the air with yellowish-red dust straight from Mexico. My four hours in the tripod stand that afternoon were grueling. I sat there for the duration with my head tilted into the wind to avoid losing my hat. As expected, not a creature was stirring.

As sundown approached, there was a reprieve from the wind. A band of seven or eight javelinas passed near my stand — a glint of hope that other animals might be seen. With less than 15 minutes of shooting time remaining I spotted an animal moving through a small clearing approximately 500 yards away. My binoculars were trained patiently on the next clearing. Sure enough, it was a buck...with very dark antlers. It may be the Cactus Buck, but I couldn't tell at that distance.

Without hesitation I climbed from the stand and began zigzagging my way along game trails through dense cover toward the buck. A windmill conveniently served as my reference point. Otherwise, there were no distinguishing habitat or geographical features.

Once in the vicinity of the windmill I stopped and glassed for the flick of an ear or the twitch of a tail in the thick brush. Something moved! Quickly fine-tuning the focus of my binoculars revealed only a set of antlers — and they were covered in velvet. I had no shot at all and twilight was advancing. It was that critical time, the shank of the evening when light diminishes noticeably by the minute.

As he continued feeding, my "stalking" wheels were turning. I didn't have the luxury of waiting for the buck to present a better view. I was the one who had to make a move. Instead of inching forward like a cat, a predator, I chose to burst noisily from cover like a charging gorilla. In response, the buck would flee to the left or right, or straight away and deeper in cover. Had he exercised the latter option, our paths never would have intersected and this story would have ended here. As it was, he ran in an arc to the right and stopped in an open lane to determine the source of the commotion. He was upwind and hadn't seen me. Curiosity is the one character flaw of whitetails that must be remembered when stalking. I sat on a bare spot of ground with my legs crossed to cradle my elbows and steady the rifle. Years of practice at the rifle range in a variety of shooting positions, especially this one, brought its reward.

When Larry Marchinton joined us at the skinning shed and inspected my Cactus Buck he remarked, "Yep, that's the one I passed up in the Horse Trap pasture." I had received a gift from the gods, and from my hunting companion. It was a hunt to be treasured and shared.

Biological Information: The buck's neck was not swollen. Rather, it had the sleekness of a doe's neck. Unlike other 5½-year-old bucks, his tarsal glands were not stained. And, although the testicles had descended into his scrotum, they were atrophied — about the size of peanuts. An animal with underdeveloped testicles (hypogonadism) or one having testicles that remain in the abdominal cavity (cryptorchidism) typically have low or nonexistent production of testosterone. Without the seasonal ebb and flow of testosterone the antler development cycle is altered. Antlers are not shed and they remain in velvet year round. Furthermore, the antlers continue to grow as the animal matures. Very old bucks with these congenital testicular deformities often have bumpy antlers with numerous abnormal points giving them a "cactus" appearance. Bucks with this condition should be removed from the population because they are incapable of reproducing. If allowed to mature, obviously they have the potential to provide a memorable hunt.
Note: *This article appeared in Quality Whitetails (V 4, I 2 -1997).*

14x14

Joe's Story

December 23, 1996, was a busy day around the Hamilton household with the usual holiday preparations. I slipped away to spend the shank of the evening in a deer stand several miles from home.

I walked the tunneled woods road to a convenient tripod stand, settled into the swivel seat, checked the wind, and placed my rifle on a sand bag along the shooting rail. As always, the scope was checked for clarity and magnification. While gazing down the woods road I was startled by motion in my scope. A huge buck stepped into the narrow road at 150 yards, turned and faced me. If I had arrived one minute later the hunt would have ended with a glint of antlers and an indignant white flag.

Without having to move my rifle, the crosshairs were centered on his swollen neck. For five long minutes I stared through increasingly blurred eyes, switching from the scoped vision to my binoculars. His brow tines were double on each side, the bez tines (G-2s) were forked like a mule deer's characteristic form, and the left main beam was broken, with about one-third of the beam missing.

During the five-minute showdown my thoughts began to race toward the possible decision to pull the trigger if he turned slowly, and back in time to an early morning stalk in October of the previous hunting season when I got a glimpse of a mature buck with forked bez tines. I was again in that once-in-a-season encounter with a denizen of

Joe's South Carolina buck taken at 5 p.m., December 23, 1996.

the thickets.

Over the years numerous broken-antlered bucks were allowed to walk because they appeared to have potential. This situation was different. The buck's buffalo shape and massive antlers were indicators of an animal at its pinnacle. Furthermore, poaching is traditional in this neighborhood. This opportunity may be the last — at least for me.

I thought of the occasions that the SHOOT • DON'T SHOOT • WAIT FOR A BETTER LOOK slide program and magazine articles had been presented to foster quality deer management. I thought of the many shed antlers found on this property and knew there must be a suitable one to use as a replacement for the missing portion of the left antler.

The decision was to SHOOT, only if a broadside shot could be taken. At precisely 5 p.m. the buck turned and a Firepot Story of coincidence was born. He was 6½ years old and weighed 175 pounds. Assuming the antlers were matched initially, the buck had 14 points and a 20-inch spread. That's exactly the way it would be restored.

The next night I called Al Brothers in Texas to wish him and Claudia, his wife, a Merry Christmas and, of course, to share my hunting story with him. Having heard the details, Al commented after a very long pause, "Jose, you're not gonna believe this. I did the same thing at 5 p.m. yesterday."

Al's Story

On December 22, 1996, a hometown friend and hunting partner accompanied me deep into south Texas for a deer hunt. Our headquarters was a remote ranch about 30 miles from the Mexico border. We would be hunting in the famous "Golden Triangle" of the Rio Grande Plains brush country.

We arrived with less than an hour to unload our gear and to do some necessary scouting. It was a dark, overcast day with a fine mist of rain. The bucks were really moving as

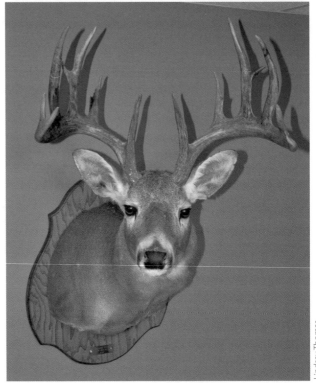

Al's Texas buck taken at 5 p.m. on December 23, 1996.

Lindsay Thomas

expected because the brush country rut usually occurs from the 17th to the 25th of December. A storm front or "norther" was due to pass through that night, clearing the cloud cover and sending the temperature down into the 40s. Our timing and the changing weather conditions made the perfect combination for hunting.

As darkness approached, we were about 300 yards from the ranch house, but there was another excellent spot to check out. A windmill provided one of the only water sources for game and cattle in that dry, sandy country. There was movement in the thick cactus and mesquite near the water trap. Through my binoculars I saw a large buck peering at me from thick cover. The only visible portion of his body was from the white spot under his chin to the tips of his massive antlers. I took a firm rest and shot for the white spot. He vanished! We followed his running tracks for a distance and found no blood. I had missed what should have been an easy shot.

Early the morning of December 23, we returned to look again and perhaps discover the reason for my misfortune. My bullet had struck a thumb-sized mesquite branch, deflecting its path from the white spot.

After lunch I returned to the windmill on my four-wheeler, which I use as a ground blind. Positioning my four-wheeler in a mesquite bush by trimming limbs and backing in, then covering the front with camouflage cloth, I settled in to wait. My blind was about 70 yards downwind of the trail the buck had used the day before. By late afternoon I had observed and "let walk" four different large bucks. A mental picture of the odd points and massive antlers was printed firmly in my mind, and it was him or nothing.

Just at 5 p.m. I spotted him walking cautiously along the same trail. Better lighting revealed a broken main beam, but there was no doubt that it was the same buck. I immediately thought of using one of my rattling antlers as the source for the missing portion of the buck's main beam. This time I waited for a clearing and a shoulder shot. He fell within 20 yards of where I missed him the afternoon before.

Why did he use the same trail at about the same time? Water sources in that very dry country are active social centers for deer. Earlier that morning I had noticed numerous scrapes and rubs concentrated in a two-acre area. Since the buck had been alone when first seen, I figured the chances of him returning were very good. For once I was right.

In looking back, I am glad that my bullet struck that mesquite branch, for if it had not, I would have missed the planning, preparation, sights and sounds, and experiences of "outlucking" or outsmarting my quarry the next day. The buck was 8½ years old and had an impressive 14-point rack.

Author's Note: Some would argue that the above incidents are mere coincidence, but serious practitioners of quality deer management realize that the odds of bucks like these reaching maturity without proper habitat and herd management are as rare as the 14-point bucks themselves.

Note: *This article appeared in Quality Whitetails (V 5, I 4 - 1998).*

Old Bucks of the New Millennium

"Hunting trails may grow cold, but the memories last a lifetime." This prophetic statement was inscribed in my treasured book, *Producing Quality Whitetails*, by its coauthor Al Brothers. A long time friend, fellow biologist, hunting companion, and mentor, Al keeps my fires burning, especially during the off-season.

Several months have passed, wildflowers are in full bloom, turkey gobblers are proclaiming their seasonal rites in the deer woods, but I still find myself reminiscing the many sagas of the 2000 hunting season. After two decades of involvement in quality deer management, my hunting seasons now are steeped in flavor from encounters with old bucks.

The framed image of an exceptional eight-pointer, bedded on a mixed pine and hardwood hillside, serves as sentinel of my office as the "Old Prentiss at Merigold" once cast a watchful eye over his southern Mississippi domain. Since my earliest years among seasoned deer hunters I have been intrigued by the names they have given particular old bucks. I can't recall anyone ever naming a young buck! If so, an adjective would have to preface each name, like "Potential Bully of the Woods." It soon became apparent that a professed respect for specific bucks bestowed an experienced hunter the honor or responsibility of naming them.

The origin of names is interesting as well. Some names are determined by the exact location of sightings, like the "Cemetery Buck," the "Sawdust Pile Buck," and the "Double Curve Buck." Often, sightings of a particularly large buck will result in that buck being named after the property. Dual names are also assigned, like the "Trillium Buck of Spring Island," the "Magnolia Buck of Bluff Plantation," and "Old Prentiss of Merigold Hunt Club," which also became the subject of an artist's brush. Physical characteristics have identified individual bucks. I remember a renowned buck from my early years that was called "Old Sloughfoot" (pronounced slew foot) because of a deformed hoof and his telltale crooked tract. About 10 years ago a Texas rancher missed a superb buck with a 44 magnum pistol. Photographer Wyman Meinzer caught the "44 Magnum Buck" on film just after the incident and presented the rancher with a framed photograph for the hunting lodge. No one saw

Scott Rhodes with the "Skyscraper Buck of Coosawhatchie River."

that buck the entire next year. Then, Al Brothers became the envy of neighborhood hunters the following hunting season when he crossed paths with this buck that had 15 points, a 25-inch spread, and scored 169 2/8 Boone and Crockett points.

Last fall while scouting in preparation for a visit from my Australian friend, Peter Stuart, I encountered a buck feeding in one of our club's aeschynomene patches. When the buck lifted his head the image was akin to a football referee signaling a touchdown. His rack was not as wide as the ear tips, but the bez tines (G-2s) were unusually long. Peter's three-day hunting visit yielded a fine 2½-year-old eight-pointer, while the newly-nameed "Touchdown Buck of Leather Britches Hunt Club" remained elusive, yet imparting a certain mystique to our outings.

Having obtained a representative sample of a southern whitetail for their new house in Australia, Peter and his wife Jean were invited to spend the last night of their visit on a nearby plantation. Owned by Mr. Tommy "Tombo" Rhodes (Charter Life Member of the QDMA), Oak Grove Plantation is a sprawling 4,200-acre property that has been under QDM guidelines for nearly 20 years. Incidentally, Al Brothers visited there several years ago and stated, "It is the best managed property I have encountered in my years as a wildlife biologist."

Scott Rhodes, QDMA Life Member and Tombo's son, toured us around the plantation the following day and raved about a buck he had seen while bowhunting several days before. A shot was not taken because of an undesirable angle, although the buck was well within range. According to Scott, the buck's rack was very narrow, but the long points gave it "a lot of character." He named it the "Skyscraper Buck of the Coosawhatchie River." As we were leaving the plantation after an enjoyable tour and numerous deer stories, Scott was preparing for a late afternoon hunt from his perch overlooking the narrow, blackwater river.

That night I received a telephone call from a very excited hunter. Scott proudly announced, "I got him!" The "Skyscraper Buck of Coosawhatchie River" was entered into the plantation's deer harvest log as a 155-pound, 3½-year-old, eight-pointer with a "green" Pope and Young score of 130. The longest points, the G-2s, measured nearly 12 inches, but the outside spread was only 12½ inches!

The next weekend I stepped into the yard well before daylight to check the hunting conditions. A high wind with a temperature in the low-30s was not what I had hoped for, but the lure of the "Touchdown Buck" was irresistible, so I headed for Leather Britches.

With the last drop of hot coffee drained from my thermos, I checked my watch — 7:56 a.m. I had decided to climb from my stand and begin stalking the thickets at 8:00. Experience was telling me that going to the deer instead of waiting for them

Our dachshunds Copper and Frogmore at the end of the trail with the "Touchdown Buck of Leather Britches Hunt Club."

was the best approach under these weather conditions. One last survey of my shooting "windows" defied my experiences. The fate of my quest was sealed! I hurried home to get my wife Donna, a camera, and our two dogs. It was a monumental occasion for the little dachshunds to try their noses at tracking. Their olfactory senses paid off and the "Touchdown Buck of Leather Britches Hunt Club" was ours! He weighed 168 pounds and was 5½ years old. His nine-point, 14⅝-inch-wide antlers sported 11½-inch G-2s and eight-inch brow tines.

Quality deer management has brought many hunters along the path of enlightenment, awareness, and understanding to the goal of respect for the wily whitetail. Consequently, due to the widespread participation in QDM, there are more older-age bucks throughout the whitetail's range than ever before — more to be named and more to flavor our pursuits in the new millennium. These are the building blocks of memories, those that will last a lifetime.

It is imperative to note that neither of the two bucks featured in this Firepot Story would have met the minimum 16-inch spread limit of many hunt clubs, although both have been mounted. In all fairness to the various antler forms among whitetails, management guidelines should offer a list of "harvestable" antler criteria so hunters will have a choice of one or a combination of characteristics. The list should include antler mass, number and length of points, main beam length, and antler spread — all based on neighborhood standards. These criteria should be considered also in conjunction with body shape. In contrast to the stovepipe bodylines of a 2½-year-old buck, bucks 3½ and older usually have better developed shoulders and necks, thus giving them a buffalo-shaped silhouette.

Remember, deer management is a dynamic endeavor. Fine tuning the guidelines will be an ongoing process. The path taken is just as important as the ultimate destination. Enjoy each step along the way.

Note: *This article appeared in Quality Whitetails (V 8, I 2 - 2001).*

The Trillium Buck

The past, present, and future of a particular South Carolina coastal island are marked by exploitation, change, and stewardship. The recent find of a Clovis arrowhead provided archaeological verification that humans have impacted Spring Island for at least 10,000 years. Following thousands of years of occupation by nomadic hunter/ gatherers, conditions changed appreciably once settlers depended on their newfound home for sustenance year-round.

A settler purchased Spring Island in 1706. Throughout the next two centuries nine generations of his family flourished on the island's bounty. By the late-1800s, two-thirds of the 3,000-acre island had been cleared for the production of corn and Sea Island cotton. Hundreds of cattle, sheep, and swine ranged freely throughout the woodlands. The plight of wildlife populations under such intensive agriculture is obvious.

Salvation of the worn-out island came in 1964 when Mr. and Mrs. Elisha Walker Jr. assumed ownership. Under the watchful eye of their plantation manager, Mr. Gordon Mobley, wildlife food plots were established, bottomland fields that were enhanced for waterfowl, and roads were improved.

Mr. Walker passed away in 1973, but Mrs. Walker remained committed to the cause until her death in 1982. Their stewardship had brought fame to Spring Island as an extraordinary property for hunting quail, doves, waterfowl, and deer.

This critical juncture for Spring Island was fraught with uncertainty, a time when security came only from the Walker Trust and the vigilance of Gordon Mobley. Would Spring Island become a residential development like nearby Hilton Head Island or was there a wealthy individual interested in furthering the Walkers' philosophy? What appeared as an either/or situation resulted fortunately in a novel blend of the two, but not before the island's natural integrity was threatened.

In 1985 the county zoned the island for 5,500 housing units and three golf courses. Development was contingent on connecting Spring Island to the mainland via a high-rise bridge. The bridge was not permitted, thus giving Spring Island a reprieve.

Visionary developers Jim Chaffin, Jim Light, and Dr. Peter LaMotte purchased the island in 1990 and secured its future by establishing the Spring Island Trust; a non-profit organization dedicated to the protection and preservation of the island's natural environment and cultural history. In keeping with this objective, housing density was downsized to 500 and only one golf course was allowed. Several nature preserves were identified and members'/residents' lots were bounded by nature curtains; thus, an "emerald necklace" was created.

The Walker philosophy transposed to the Spring Island philosophy with the vision of a "nature park," a harmonious blend of human settlement and the natural environment. With the guidance of Mrs. Betsy Chaffin, founder and director of the Spring Island Trust, a nature lab was established and a naturalist was added to the staff. It was the first duty of the naturalist to help the developers know which special "nature places" should not be changed. Those places were mapped so that the human footprint on the land would not compromise the island's natural amenities.

While in the "limbo" period, those seven years under the Walker Trust, Gordon Mobley sought my advice in managing the deer herd, which had increased markedly as a by-product of intensive habitat management for quail. Realizing that development of the island was inevitable, we agreed that a dramatic population decrease was necessary. Comments from visitors — hunters and non-hunters alike —revealed a high level of interest in observing mature bucks with well-developed antlers. Both objectives could be satisfied by following the basic tenets of quality deer management; maintaining herd density in balance with existing habitat conditions, while allowing more bucks to reach maturity.

Spotlight surveys were conducted prior to each hunting season to determine herd density, sex ratio, number and distribution of mature bucks, and therefore the desired harvest. After several years of surveys we noticed a pattern regarding the whereabouts of mature bucks. A particular region near the island's south end had been dubbed the Trillium Garden because of a profusion of the garnet-colored wildflowers, relics of the Ice Age, with three, mottled, and drooping leaves. It was in the vicinity of the Trillium Garden that most mature bucks were observed. Mr. Mobley had the answer. This area was not subjected to prescribed fires or bush hogging as was the remainder of the island; therefore, it had become somewhat of a jungle. Obviously, cover of this degree afforded bucks more protection and allowed them to grow older.

Naturalists were added to the staff to accommodate an increase in new residents and participation in nature-related activities. In an attempt to involve everyone in the deer management program a special event was planned for a December evening in 1994. The first annual Venison Appreciation Night featured a variety of exquisitely prepared dishes. The ultimate expression of respect for wild game is to share it with family and friends at the dinner table. This gesture is symbolic of early encounters between our forefathers and Native Americans. It is a time of thanksgiving and completing the circle of wildlife management.

Popularity of the Venison Appreciation Night has grown as more people call Spring Island their home. The number of non-hunters who participate has increased each year. Now more than a dozen recipes provide the gastronomic enticement.

Last December, at the sixth annual dinner, another tradition was launched. The

Michael Perry

Brian McCafree's 11-point buck taken on Spring Island in 2008. This is an exceptional specimen from a coastal island habitat — a testament to the QDM program that produced it — and a true Trillium Buck!

deer management committee decided to formally recognize the best buck taken during the previous hunting season; its title was derived from the area renowned for producing mature bucks. A plaque presented at the dinner bore this inscription:

THE TRILLIUM BUCK OF 1998
A Tribute To Spring Island's
Quality Deer Management Program
In Recognition Of The Hunter
Geoff Applegate

Wildlife populations on southeastern coastal islands usually reflect the seasonal and annual fluctuations in natural foods unless properly managed. Average weight per age class, fecundity (fawns per doe), and antler development serve as barometers for deer health. On Spring Island, does normally produce twins, yearling bucks average 108 pounds (live weight), and antler development among adult bucks is comparable to that on well-managed properties on the mainland. In fact, several state records (minimum Boone and Crockett score of 125), including the 1998 Trillium Buck, have been produced here. By comparison, on a neighboring, unmanaged island the yearling bucks averaged less than 70 pounds, twins were never observed, and most adult bucks had spindly, narrow racks with short points.

Wild turkeys (10 hens and 5 gobblers) were stocked in 1996 by the South Carolina Department of Natural Resources and currently number over 100. The density of southern fox squirrels is the highest in the range of the species. Henry David Thoreau's dictum certainly applies to Spring Island: "In wildness is the preservation of life."

Spring Island's future as viewed by its developers and residents is an opportunity and an obligation. The relationship between the residents and the island's ambiance, cultivated in large part by the three naturalists, has resulted in a further scaling down of home sites. Now, only 410 will be allowed, following a buy-back of 90 lots by island residents. It is comforting that a property with such a bounty of natural treasures will travel into the future very much as it is now.

Smart growth of this sort must become the norm rather than the exception. Unfortunately, the demands of our spreading civilization are consuming "natural" areas, wildlife habitat, across the nation at a rate measured in acres per second.

Conservation organizations including Ducks Unlimited, The Nature Conservancy, and local land trusts along with state and federal wildlife agencies are working fervently to secure our nature-based traditions through land conservation. Invest in your future as a sportsman by supporting local, state, and national efforts to protect vital wildlife habitat. **Note:** *This article appeared in Quality Whitetails (V 7, I 3 - 2000).*

Foreigners

A classmate of mine in the second grade made the announcement that her family was going to have a visitor, a rancher from South America. Her father operated a dairy, so apparently this rancher was on a fact-finding mission to the states. Our teacher asked Nellie Kaye if she would bring her guest to school so we could meet someone from another continent, another culture, another world. The very mention of the word continent sparked my imagination.

In those days, I measured distances in bicycle miles. A quick glance of South America's place on the globe in relation to North America, and particularly North Carolina, and I realized that a genuine foreigner was about to be in our presence. By my perspective, someone from that far away was just short of being an alien, and that notion was soon adopted by all of my classmates. We anxiously awaited the day of the visit 'cause none of us had ever encountered a foreigner.

The day finally arrived and Nellie Kaye entered the classroom smiling from ear to ear. Following her was a man dressed in black, standing nine feet tall. Well, he was at least twice as tall as us second-graders. His hat, shirt, pants, and boots were adorned

The antlers from this fallow deer were collected as sheds in the Land Between the Lakes in Kentucky. The skin was provided by a friend in Hobart, Tasmania, Australia.

with silver medallions. Must have been the best cowboy regalia his country had to offer. Sort of reminded me of Zorro — with glitter. He sure looked like a foreigner, and when he spoke there was no doubt. Obviously, the impression was lasting, for me anyway.

It wasn't until my college years that foreigners were a part of every day life. Then, in 1987, while working in South Carolina as a deer-research biologist I received an invitation to visit the land down under as a guest of the Australian Deer Association (ADA). When applying for a passport and visa it dawned on me that I was on the verge of becoming a foreigner myself. All of a sudden there were feelings of uncertainty about fitting in, being accepted as a fellow deer hunter and appearing as different as the visitor of my second-grade class.

My apprehensions were soon quelled. I was treated like Royalty 'cause most Australian deer hunters had never met a wildlife biologist. During this initial visit and several that followed, I was introduced to three of the six deer species that now reside in Australia. We toured their habitat by day and I presented slide programs on wildlife management in the USA to interested groups at night.

On a historical note, back in the mid-1800s there were 17 deer species brought to Aus-

The antlers from this sambar deer were collected as sheds on St. Vincent Island in Florida. The skin was provided by a friend in Moe, Victoria, Australia.

tralia and 11 were liberated into the wild. Since deer are considered as "introduced" wildlife, they generally have been treated accordingly. The Australian Deer Association (ADA) was founded in 1969 in an effort to unite deer hunters toward deer conservation. A primary driving force behind that movement was Arthur Bentley, later renowned as the "Father of the Deer." Had it not been for the ADA there likely would be no legal hunting of deer. Furthermore, deer would have been relegated to the status of vermin. But that is not the case because deer hunters in Australia have the same convictions to their quarry as they do the world over.

The stature of the ADA regarding deer conservation became a guiding light for the development of our Quality Deer Management Association in 1988. The overwhelming success of quality deer management in the USA spread to the fallow deer herds in Tasmania, Australia. Hunters/managers there will soon be celebrating their 10th anniversary of a quality deer management program spearheaded by QDMA's Brian Murphy.

The friendships that developed from my trips to Australia will be treasured forever. What I learned from Australian deer hunters has affected my hunting, my profession, and my life in general. As an expression of my appreciation I have "assembled" two foreign deer heads to watch over my home.

The sambar, originally from India and representative of Australia's number one game animal, is a combination of skin from the high country of Victoria, Australia and antlers from St. Vincent National Wildlife Refuge in Florida. Sambar deer were released on St. Vincent Island in 1908. Ownership of the island changed several times until The Nature Conservancy bought it in 1968 and transferred title to the U.S. Department of Interior for addition to the national wildlife refuge system. The sambar population has flourished and public hunting is available.

Originating in Europe, the adaptable fallow deer has become established on numerous continents. The specimen in our home is a combination of skin from Tasmania, Australia and antlers from the Land Between the Lakes in Kentucky.

These foreign diplomats are symbols of hope for our future. In the universe, neither man nor beast is a foreigner, and that is the common ground upon which we must stand.

Note: *This article appeared in Quality Whitetails (V 10, I 5 - 2003).*

The Silhouette Buck mount with jawbone and left antler.

The Silhouette Buck

We had made several passes through the 8,000-acre ranch and there was no doubt that a deer hunter's greatly anticipated window of opportunity had opened. Al Brothers turned to me and said, "Jose, the bucks are runnin'!"

It was in the early 1980s and I was encountering for the first time a well-managed deer herd during the zenith of the breeding season — the rut. Heretofore, all of my experiences with this form of deer behavior had been with traditionally-managed herds; those with a disproportionate sex ratio (more adult does than bucks) and a young age structure among bucks. I had never seen multiple bucks pursuing a doe in heat. Conditions were different on this property in the renowned Golden Triangle of the south Texas brush country.

It's like observing a different species of animal when comparing the physical characteristics, particularly antler size, and behavior of whitetails subjected to contrasting management strategies. What was my response to this novel, Texas-style of management? I was excited, exhilarated, envious, and challenged. Why challenged? Al told me that my responsibility was to return to South Carolina as Johnny Appleseed with the "seeds" of hope for neighborhood deer hunters.

Back on the ranch, Al would stop his truck at the intersection of "senderos," swaths cut through thick brush as seismographic survey lines for oil and gas exploration. In that position he could watch ahead and to each side with his binoculars. The rear view mirror was checked often as well for deer crossing behind us. The deer activity was nothing short of phenomenal. We changed locations after 15 minutes or so. About mid-morning we noticed one group of seven bucks standing nervously in a semicircle as a hot doe lay bedded against a cluster of prickly pear cactus. A tending buck, obviously the dominant one, was pacing to and fro between his temporary mate and his competitors. Al drew my attention to the most distant buck. He had a wide, unbalanced rack and a sagging belly. He seemed to be a satellite, a non-threatening observer, to the event. We continued our tour, but decided to have another look at this group later in the day.

Lunch was filled with chatter about all that we had observed that morning. I had seen more buck/doe chases since breakfast than I had observed in all of my years of deer hunting in the Southeast. Lunch was brief, driven by anticipation of resuming our tour of the property.

By mid-afternoon we returned to the location of the buck group with the hot doe at bay. She remained bedded and the bucks were still there. Al gave me the option of taking the satellite buck. Without hesitation I transitioned into the hunting mode and took the shot. We headed to the skinning shed with my old-timer. His jawbone revealed that he was 8½ years old. The rack, with four points on the right and three points on the left, measured 21 inches wide. This was by far the oldest buck I had ever harvested.

For nearly 20 years this buck's rack and jawbone were displayed in my office as reminders of my hunt with Al Brothers. Then I decided to mount this buck in a unique way of showing his better side. I contacted my hometown friend and accomplished taxidermist, Steve Guyton, and asked him if he would consider mounting half a deer head. You can imagine his initial response, but he agreed to take on the task. A straight-forward form was cut in half with a band saw. The finished product was a mounted deer head with one eye, one ear, and the right side of his rack. My over-the-hill buck from south Texas finally had a name — The Silhouette Buck.

Note: *This story has never been published.*

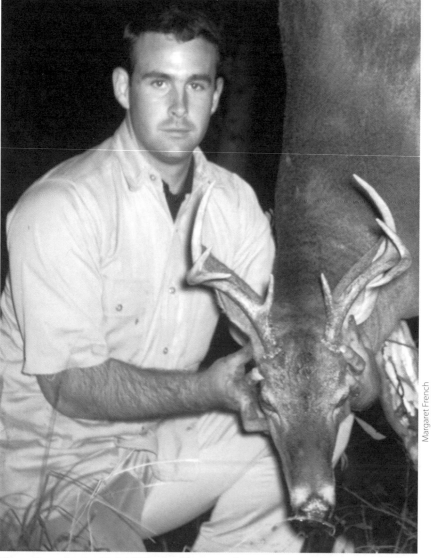

The author with the High Hill Buck of Sugar Loaf.

The High Hill Buck of Sugar Loaf

Our club hunted twice a week — Thursday afternoons because the stores in town closed at noon, and all day on Saturdays. As luck would have it, I had only morning classes on Thursdays at Southeastern Community College, so I could usually make the 30-mile drive back home in time for the afternoon dog drive.

On my way home this particular Thursday afternoon, I was still flying high from the life-changing events that occurred the previous week on Halloween Day, 1968. I had joined the hunting group late, but I still had enough in time for the afternoon dog drive in the Kemp Woods, less than a mile from the courthouse in my hometown, and across the Cape Fear River.

But the price I paid for being late was to take a "back" stand. That meant that everyone else had chosen their favorite stand and I was to cover the back door in case the chase went in the wrong direction — not down river as usual. Well, the dogs hit a hot track and within a minute or so the deer was up and running. A cacophony of hound voices alerted the hunters. They headed down river as expected, but there were no shots. I thought it must have been a doe they were running since deer hunting in those days was for bucks only.

As the hound voices began to fade, I heard a crash and there he was! The buck of my dreams was bounding in 20-foot leaps in the opposite direction of the dog drive. Old timers would have said he was "slippin' out" or "skulkin'." Well, this old buck was not slipping out — he was heading hell-bent-for-leather away from the commotion, and he was not quiet about his departure. My dove-hunting skills came into play and I swung as the buck was in mid-stride about six feet high — I pulled the trigger and he slid along the sugar-sand ridge as a baseball player slides into home plate. That buck had an eight-point rack with an outside spread of 21 inches. He weighed 195 pounds. The jawbone revealed that he was 3½ years old. It was and still is the largest buck I have ever taken in my home state.

Now, a week later, I was joining the club for an afternoon hunt at Sugar Loaf. Folks were on their stands before I arrived. I drove to the back corner of the tract, to a location called the High Hill. You have to be a flatlander to appreciate the term "high hill." The elevation change is slight at best, but it is a hill, and deer seemed to use this geographical feature as a travel corridor. I knew that and this is where I wanted to spend the remainder of the afternoon. The problem was that someone was already there. I drove past, turned around and stopped to apologize for the disturbance. "Your timing is perfect," he said, "I have a meeting in town and must leave now."

During frequent visits to the Sugar Loaf area I had paid close attention to the deer crossings along the sandy, two-rut road from the high hill nearly a half mile to the Wright family cemetery on a bluff over the Cape Fear River. There were two places with the most tracks — the High Hill and the Double Curve. I was informed that Jack Cross was covering the Double Curve, so I was thrilled to fill the vacant stand at the High Hill. For those unfamiliar with a dog drive, the stands hunters select are at well-used deer crossings. The stand is simply a "place" to position yourself that provides cover, yet offers a good vantage point near a crossing.

Reenactment of the hunt for the High Hill Buck using the mounted head.

I backed into some shrubby vegetation, dropped to my knees, and faced the road with my back to the river lowlands. The drone of distant hound voices in the lowlands was barely audible, but at least there was activity. Although I was 21, I had deer hunted this way enough to know that constant vigilance was an absolute necessity. Deer can appear at any time — not just when the hounds are heading in your direction. There were countless times that, as a younger, less experienced hunter, I was preoccupied with peeling an orange or cutting an apple into thin slices and glanced up to see a deer from nowhere staring at me like a laser beam. Needless to say, the deer always seems to elude you in such situations.

Looking up and down the road reminded me of my first trip to Sugar Loaf with my Father when I was only three years old. It was one of his favorite haunts in our home county. Then, there were no deer, black bears, or wild turkeys — only squirrels and rabbits. Now, deer were there, but in low numbers. Bears and turkeys would appear on the scene years later. Dad lost his battle with cancer at a very young age and would not be around to witness these changes or to cheer my involvement. During our short time together though, he did set my ship assail in the right direction.

Vigilance means listening to the slightest sounds in the woods. The snap of a twig or rustle of leaves could signal the approach of something worthwhile. More often than not though, the faint sounds are made by birds or squirrels. Maintain your guard. An animal the size of a deer can glide through the woods as silently as a slight breeze.

Having been on my stand for less than 15 minutes I detected the footsteps of something approaching the road only 10 yards to my right. In a millisecond the nose of a deer emerged from cover. I slowly raised my shotgun and the deer, A BUCK, took another step, revealing his eight-point rack and the upper portion of his neck. My vigilance paid off this time and I shot a "skulking" buck!

This was the only shot fired during our afternoon dog drive. Within an hour the crowd assembled to hear my story and view the fine buck. We loaded the deer into the back of a pickup and headed, in a caravan, to our camp on the south end of town. There was no skinning shed in those days, just dog pens. A 2 x 4 had been nailed horizontally to a large oak tree and the board had a notch near the end. We would put a stout section of tree limb through the deer's hamstrings and hang him in the notch on the horizontal board for skinning and dressing.

Among the crowd of onlookers was my Mom. Someone had called her about the successful hunt, and she came with her camera to capture the moment. Mom remained on the front line of my supporters until she became an angel at age 93. I was interviewed a while back by a young, fellow Eagle Scout about my career in wildlife management. He asked who most influenced my life. Without hesitation I said it was my parents, scoutmaster, and major advisor in college. I found that the harder I worked to make them proud, the more I accomplished. It was my drive to thank them, to pay them back, that forged my life as a wildlife biologist.

Forty years later a cabin was built at Sugar Loaf and the mounted head of the High Hill Buck was donated to hang on the wall as a reminder of the progress we have made in deer management. Bucks like this 2½-year-old, commonplace now, are allowed to "walk." Larger bucks, black bears, and wild turkeys are abundant on the Sugar Loaf tract — a testament to wise management, proper mentoring, and changing times.

Note: *This story has never been published.*

The Magnolia Buck: A Eulogy

Deer names originate from hunters' respect for an individual and are assigned on the basis of physical oddities, a particular hunting area or community where they were harvested, or simply because they were obviously old.

I was always envious of someone who had gained (or assumed) the privilege of naming deer, moreover of someone associated with a famous deer. My time was to come, and it was to have a profound effect on my life as a deer hunter/manager.

He was first encountered in October 1985 during a routine spotlight survey on the South Carolina lowcountry plantation where I resided. The area had been hunted with dogs for bucks only through 1984, so we were surprised to see a mature, eight-point buck. He was chasing a doe and appeared oblivious to our presence. The next morning I scouted that woodlot and found a cluster of six magnolia trees that had been marked in a unique fashion. A buck had rubbed each tree straight forward, leaving deep furrows in

Trail camera image of the Magnolia Buck and the magnolia tree bearing his markings.

a vertical pattern. Apparently the brow tines were used to create this unique rub design. Only a mature buck would attack trees of such diameter (8-10 inches).

Just before dark that same day I returned to the woodlot and positioned myself on the ground at the base of a large red oak. Within a matter of minutes he appeared in a clearing about 75 yards away and began zigzagging in my direction. He seemed tense, preoccupied. The rut was in full swing and he had quite a harem nearby with no competition, at least from bucks in his age class. He stopped often and looked in all directions, but continued toward me. Several heavily browsed greenbrier shoots only five paces from me caught his attention and he paused for a few bites of succulent, new growth. I had never been this close to a mature buck before. Hiding behind the stock of my Marlin 30-30, I studied his antlers in detail. He had nearly a 16-inch spread and eight typical points with a one-inch point originating straight forward from the burr of each antler. A rack that distinct could be recognized easily, and it was later.

Judging by body shape, with bulky shoulders and swollen neck, the buck was at least 3½ years old. He must be the one that marked those magnolias so distinctively, I thought as he walked past, presenting a memorable broadside view. He made a bee-line for the cluster of magnolias, thus marking the beginning of the Magnolia Buck story.

Several hunters caught glimpses of the Magnolia Buck during the '85 deer season, but we had launched full-bore into a quality deer management program and were harvesting does only. Anyway, he needed a respite from the storm of extreme hunting pressure from houndsmen and the high deer density that resulted from a history of doe protection.

One Sunday afternoon in February 1986, a shed antler was found near the site of our first encounter. The antler had four typical points and a one-inch point on the burr. He had survived our initial season of quality deer management! We searched ardently for the matching antler, but to no avail. Then in July a farm worker showed up on my doorstep with a bleached antler — the long-missing half of the Magnolia Buck's rack.

Five deer seasons passed and although many quality bucks were brought to our skinning shed, none exhibited the antler characteristics of the Magnolia Buck. Discussions of his movement patterns and favorite haunts dominated our visits around the firepot.

The Magnolia Buck had become a neighborhood legend. His presence imparted a certain flavor to the woodlot bearing those personal, vertical rubs on magnolias. Shed antlers with burr points found during successive winters bore testimony that he was still around. Pursuing such an elusive animal taught us the true meaning of a quality hunting experience.

During the summer of 1991, Grant Woods, a doctoral candidate in wildlife biology from Clemson University, began a study of rub behavior on Bluff Plantation. This site was chosen primarily because we had practiced quality deer management since 1985 and had noticed an increase in the density and size of rub trees. Although no one ever admitted it, the Magnolia Buck also had a "hand" in determining the research site.

Nine infrared-triggered cameras were put into position to monitor rub activity. One such camera was located near a large magnolia tree, obviously within the home range of our renowned buck. Another camera near a 10-inch diameter sassafras (a preferred rub species due to its aromatic character) was particularly busy "capturing" visiting bucks. Thirteen different bucks were photographed at the sassafras rub on Cemetery Hill. The camera that most interested our hunters "watched" the magnolia tree. Only one buck was photographed there during the fall of 1991 and 1992. Guess which one?

The Magnolia Buck managed to elude hunters season after season. Then, on the morning of October 12, 1993, one of the property owners was sitting in his portable tripod stand when a large-antlered buck materialized in thick cattails along an old rice-field. The density of cover prevented a shot. A quick glance with binoculars revealed that the buck was trailing a doe. She slowly emerged from cover and he followed. They were traveling parallel to a ditch that angled toward the stand and the awaiting hunter. Seconds turned to minutes and seemingly to hours, but the pair approached. They stopped in a clearing only 60 yards away. Antlers coated with early morning dew glistened in the sunlight — truly a mesmerizing sight.

The Magnolia Buck and a hunter had finally crossed paths in an age-old drama that stirs the deepest of emotions. With heart pounding, the hunter readied his rifle as best he could. A shot rang out and the Magnolia Buck vanished, unscathed.

Marker of the Magnolia Buck's grave with a magnolia flower and his life span.

Ironically, two mornings later a non-resident motorist, speeding through deer country during the peak of the rut, struck an animal. The Magnolia Buck lay dead on a highway roadside at 5:30 a.m. on October 14, 1993.

Majestic to the end, with a perfectly matched 10-point rack scoring 138 Boone and Crockett points, and a weight of 175 pounds, he was the epitome of a quality buck, even at the ripe old age of 11½. I buried him between two magnolias. His signature on each tree is a fitting epitaph.

During the span of time we shared an address, there were 415 deer (116 bucks and 299 does) harvested on this 3,200-acre property. Also, each year several deer were shot from the highway by poachers — an absolutely deplorable yet common activity.

Nevertheless, the Magnolia Buck slipped through this gauntlet, a tribute to his elusiveness.

It was his behavior, the phantom-like nature and preference for magnolias as jousting partners that yielded his name and later created his legendary status.

Considerations of whitetail genetics are usually antler-related. Have we not overlooked a more important heritable trait — that of behavior? The Magnolia Buck personalized his woodlot with constant reminders that he was still around. Now, after nearly two decades of breeding, he and his progeny have spread that unique behavior throughout the neighborhood, assuring many quality hunting experiences to come.

Herein lies but one of the rewards of participating in quality deer management. We revere the Magnolia Buck for pioneering our emotions through the early stages… most of all, for the mystique, those intangibles we learned to savor.

Just last year his antlers were combined with the cape of a 7½-year-old buck from the neighborhood. The mount graces a wall in the home of the hunter who missed him. The Magnolia Buck will not be forgotten!

Note: *This article first appeared in the Summer/Fall 1994 issue of Quality Whitetails and was revised for Quality Whitetails (V 9, I 3 - 2002).*

CHAPTER 6

INDIVIDUAL TRIBUTES

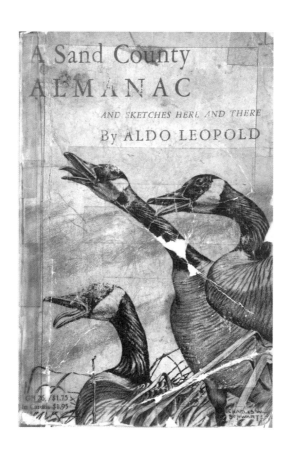

My original copy of A Sand County Almanac has traveled with me to New Zealand, Australia, Africa, Canada, and throughout the United States. The author, Aldo Leopold, has had a profound influence on my life and profession as have other noteworthy individuals.

Arthur Bentley with a fine fallow buck in Tasmania, Australia on March 16, 1979.

A Tribute to Arthur Bentley – Educator and Hunter

D eer hunting exists today because some special person gave each of us the opportunity to participate in this time-honored tradition. Young American Indians accompanied their elders on trips afield to secure venison for their families. This form of apprenticeship carried throughout the colonial period in America and continues as the foundation of deer hunting as we know it today. We follow the footsteps of our elders, usually those of grandfathers, fathers, uncles, or older brothers. Once deer hunting becomes the "fire in our belly," our appetite for more knowledge is never whetted. Wisdom gained from our fellow hunters is invaluable, but there is a vast storehouse of knowledge elsewhere in the written word.

American hunters have been exposed to a wealth of information provided by an endless list of authors. Familiar names and their classic works include James Fenimore Cooper, *The Deerslayer* (1841); William Faulkner, *Big Woods* (1955); William Monypeny Newsom, *White-tailed Deer* (1926); Archibald Rutledge, *An American Hunter* (1937); and Robert Ruark, *The Old Man and the Boy* (1957). A bibliography of hunter/writers would cover pages. We have been and continue to be blessed with a variety of writings ranging from folklore to scientific information.

The profession of wildlife management was pioneered by Aldo Leopold in 1937 when he became the first professor in a one-man department at the University of Wisconsin. That same year The Wildlife Society was formed under the watchful eye of Leopold. The Pittman-Robertson Program, initiated in 1937 as the Federal Aid in Wildlife Restoration Act, is the world's premier wildlife conservation effort. The well-being of most wildlife in the U.S. today can be traced in some way to this phenomenon. Through this program sportsmen have continued to provide the vital fuel that has kept the fires of conservation aglow.

Half way around the world, in the land down under, the situation is quite different. Soon after the colonization of Australia an Acclimatization Society was formed to bring certain plants and animals from other parts of the world, primarily Europe, to simulate familiar living conditions in a strange land. Cattle, sheep, and agricultural crops were the most common introductions, but the list included 17 species and subspecies of deer. Eleven deer species were liberated into the wild during the mid- to late-1800s, and six of those are present today. There were no deer in Australia prior to the efforts of the Acclimatization Society and several independent parties.

Since deer are considered as "introduced" wildlife, they generally have been treated accordingly, with little or no attention from professional conservation agencies. The state of affairs concerning deer was destined to change. Deer hunting produced a pioneer, a man who would become respected as the "Father of the Deer." Arthur Bentley, in his early 20s, became interested in deer in 1937. Except for the time spent serving his country in World War II, he has been actively involved in improving the status of deer in Australia ever since.

In 1952 he became a member of the Australian Crocodile Shooters Club, which in 1954 changed its name to the Australian Crocodile and Big Game Hunters Club because of the increasing interest in deer and deer hunting. He was elected secretary of the club in 1952 and held that position until 1959.

In 1956 he established a Conservation Committee within the Australian Crocodile and Big Game Club long before conservation became a familiar word, or the cause for conservation was fashionable. He was the committee's only secretary.

In 1960 he established the Victorian Conservation Committee, an organization which focused on deer. In 1962 the committee became known as the Victorian Deer Conservation Cooperative Ltd. and functioned until 1984 as an active organization. In its long history the Cooperative had only one secretary — Arthur Bentley.

In 1967 his book, *An Introduction to the Deer of Australia*, was published. This book remains the only comprehensive reference work on the deer of Australia.

The Australian Deer Association (ADA) was founded in 1969 in an effort to unite deer hunters toward deer conservation. A primary driving force behind this movement was none other than Arthur Bentley. The ADA logo bears this quote by Aldo Leopold: "Conservation is a state of harmony between men and land." Our "Father" of wildlife management is theirs, too, thanks to Arthur Bentley.

He advocated the establishment of a government-sponsored agency to advise on deer management in Victoria. In 1973, largely as a result of this advocacy, the Minister of Conservation established the Deer Advisory Council of Victoria. Arthur Bentley was the Victorian Deer Conservation Cooperative's original delegate on the council. The establishment of the Deer Advisory Council in Victoria promised to be one of the most significant moves toward improving the status of deer in Victoria. But after only five years of success, the government used the council to frustrate the deer management and conservation efforts of the hunting groups. As a result, the ADA resigned from the council in 1977. One year later, the Wildlife Department abolished the council. The ADA remained faithful to the cause and can be credited for the only long-term improvements in the status of deer in Australia. Since 1984, the ADA has been the single organization representing deer and deer hunters.

Arthur Bentley was awarded the British Empire Medal on the Queen's Birthday Honors List in 1975 for long and valuable services to deer conservation. The citation reads, in part: "His work in deer preservation has been an inspiration to all those who have come in contact with him." No other Australian has been honored in this manner for services to deer.

His service to the Australian Deer Association has been dedicated and distinguished throughout the history of the organization. He has been an inspiration, and given guidance, through the many executive positions he has held.

In addition to his many activities and achievements, Arthur Bentley has contributed to the promotion of deer management in Australia through the presentation of papers at various conferences and the writing of technical publications. He serves as chairman of the Australian Deer Research Foundation Ltd. This organization has published numerous books, written by local hunters, funded projects involving several species of deer in Australia, and was instrumental in the recent Tasmanian fallow deer project directed by Brian Murphy.

Arthur Bentley is a man of many talents: author, artist, poet, sculptor, and conservationist. He became the first to be granted Life Membership in the Australian Deer Association in 1977. This was a well-deserved honor for an individual with no formal biological training and one who has always served as a volunteer. Two other stalwarts, Mike Harrison and Peter Stuart, of the ADA have joined Arthur as Life Members. Arthur Bentley has been a father figure and mentor of Mike and Peter for many years. In fact, he is regarded in such capacity by anyone who meets him. He is truly one of the Deer People, devoutly committed to deer and deer hunters the world over. We should be challenged to emulate his example.

Many of his hunting companions (mates) from the distant past refer to him simply as A.B., a title that seems appropriate for such a modest gentleman. A feature of ADA's Annual Hunters' Dinner is the presentation of the Arthur Bentley Trophy to the hunter who has taken the best sambar deer stag during that year. Before receiving the circulating trophy, the fortunate hunter must recount his hunt in detail, and in doing so pays

Left to right are: Mike Harrison, Arthur Bentley, and Peter Stuart —
Life Members of the Australian Deer Association.

tribute to his quarry. As a keepsake the hunter receives a medallion, inlaid in wood, bearing the bust of a magnificent sambar stag and the signature "A.B."

My pilgrimage to Australia occurred in 1987. Aside from the expected fascination for Australia's unique animals and landscape, the highlight of the visit was an introduction to Arthur Bentley and the Australian Deer Association. The stature of the ADA regarding deer conservation became a guiding light for the development of our Quality Deer Management Association in 1988. A monumental international trade had taken place. The ADA is based on the "Land Ethic" principles extolled by Aldo Leopold, and now, Australia's "Father of the Deer" had inspired a similar movement in the States.

Our established relationship continues to be symbiotic. The overwhelming success of quality deer management in the USA has spread to Tasmania, Australia and is destined to reach other corners of the world.

During a recent return trip to Australia I had the fortune of an extended visit with Arthur Bentley. Before parting, Arthur commented, "You know, Joseph, I dreamed that I was sitting at your Firepot, and you'll never guess who was sitting across from me — Al Brothers!" I told Arthur that such pioneers were always there in spirit. That's the role of mentors.

Note: *This article appeared in Quality Whitetails (V 2, I 3 -1995).*

Dr. Larry Marchinton will always be a hunter because the "fire" is in his heart and soul.

A Tribute to the Marchintons

D r. Larry Marchinton officially retired from The University of Georgia's Warnell School of Forest Resources in November 1996. During his stay at the university, Larry served as major professor for 45 Masters and PhD candidates. In addition, since 1967, he taught a marathon course in Wildlife Management Techniques to hundreds of students. His impressive list of technical and popular publications, while focusing on the white-tailed deer, includes basic research and management of black bears, wild turkeys, foxes, rabbits, opossums, feral hogs, alligators, and dusky seaside sparrows.

Larry Marchinton was the type specimen of wildlife professors. In academic terms he was the one who best represented his kind — the one other professors aspired to emulate. The friendships Larry established with his students carried through into their professional careers. In short, Larry assumed the major professor title for life. His students ultimately became his family and he is revered as our mentor.

I had the distinct pleasure of visiting the Marchintons at a fireside celebration of his retirement. While there I read the compilation of letters from his many students. Without exception, Betty, Larry's wife was mentioned as a primary reason for his success as an educator. Betty Marchinton is the consummate team player. Her duties extended well beyond the responsibilities as hostess for their numerous gatherings of graduate students to include office manager, activity planner, editor and even co-author. Larry and Betty have always performed as a team.

This is what I wrote in his retirement letter: " Nearly three decades have passed and the time has come to pay tribute to someone I have known as an educator, major professor, hunting companion, fellow QDMA member, and friend. You have served admirably in each category and I have benefited every step of the way.

"We shared common origins as coastal deer houndsmen, brought together by a mutual admiration of the whitetail and a quest for more knowledge. Our paths have crossed so many times since September 1967 that the quagmire of stories is difficult to unravel. Suffice it to say that if we retired to rocking chairs on the front porch we would have a storehouse of memories to keep us entertained from now on.

"Although you're retiring from the hallowed halls of learning, this is but a milestone from which to begin another chapter of outdoor experiences. The advantages are that you can participate full-time and you have amassed an inexhaustible list of hunting companions — your former students. Allow the endurance of the beagles and your most faithful companion Betty to serve as your activity barometer.

"Years ago you impressed upon me the importance of writing. While gratifying when finished, the process of conveying my thoughts on paper remains arduous. Choosing the appropriate setting does loosen the thought process. For this special occasion I waited until I was on a deer stand and the hounds were in full cry. During the course of the morning's deer drive I passed up shots at two four-pointers and a large eight-pointer, and took a doe instead — it was an antlerless hunt. How times have changed! Wish you could have savored the pleasures of this hunt with me, but there will be other opportunities.

"Best wishes to my mentor and friend! Our firepot will always have a special bench reserved for the Marchintons."

The Deer Committee of the Southeastern Section of The Wildlife Society bestowed Dr. Larry Marchinton with the Deer Management Career Achievement Award at the annual meeting of the Southeast Deer Study Group in Charleston, South Carolina in February 1997. Although only Larry's name was inscribed on the prestigious plaque, those of us who know the Marchintons are aware of the role Betty played in making this a reality. Their influence has spread internationally through the many students they have touched.

In 1991 the Marchintons traveled to the land down under as guests of the Australian Deer Association. Larry was invited to deliver the keynote address at the second annual banquet of The Keepers of the Hunting Spirit in Melbourne. Excerpts from his address divulge Larry Marchinton's insight.

"What is the mystical Spirit to which we refer? Is it natural or supernatural? I think mostly the former. Is it not a biological thing — an instinct, one that pervades the soul of mankind — an innate characteristic fostered by more than a million years of necessity? If so, can this desire to hunt be a bad thing as many would have us believe? Having the instinct to hunt is not optional among those of us that do, and therefore cannot be wrong. Remember, this instinct, this Spirit of the Hunt is as deeply ingrained as more than a million years of necessity can make it. Hunting is not so much what we do, as being a hunter is what we are!

"The Spirit of Hunting, although a very natural and honestly acquired instinct, must only be expressed in the most ethical and environmentally responsible ways. And yes, I think that this is the very reason The Keepers of the Hunting Spirit are meeting tonight — to help establish the highest ethical standards for the hunting fraternity and

Larry and Betty Marchinton visiting a swamp in South Carolina along the Savannah River.

to provide them with a moral anchor in the rapids of society's changing values.

"Hunting breathes vitality. Life is part of death, and death is part of living. An ecosystem has plants and animals that have 'created' each other. Once created will predator and prey remain as they are forever? Hardly! The prey must have the predator, just as the predator needs the prey. One without the other eventually becomes something less. The wolf becomes a dog. The deer becomes a cow. And what does man become? That's a question that each of us must answer for ourselves by reaching deep into our minds, our hearts, and our souls. By stopping natural processes, preventing normal predator/prey relationships, we inadvertently start down another destructive pathway. The science of modern wildlife management should be, and is, designed to prevent this by nurturing and maintaining the delicate relationships between the hunter and the hunted.

"Yes, we must search our genes, the very recesses of our antiquity, to see if the Spirit of the Hunt has survived. But it is as rational, informed present-day human beings armed with all the facts that modern biological science can provide us, that we ultimately must decide what is the appropriate biological and ethical expression of this ancient legacy — this Spirit of the Hunt. The thing to remember is that the Spirit is important and necessary to both man and his prey. Without it, both inevitably must fall back from the evolutionary pinnacle, from the keen edge honed by our ancient relationships."

Note: *This article appeared in Quality Whitetails (V 4, I 1 - 1997).*

Uncle Clennon

Recently while attending a meeting at my alma mater, The University of Georgia, a former classmate was reminiscing about the hunting and fishing stories that added spice to our rigorous academic schedule. He asked about one of my hometown friends who had the name of a disease. I drew a blank. Who would label their son with a disease name, anyway?

My friend said he vaguely remembered Rabies as the person's nickname. Suddenly a light came on. It must have been my southern drawl. Many of us from rural neighborhoods south of the Mason-Dixon Line speak lazily, typically slurring the end of a multi-syllable surname. I often mentioned my friend Ray Beasley, 'cause he and I had hunted, fished, and camped together since our careers as kids.

During the mid-1960s Ray accompanied his parents to his father's home in Barbour County, Alabama. Ray's uncle Clinton (pronounced Clennon) Beasley was bragging about a buck he has shot the week before. "These Alabamer deer are way yonder bigger than your Carolina deer." Uncle Clennon was trying to be serious, but his reputation as a jokester and an ever-present devilish smile prompted Ray to ask about the horns' whereabouts. "Oh, I hauled the head around in the bed of my truck for several days making certain all of my hunting buddies got a look at it. The weather was mighty warm and that old head turned kinda smelly, so I stopped on the bridge down the road a ways and throwed that darned thang in the creek."

"Which bridge, and uh, just how deep is that creek?" Ray wanted to get his hands on those antlers 'fore his curiosity got the best of him. One of his cousins drove him down to the bridge and they used a long bamboo pole with a length of string to entangle the antlers and rescue them from the creek. Uncle Clennon told Ray that since he had gone to all the trouble of fetching the rack he may as well keep it.

When Ray returned to North Carolina with the massive antlers it caused quite a flurry of excitement. One thing was for sure, Uncle Clennon's comparison of "Alabamer" and Carolina deer was accurate. We had never encountered such a rack of antlers and also couldn't believe he had tossed it into a creek.

Several years later Ray announced that Uncle Clennon was coming to North Carolina for a visit. "He's a storytellin' character," was the only introductory comment Ray offered. What an understatement that would turn out to be.

Ray and Uncle Clennon were standing out in the yard when I arrived. He didn't look at all like I expected. He was much taller than his brother (Ray's father) and he was cross-eyed. In fact, Uncle Clennon said he was so cross-eyed that he could stand on their front porch and count the chickens in the back yard. "My family thinks I'm crazy, and I believe they're probably right," he exclaimed behind that devilish grin. I solidified our friendship by asking him to tell the story about his big "Alabamer" buck.

Without batting an eye Uncle Clennon turned his back to Ray and me and gazed across the yard. I was on the verge of learning that Uncle Clennon was more of a mime than a storyteller. Still gazing across the yard he leaned forward a bit and began bobbing his head as if he was watching an approaching deer. He extended his arms like he was holding a gun and flinched three times without uttering a word. Ray said, "I think he

Ray Beasley with Uncle Clennon's "Alabamer" antlers.

just fired three shots at the buck!" Uncle Clennon walked in the direction he had "shot." When he was about 40 steps away he looked to the ground and hesitated. He took a couple more steps and bobbed his head like a chicken pecking grains of corn. "He's on the blood trail," Ray chuckled. Well, Uncle Clennon walked out of sight. Minutes later we saw him round the corner of the neighbor's house, still moving his head in that corn pecking fashion. Gradually, he turned our way and walked past us about 20 steps. All of a sudden he stood straight and held his extended arms to the sky. Ray and I realized that Uncle Clennon had just found his buck. When he joined us I fully expected him to ask for assistance in loading the buck into his pickup truck. Instead he said, "That's the way it happened. Pretty good story, don't you think?"

In early January 1977, I was on a road trip through east Alabama and noticed the name BEASLEY on a mailbox. A quick glance at my map revealed that I was in Barbour County, Uncle Clennon's stomping grounds. A nearby country store seemed to be a good place to begin my search for Uncle Clennon. I entered and much to my surprise was standing face to face with a tall, cross-eyed character wearing a devilish grin. It was Uncle Clennon in all of his splendor. My search was short-lived. He owned the store!

"Hold still, let me tell the wife you're here." He was back in a flash. "You might as well spend the night and get a fresh start in the morning." I graciously accepted 'cause the afternoon's sleet storm had created treacherous driving conditions. "We can come back out to the store after we eat a bite and tell some hunting stories 'til bedtime."

Within an hour after supper the small store was filled with Uncle Clennon's friends. There were no chairs or benches for seating. Each person was perched precariously on a wooden drink crate.

The proprietor, my host, launched into a discussion about an article on antler rattling he had just read in a sporting magazine. Although the article originated in Texas he decided to try this newfangled technique on his "Alabamer" bucks. The atmosphere was akin to a tent revival complete with the ritual of communion. Before Uncle Clennon embarked on his hunt the visitors, one by one, stepped behind the counter and took a nip from little half-pint bottles concealed in brown paper bags. They were so discrete with this activity that I doubted its legality, but asked no questions. Eventually all eyes turned toward Uncle Clennon.

He took the cue and began rattling his imaginary antlers as deftly as Marcel Marceau, renowned French mime. For the next 10 minutes he simulated several rattling sequences characteristically with no words uttered. His audience, apparently accustomed to this style of storytelling, remained quiet, except for frequent trips behind the counter. Since the rattling elicited no responses, Uncle Clennon decided to take a nap. He pulled the bill of his cap down to the bridge of his nose, leaned back against the wall while sitting on his drink crate, and acted as though he was snoozing. I was utterly amazed at the reverence of his friends.

Uncle Clennon emerged from his make believe nap, repositioned his cap, and resumed his rattling antics. With that sequence completed he piped up and extolled, "Them Texans can keep their rattling horns in Texas, our 'Alabamer' bucks is too crafty for such trickery!"

I am indebted to my friend Rabies for sharing his Uncle Clennon with me. Such relationships are among the genuine treasures of hunting.

Note: *This article appeared in Quality Whitetails (V 8, I 1 - 2001).*

In the Shadow of the Iron Horse

By Joe Hamilton And Gerald Moore

Only 15 miles, as the crow flies, from the QDMA's headquarters in Watkinsville, Georgia, an iron horse stands atop a pastured hillside. The equine statue, an ominous man-made figure over 10 feet tall, was permanently located there in 1959 following its unceremonious debut on The University of Georgia campus. Why the move? Rumor has it that a bale of hay positioned under the horse's head by pranksters was the final "straw" in a series of character defamations which prompted the sculptor to seek a resting place of solace for his creation. Now, its stately prominence graces the rural neighborhood, including nearby deer woods.

In 1969 a wildlife graduate student from south Georgia sat in his homemade climbing tree stand overlooking a creek bottom within shouting distance of the Iron Horse. Deer season was in full swing and the chance of seeing a better-than-average buck was good because this region of Georgia had been stocked in the 1950s with whitetails from Wisconsin. At that time, the deer population was well within the carrying capacity of

The equine statue, an ominous man-made figure over 10 feet tall.

its habitat and foods were abundant. The prospects of a good hunt were all in place. This November hunt was destined to chart the course of Larry Corbett's life as a deer hunter. Incidentally, Larry was known to close friends and classmates by his last name.

We visited Corbett recently at his home in Echols County, Georgia, where he worked until retirement in 2001 as the County Extension Agent. In fact, the pickup truck (with a QDMA decal in the rear window) parked in his yard was presented to him as a token of gratitude from the landowners he served throughout his career. Stories were told of our graduate school experiences with difficult courses, field trips, and the professors that taught us the way of wildlife management. But the story that dominated our visiting time was Corbett's recounting of his hunt.

He had found some promising sign while scouting the area and decided to invite his major professor, Dr. Larry Marchinton, to accompany him on the maiden hunt. They arrived in the wee hours of the morning so they could be in their stands well before daylight. According to Corbett, not long after sunrise he heard something approaching from behind, and turned slowly only to see two young boys, clad in hunter orange, ambling along as they talked quietly. A wave from Corbett got their attention and they politely backtracked. Disgusted, he thought, "Well, there's not much chance of seeing anything now that human scent is all around my stand." Within a few minutes, though, the sound of a cracking limb revealed a small doe about a hundred yards away. She approached to within 70 yards, hesitated momentarily, and retreated quickly into dense cover. Another snap of a limb and a huge buck appeared where the doe was first seen. Corbett shouldered his 30-30 rifle and attempted to line up the buck in his iron sights.

Corbett recalled, "It was the largest buck I had ever seen in the woods and I just didn't feel comfortable with taking a shot at that distance. He stood there like a statue for what seemed a lifetime. Then he followed the doe's trail and stopped 70 yards away. I took careful aim at his massive neck and pulled the trigger. He fell to the ground immediately. While I was climbing down, I glanced over my shoulder to make sure the buck was still there — he wasn't! I caught a glimpse of his tail as he disappeared. Once on the ground, I walked over to where the buck had been to check for blood. There was a little blood where he fell, but none in the direction he had run. It wasn't long before Dr. Marchinton showed up and asked what I had shot. All I could say is that it was a monster. It was the largest buck I had ever seen in the woods. We drove back to Athens, got one of Dr. Marchinton's trailing hounds, and returned to the site. The dog picked up the scent and took us straight to the buck. He had gone only a couple a hundred yards." The buck weighed 255 pounds live weight, had 14 points and, although never officially measured, it was thought to have grossed 158+ and netted around 151 Boone and Crockett points."

The "Corbett Buck" was certainly a very impressive trophy and all the wildlife students raced to see it first hand. With such a fine specimen to his credit, Larry Corbett vowed to hunt only mature bucks. He stuck to his conviction. During his working career he influenced many local and regional sportsmen to enhance their hunting experiences by passing up young bucks. Although he never put another deer in the cooler the size of his famous buck taken in the shadow of the Iron Horse, all the deer he took had one thing in common — maturity.

During our visit the mounted head was admired and photographed, but the collection of large antlers amassed since 1969 was equally impressive. Corbett proved time and again that letting them go so they can grow is a well-founded concept. He has been a stalwart member of the Quality Deer Management Association and the kind of person anyone would be proud to hunt with and to call a friend.

Author's Note: *Gerald Moore is the regional wildlife biologist in the Central Piedmont with the South Carolina Department of Natural Resources. He and I were classmates of Larry Corbett at The University of Georgia's School of Forest Resources during the late 1960s and early 1970s. Larry Corbett departed this realm and entered the Happy Hunting Grounds shortly after our reunion. Larry was a disciple of buck management. He taught me a lesson in traditions and respect for your elders. Larry would smile to the point that his eyes nearly closed, but when pressured about harvesting does, he simply said he just wasn't raised that way. Whether you agree or not with a friend's convictions you must place your friendship above any differences you may have on any issues. Larry Corbett was a long-time deer hunter and he never harvested a doe — not even with a vehicle! It is rare to encounter someone who will stick with their guns to this degree.*

Note: *This article appeared in Quality Whitetails (V 10, I 3 - 2003).*

Aldo Leopold at the family's beloved shack.

The Compleat Conservationist: Aldo Leopold

Aldo Leopold, founder of scientific wildlife management, is regarded as the 20th Century's most influential spokesman for conservation and environmental quality — his teachings left a message for our times. He spoke of developing an ecological conscience to reflect individual responsibility for the health of the land and the animals and plants which grow upon it. He predicted that this "Land Ethic" would be long in coming but warned that its birth was an ecological necessity.

In the late-1960s an aspiring college student was introduced to Aldo Leopold's classic book, *A Sand County Almanac.* The eloquence of this renowned pioneer in the conservation movement inspired the student to pursue a career in wildlife management. Leopold spoke of mankind's relationship to things natural, wild and free, spurring the student on to a quest for more knowledge of the father of his profession.

I was that college student, and I remain a student of the man whose teachings, philosophies, and dedication to wise use of our natural resources provide the guidance

Photo courtesy of the Aldo Leopold Foundation

needed for understanding and appreciating man's role in life's drama. "Conservation," he wrote, "…is a state of harmony between men and land. Despite nearly a century of propaganda, conservation still proceeds at a snail's pace…"

Many voices have cried to us from the wilderness, most noted among them Henry David Thoreau, John Muir and, more recently, Rachel Carson. Although few recognize the significance of his contributions, the name Aldo Leopold deserves a place among the list of those who sought to enhance our lives through ecological enlightenment.

Leopold is best known to natural resource managers and participants in the environmental movement. In a poll of such a group (by *Sierra* magazine, May-June 1986) including writers, scientists, activists, educators, politicians and others asked to identify the book that had been most meaningful to them, *A Sand County Almanac* was cited first.

Aldo Leopold has been described as a professional forester, game manager, scientist, teacher, philosopher and writer – a prophet for all seasons, but one called by critics a man ahead of his time. The time for his message to be acknowledged and acted upon has arrived. As we see habitat and resource loss and abuse, we recognize that the quality of life ultimately will be measured by how we advance rather than by how much. Leopold's "ecosystem thinking" left a message for a "more enduring civilization."

Rand Aldo Leopold was born January 11, 1887, in Burlington, Iowa. Located on a high bluff overlooking the Mississippi River, the homeplace provided the perfect setting for a young boy to explore and ponder the natural world. His parents, Carl and Clara Starker Leopold, nurtured Aldo's aesthetic sense through their traditional German heritage.

As a youngster, Leopold accompanied his father on frequent enjoyable hunting trips, that more importantly, – were educational. Carl Leopold taught his son to read sign, but he took such learning experiences a step further by asking, "Why? What does this mean? What has this animal been doing? Why does this plant grow here and not there?"

This approach to understanding the intricate relationships between animals and their environment was one which Aldo would culture throughout his life. Ultimately, he would expand this approach to explain man's functional role as part of the environment, or land community, rather than ruler or despoiler of it. In the interim many events and experiences channeled the development of his philosophy.

During the 1890s, spring duck hunting was still in practice, but Carl Leopold had observed a decline in waterfowl populations and refrained from spring hunting. This act of self-restraint provided young Aldo a foundation for his own ethical development. Years later, he regarded his father as a pioneer in sportsmanship.

A good English teacher taught Aldo the basics of writing, but it was his mother who stimulated the development of his writing ability when he entered preparatory school in Lawrenceville, New Jersey. Leopold frequently went on long tramps into the surrounding countryside to observe and discover, much as he had done in his younger days at home. He took extensive notes and wrote home to Clara about the plants and animals he encountered.

He continued his habit of letter-writing when he went on to the Sheffield Scientific School at Yale University, penning over 10,000 pages of letters, mostly to his mother, and thus sharpened his communication skills. Leopold was deeply involved with his academic interests in the burgeoning field of forestry, and his early conviction to conservation was evident in one letter he wrote to his father concerning the ongoing spring shooting of ducks: "I am sorry that the ducks are being slaughtered as usual…when my turn comes to have something to say and do against it and other related matters, I am sure nothing in my power will be lacking to the good cause."

With a master's degree in forestry from Yale, Leopold went to work with the newly designated U.S. Forest Service under the direction of Gifford Pinchot and was assigned to the Arizona and New Mexico territories. During 15 years spent in the Southwest, he became enamored with the idea of managing wildlife. He started founding game protective associations that promoted predator control, establishment of wildlife refuges and the hiring of non-political game wardens. President Theodore Roosevelt in 1917 commended Leopold's efforts in game management, stating that the game protective associations in New Mexico were "…setting an example to the whole country."

Initial endeavors in this unconventional field unfortunately presented perhaps one of the greatest dilemmas of Leopold's professional career. Leopold became a staunch advocate of predator control, modeling his game management philosophy after Pinchot's utilitarian, or commodity-oriented, approach to forest management. The commodity wildlife species like deer and turkeys were to be preserved for hunting while the varmints – wolves and mountain lions – could not be tolerated and were eradicated.

Leopold's sudden realization of his short-sightedness and failure to recognize the importance of predators' role in the ecosystem came one day when he shot a wolf high in the mountains and saw it die.

Years later he described the experience in *A Sand County Almanac*. "We reached the old wolf in time to watch a fierce green fire dying in her eyes. I realized then, and have known ever since, that there was something new to me in those eyes — something known only to her and to the mountain. I was young then, and full of trigger-itch; I thought that because fewer wolves meant more deer, that no wolves would mean hunter's paradise. But after seeing the green fire die, I sensed that neither the wolf nor the mountain agreed with such a view."

In the wake of predator control, Leopold observed the plight of a wolfless mountain. "Such a mountain," he wrote, "…looks as if someone had given God a new pruning shears, and forbidden him all other exercise." The deer herd succumbed of its own "too much." He reflected, "…too much safety seems to yield only danger in the long run."

A mistake had been made, and Leopold admitted it. He began to look at the natural system as a whole, a complex of interrelated and interdependent parts. Thus, his ecosystem thinking was in the infancy of development.

He turned his energies toward the preservation of the wilderness, and his driving force in this movement was two-pronged. Wilderness, he thought, had "expected importance as a laboratory for the study of land-health." Remnants of healthy land must be preserved to serve as a basis of comparison to identify sick lands, those in need of human stewardship.

The other reason behind his efforts comes forth in these words: "Man always kills the thing he loves, and so we the pioneers have killed our wilderness. Some say we had to. Be that as it may, I am glad I shall never be young without wild country to be young in.

"Getting up too early is a vice habitual in horned owls, stars, geese, and freight trains. Some hunters acquire it from geese, and some coffee pots from hunters."
– Aldo Leopold

Of what avail are forty freedoms without a blank spot on the map? …To those devoid of imagination, a blank space on the map is a useless waste; to others, the most valuable part."

A transfer to Madison, Wisconsin, in 1924 began four frustrating years as assistant director of the U.S. Forest Products Laboratory. Leopold found his concerns with the living forest at odds with the interest of his co-workers who dealt with harvested trees.

In 1928 Leopold left the U.S. Forest Service to change his hobby of game management into a profession. Game populations were plummeting during the 1920s and action had to be taken if hunting or even casual observation of game were to remain a viable proposition. Funded by the Sporting Arms and Ammunition Manufacturers' Institute, Leopold began conducting game surveys in nine north-central states to gather information on animal species' ranges, food and habitat needs, population status and susceptibility to hunting pressures. Through these studies, Leopold developed a radical and unproven notion that wild game could be produced on a sustained yield basis, much as foresters had raised trees. The shift of emphasis was from the old idea of artificial propagation and simply restricting the harvest of game to a new idea of habitat management so that the game would raise itself.

Game management was in an embryonic state, and Aldo Leopold had become one of the country's foremost authorities on the subject. He was chosen to serve as chief draftsman and chairman of a committee to draw up a national game policy. Adopted in 1930 by the 17th American Game Conference, the policy was a major undertaking destined to guide the wildlife profession for the next 50 years. Its basic premise was that only the landowner could practice management efficiently, because he is the only person who resides on the land and has complete authority over it. It summarized, "In short, make game management a partnership enterprise to which the landowner, the sportsman and the public each contribute appropriate services and from which each

I proposed to my wife Donna at the Leopold Shack in November 1993 by giving her a ring I made from a shed deer antler.

derive appropriate support."

While unemployed during the Depression, Leopold prepared a textbook for the new field. *Game Management* (Charles Scribner's Sons 1933) established wildlife management as both an art and a science in this country, and the book's basic concepts are still sound and useful.

Another career opportunity arose in 1933, when Aldo Leopold became the first professor of game management, accepting a position in the Department of Agricultural Economics at the University of Wisconsin. Four years later, a one-man Department of Wildlife Management was established by the university. In a short course, the professor introduced his students to what he called land health. "What conservation education must build is an ethical underpinning for land economics and a universal curiosity to understand the land mechanism. Conservation may then follow."

Leopold had strong ties with the farmers of America, believing them to be on the front lines of conservation. His interest in agriculture arose initially from his concern for soil erosion and also the impact, good or bad, that farming could have on wildlife habitat. As a conservation philosopher, he sought to define the role farming played in the greater equation of man's relationship to the natural environment.

Leopold's career put him in touch with people from all walks of life, and he kept his convictions before the public through several books and more than 350 articles. While his ideas were novel and he often met opposition, he was recognized within certain circles. He was an organizer of The Wildlife Society and the Wilderness Society and served on the governing bodies of several national conservation organizations.

Problems of overpopulation in Wisconsin's deer herd during the late-1930s and early 1940s forced Leopold into a confrontation with public opinion. In 1942 the state Conservation Commission appointed Leopold to the Citizens Deer Committee, which was challenged to inform the public of a need to alleviate the unsightly and wasteful winter die-offs of deer.

Prevailing herd conditions were characteristic of overpopulation, resulting from years of buck-only hunting seasons. Low body weights, poor antler development and high fawn mortality reflected nutritional stress. A young age structure caused by heavy hunting pressure contributed to the preponderance of small antlers. Herd reduction appeared to be a biological necessity.

Drawing from his experiences in the Southwest in the 1920s when he had supported buck-only hunting, Leopold now advocated the harvest of antlerless deer, temporary elimination of the usual buck season and lifting the bounties on wolves and coyotes. A public outcry resulted, mainly from those in the tourist industry whose livelihood depended on maintaining a high-visibility deer population. Concerned citizens felt that emergency feeding programs would solve the problem of winter starvation. Leopold's concern about overpopulation was not just for deer herd health, but rather for the long-lasting effects of too many deer on habitat composition or land health.

For years his pleas for research on habitat requirements had gone unheeded by the state Conservation Commission. He felt there should have been a gradual education of the public to the need for proper deer herd management, which would entail the harvest of antlerless deer.

The events that followed would haunt Leopold for the remainder of his professional career. Two months after his appointment to a six-year term on the Conservation Commission, that body proposed a split-season plan (four days of buck followed by four days of doe), although Leopold had favored a strictly antlerless hunt, but there was no system for controlling hunter numbers. Herd reduction was accomplished — the harvest was nearly three times as large as ever before — but the public had not been adequately informed of the reason for the reduction.

Wisconsin's first season allowing harvest of antlerless deer came to be known as the "crime of '43." Because of his outspoken support for a change in hunting tradition, Leopold became a scapegoat, shouldering the blame for the slaughter. His continued efforts to sway public sentiment toward maintaining the deer herd within the habitat's carrying capacity were to no avail. He would not live to see another antlerless deer season in Wisconsin. (The state eventually adopted deer management practices to maintain a healthy deer herd, but most importantly, the environment was given a chance to restore its integrity).

Unquestionably ahead of his time, Leopold tried to provide us with a direction and the proper attitude to prosper as a "more enduring civilization." The final chapter in his life teaches that our environmental attitude will be the test of time.

Two years after Leopold began teaching he sought an opportunity to practice land husbandry, which he believed "…unknown to the outdoorsman who works for conservation with his vote rather than with his hands. It is realized only when some art of management is applied to land by some person of perception."

He purchased a 120-acre farm north of Madison, Wisconsin, and it became Leopold's "refuge from too much modernity." The family converted an old chicken house into rustic living quarters and affectionately called it the Shack. Weekend retreats and vacations to the shack provided solitude, family togetherness and an opportunity to participate in the healing process of the land, to restore its ecological integrity.

After spending three months in Germany studying what he considered the ultimate in forest and game management, Leopold returned to the university and his "sand-county shack" to ponder and write on the ecological and aesthetic costs of extreme environmental control. The shack and its surroundings were to become the setting for the compilation of a lifetime of experiences, observations and philosophies into his classic *A Sand County Almanac*, foreworded by these comments: "There are some who can live without wild things and some who cannot. These essays are the delights and dilemmas of one who cannot."

The shack sketches reveal Leopold's ability to feel the land's pulse and his eloquence in conveying his deep and ethical regard for things natural, wild and free. During one vivid essay on the joys of a time spent fly-fishing for trout, he muses, "I sit in happy meditation on my rock, pondering, while my line dries again, upon the ways of trout and men. How like fish we are: ready, nay eager, to seize upon whatever new thing some wind of circumstance shakes down upon the river of time! And how we rue our haste, finding the gilded morsel to contain a hook. Even so, I think there is some virtue in eagerness, whether its object prove true or false. How utterly dull would be wholly prudent man, or trout, or world!"

Throughout his writing run the themes of savoring the sporting experience and fully appreciating the intangibles, he emphasized the pursuit rather than the prize. After his morning at the trout stream he confessed, "…none of those three trout had to be beheaded, or folded double, to fit their casket. What was big was not the trout, but the chance. What was full was not my creel, but my memory."

His words about his farm's woodland express his view of each natural thing and occurrence as a vital part of the whole: "Soon after I bought the woods a decade ago, I realized that I had bought almost as many tree diseases as I had trees. My woodlot is riddled by all of the ailments wood is heir to. I began to wish that Noah, when he loaded up the Ark, had left the tree diseases behind. But it soon became clear that these same diseases made my woodlot a mighty fortress.

"A flock of a dozen chickadees spends the year in my woods. In winter, when we are harvesting diseased or dead trees for our fuel wood, the ring of the axe is a dinner gong for the chickadee tribe…every slab of dead bark is, to them, a treasury of (ant) eggs, larvae and cocoons…it lightens our labor to know that they, as well as we, derive aid and comfort from the fragrant riches of newly split oak…but for diseases and insect pests, there would likely be no food in these trees, and hence no chickadees to add cheer to my woods in winter."

Aldo Leopold died of a heart attack in the spring of 1948 while fighting a grass fire on a neighbor's farm. At his death the collection of essays and shack sketches was still in manuscript form and was later published as *A Sand County Almanac*.

Leopold's last essay, "The Land Ethic", was perhaps his most enduring contribution to our society and our environment. He spoke first of the ethical sequence. "The first ethics dealt with the relation between individuals. Later accretions dealt with the relation between the individual and society. There is as yet no ethic dealing with man's relation to land and the animals and plants which grow upon it. The land-relation is still strictly economic, entailing privileges but no obligations. The extension of ethics to this third element in human environment is an evolutionary possibility and an ecological necessity.

"A land ethic, then, reflects the existence of an ecological conscience, and this in turn reflects a conviction of individual responsibility of the health of the land. Health is the capacity of the land for self-renewal. Conservation is our effort to understand and preserve this capacity."

Aldo Leopold's "Land Ethic" must be accepted and applied universally if the quality of life we now enjoy is to be carried through future generations. He leaves us with a sense of optimism about our future: "I have no illusion about the speed or accuracy with which an ecological conscience can become functional. It has required 19 centuries to define decent man to man conduct and the process is only half done. It may take us long to evolve a code of decency for man to land conduct. In such matters we should not worry too much about anything except the direction in which we travel."

Author's Note: *Reprinted by permission from SOUTH CAROLINA WILDLIFE magazine, May-June 1987; copyright 1987. This article appeared in Quality Whitetails (V 2, 13 - 1995).*

Changing of the Guard

During the live auction in August 2010 at the Bladen Lakes Branch REACH banquet (Elizabethtown, N.C.) a long-time friend and hunting companion turned to Donna and me and asked if we were interested in going to Africa. Donna quickly replied with an emphatic YES! Walter McDuffie was the successful bidder for the Africa Maximum Safaris hunt package for four — two hunters and two observers/photographers. Plans for the trip were in the works before we left the banquet that night.

Donna and Walter's wife, Diane, decided that the long flight to Africa should be "softened" by a stopover in London for a couple of days. May 2011 rolled around and we were off to Africa via London. We crammed a fair bit of sightseeing into those two days. The highlight was a visit to Buckingham Palace to witness Great Britain's main tourist attraction, the renowned Changing of the Guard ceremony. It was a spectacle laced with pomp and circumstance — fancy to the nth degree. With a heavy dose of history and tradition, we were off to Africa.

On August 15, 2011 a more personal experience regarding the Changing of the Guard occurred. I arrived at home from the QDMA's National Convention that day just in time to freshen up a bit, change clothes, and head to our local hospital in Walterboro, SC. Our daughter Moya and son-in-law Charlie were poised to present Donna and me with our first grandchild. Within an hour of my arrival the initial cry of Baines Hamilton Pierce could be heard from the nearby waiting room. WOW! Only 30 minutes old, he was whisked away to the nursery in a plastic tray, like a tournament bass, for the obligatory weighing and measuring — eight pounds and 21 inches long were his first stats. As he lay there in his birthday suit, squalling, and thrashing his four appendages like

The author's hunting mentor from his youth, Clarence Leo "CL" Turner.

an upside-down turtle, I reached over and shook his tiny hand and said, "Little fellow, it's good to meet you and I look forward to shaking your hand on this date, your birthday and the first day of deer season, for a long time.

Baines will soon become one of the QDMA's youngest Life Members and arrangements are underway to present him with a lifetime hunting/fishing license from the S.C. Department of Natural Resources. That's about all I can do for him now, but there will be much more to come as he grows older. I'll have a ringside seat in the development of this future hunter. As a grandfather and fellow hunter I will serve with his father and his uncle Hunter as his mentor.

Something gained and something lost. The next morning I received the sad news that a close family friend was on his journey to the happy hunting grounds. I was reminded of a poem by Robert Louis Stevenson that seemed appropriate for Mr. Turner, a seasoned outdoorsman and sportsman.

REQUIEM
Under the wide and starry sky
Dig the grave and let me lie.
Glad did I live and gladly die,
And I laid me down with a will.
This be the verse you engrave for me:
Here he lies where he longed to be;
Home is the sailor, home from the sea,
And the hunter, home from the hill.

Clarence Leo Turner, 89, was among my earliest mentors. My Father lost the battle with cancer at the young age of 37. I was six years old, and Mr. Clarence, we called

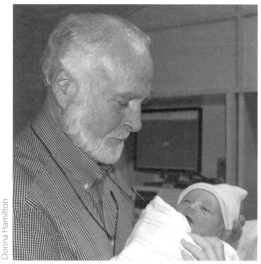

Donna Hamilton

First grandchild, Baines Hamilton Pierce. He was granted a Life Membership in the QDMA within minutes of his birth, as was his brother, Baylor Lucas Pierce, three years later.

him CL, along with other mentors stepped up to the plate and made sure that I was involved in scouting and hunting. CL was a scout master for one of our local troops and he was insistent that I join the Cub Scouts. When the time came, I progressed to Boy Scouts. The scoutmaster of my troop was Mr. Doug Waller. He had two daughters, but he treated each of us in his troop as a son. Regardless of the weather, we camped one weekend each month year round. Mr. Waller was a devout squirrel hunter. On several occasions he prepared a squirrel stew in a large cast-iron pot for the entire group of campers. The culinary delight of squirrel and rice was the impetus for me to take up squirrel hunting.

CL was on hand to teach me the art of squirrel hunting. We trudged through the bottomlands of the Cape Fear River and pulled vines to make the critters move into view. He would also ask me to stand still and look upward as he walked past a large oak or hickory to send a squirrel to my side of the tree. His techniques worked and I was hooked on squirrel hunting. In typical boyhood fantasy, I wanted to return to my "roots" and live off of the land.

It was CL who took me to South Carolina in 1956 for my first deer hunt at the age of nine. That event was life changing for me. I was so taken by the ambiance of South Carolina and BIG GAME hunting that I promised my hosts I would live here when I grew up. I did just that — because I had learned in Boy Scouts that it's important to be a man of your word. In fact, the 12 Points of the Scout Law begins: A scout is trustworthy...

Throughout my high school years I was a member of the Waddell Hunting Club. Since we were a single-car family. one of the older gentlemen from the club, usually Tootie Butler or Simp Singletary, would pick me up every Saturday morning for a day of deer hunting. There were others as well who made sure I got to the deer woods. They were Walter McDuffie, David Cross, and Glenn Parker, to mention a few.

The point is that my early development as a scout and hunter was influenced by a host of mentors including my Mom, who let me follow my dreams. Most have been joined in the happy hunting grounds by CL. Now, as a grandfather and staunch supporter of the QDMA's Mentored Hunting Program, I realize my responsibility to take my position in this traditional Changing of the Guard.

Note: *This article appeared in Quality Whitetails (V 18, I 6 - 2011).*

CHAPTER 7

WILDLIFE BIOLOGY & MANAGEMENT

Education through trial and error, often backed by research, has influenced the profession of wildlife biology and management since the mid-20th century. As a result, the white-tailed deer and those who pursue this noble game animal, have benefited immeasurably.

Kyle Harding

To this hunter the entire package was one of trophy status.

Management for Trophy Deer in South Carolina

Management for trophy white-tailed deer had its beginning in Texas during the late 1960s. Al Brothers and Murphy E. Ray Jr., authors of the book *Producing Quality Whitetails*, are acclaimed as the pioneers for developing and practicing proper deer herd management techniques which produce trophy bucks. Their book was soon followed by a similar one entitled *Hunting Trophy Deer* by John Wooters and a rash of popular magazine articles on the topic. As a result, a wave of excitement about "instant" trophy bucks spread through the deer hunting fraternity. Unfortunately, when considering initiating a trophy management program on their hunt clubs, many members have become disillusioned by the commitment of time, energy, money and the change in harvest techniques required to produce trophy bucks. However, it must be emphasized that the quality of deer harvested in a given area is directly proportional to the intensity of management.

This paper discusses the objectives of Texas-style trophy deer management and the degree to which these practices can be applied to deer herds in the Southeast, particularly in South Carolina.

First, the term TROPHY must be defined. I am reminded of the adage, "beauty is in the eyes of the beholder," when attempting to qualify just what constitutes a trophy buck. To the purist, a trophy is gauged only by antler measurements according to the Boone and Crockett or Pope and Young standards. Other hunters judge a trophy buck's antlers by number of points, wide "square" racks, or high "round" or "basket" racks, or even a personally conceived recipe combining several characteristics. A four-point buck or "forkhorn" that falls to the gun of a 12-year-old hunter is a trophy if it is a first. Many seasoned hunters, accustomed to hunting in a situation with a high deer density (too many does) and heavy pressure on the bucks, will consider a 2½-year-old buck with eight points and a 14-inch antler spread a trophy. Obviously, the management practices involved in producing a so-called trophy buck vary according to the criteria established by an individual or group. Actually, in the strict sense of the definition, a white-tailed buck will not reach his potential in antler development until he has attained an age of 5½ to 7½ years. In addition, the combination of habitat quality and genetics must be optimal for that buck to reach the trophy class.

Trophy Deer Management in Texas

Two unique factors contribute to the success of trophy management in Texas. These are the intensively managed ranch system and the use of deer-proof fences. High fencing affords a manager the opportunity of manipulating a "closed" deer herd. Through this system the loss of deer to hunters on adjacent property is minimized, hence, population control is left to the discretion of the manager and Mother Nature. Following is a brief discussion of the management practices employed in Texas for the production of trophy white-tailed deer.

Deer Census

Annual inventory of a deer population is absolutely necessary for proper management. The degree to which this practice is executed depends upon available manpower and funds, the total acreage involved and the habitat types to be surveyed. Basically, three survey methods are used. These are (1) aerial surveys, usually conducted from a helicopter; (2) night surveys conducted by a team of observers using a pickup truck and hand-held spotlights; and (3) incidental observations, which are usually recorded over a defined period of time by resident managers and are used primarily as supplementary data for either of the other two survey methods.

Surveys are routinely conducted during late summer or early fall, prior to the opening of the hunting season and at a time when bucks, does and fawns are easily distinguishable. Information is recorded on deer density and herd composition. The buck/doe ratio and the doe/fawn ratio are monitored on an annual basis to determine recruitment rates and to facilitate making decisions on the harvest strategy. Also, aerial surveys in the Texas brush country enable observers to inventory and photograph trophy bucks.

Harvest Strategy

Carrying capacity is defined as the ability of a given area of land to support a certain number of animals of a particular species. A primary consideration in trophy management is to increase or decrease deer numbers to a level just below the carrying capacity of the habitat. Maintaining deer density at this level will maximize body growth, antler development and reproductive performance.

Buck/doe ratios vary, depending on habitat condition and intensity of management practices, from extremes of one buck to 10 does on some areas to an even sex ratio on others. According to Brothers and Ray, a desired objective of trophy management is to maximize buck numbers and minimize doe numbers. Maintaining a buck/doe ratio of 1:1 or 1:2 requires a considerable effort, but is imperative in trophy management. When harvesting antlerless deer, hunters are cautioned to take only adult does to avoid including button bucks (six months old) in the harvest.

If an even sex ratio has been attained, Brothers and Ray contend that the next most important aspect of herd composition is the proper distribution of bucks within age classes. The quality of bucks within each age class is also important. Under a trophy management regime, the three categories of bucks harvested are: spikes, trophies and culls.

It is common knowledge among wildlife biologists that as deer population density increases, the percent of yearling bucks (1½ years old) with spike antlers increases. However, a spike-antlered yearling on good range is considered genetically inferior and should be harvested. During the 1970s, Texas Parks and Wildlife Department biologists demonstrated with penned deer that the antler growth potential of spike-antlered yearlings was inferior to that of branched-antlered yearlings. Furthermore, their studies indicated that bucks that were spikes as yearlings sired more offspring that were spikes as yearlings than did bucks that had branched antlers as yearlings.

Equally important as genetics for the development of trophy antlers are age and proper nutrition. Since most of the food consumed by a buck during the first two years of his life is used in body growth, the proportion of "leftover" nutrients for antler development is minimal. Most antler characteristics such as branched points, drop points, and lateral points or "kickers" do not develop until a buck attains his third or fourth set of antlers. In Texas most mature bucks taken as trophies are in the 5½ to 7½ year age classes; a few older bucks are harvested, but it is during this stage of life that antler quality begins to diminish.

The term "cull buck" is perhaps as difficult to define as is the term trophy. For the average hunter, a small-bodied spike is probably the only age buck that can be distinguished in the field as being inferior. Cull bucks can be placed in two broad categories: ostensibly mature bucks with a large antler frame and few points, and mature bucks with unusually small racks. Recognizing an inferior mature buck requires an eye for detail and a genuine knowledge of deer, therefore, "culling" should be left to the scrutiny of the most experienced hunters.

As a general rule in Texas, trophy deer hunts are on a fee basis with clients hunting under the supervision of a guide and paying up to $3,000 to harvest an exceptional trophy. Antlerless deer harvests on such areas are necessary to control population density and maintain a balanced sex ratio. These harvests are usually conducted by other hunters paying considerably lower fees. In many situations the monetary returns from antlerless harvests may exceed that from trophy buck hunting or domestic livestock operations.

Record Keeping

Maintaining a complete set of census and harvest records is as essential to proper deer management as it is in any business venture. By closely monitoring the annual trends in his data, the manager has a foundation on which to plan his harvest for the following season. Accurate records will also serve as a measure of management efforts over a period of time.

Harvest records should include weights and ages of all deer. Since most hunters are unable to age deer accurately, a jawbone should be collected from each deer and appropriately labeled. Aging is usually done by an experienced biologist or manager. Lactation and/or pregnancy should be noted in the does. Recording antler measurements of the bucks is an absolute necessity. Antler measurements should consist of number of points, greatest spread measured inside or outside the beams (be consistent), length of each main beam, and antler diameter one inch above the burr. Additional information may include date and time of kill, location of kill, condition of the animal, type weapon used, number of shots, and the name and address of the hunter. Crippling loss should also be recorded. It is helpful to plot the kills on a map throughout the season so the harvest can be evenly distributed over the property.

Habitat Management

Planting of fields for deer use is quite common in the Texas brush country. Oats and wheat are planted as winter crops, but wheat is higher in nutritive value and more beneficial to deer. Spring and summer plantings include peanuts, peas, beans, red-top cane, hygeria, milo and corn. Alfalfa is one legume which, once established, provides a nutritious deer food all year.

Automatic feeders are used on many areas to attract deer for hunting purposes or to "hold" deer so they will not be harvested on adjoining property. Most supplemental feeding is done prior to and during the hunting season. Rarely is it continued through the winter, spring and summer — a critical period of nutritional stress during pregnancy, fawn rearing and antler development. Some very intensively managed deer herds are provided supplemental food year round.

Extensive brush removal for the benefit of domestic livestock operations is detrimental to native wildlife. Wildlife managers are often forced to compromise, even though the livestock operation may be the less profitable of the two enterprises. Brush removal is done in varying degrees and patterns. Of the patterns used — strip, block or irregular "natural" clearings — the latter has proven most beneficial to deer.

Trophy Deer Management in South Carolina

Deer hunting conditions in South Carolina are vastly different than those encountered in the Texas brush country where trophy management is so widely practiced. Two major differences are land ownership and traditional hunting methods. Trophy deer management in Texas is an integral part of the large ranch system where high-fencing is equally important to domestic livestock operations. The expense of installing a deer-proof fence on South Carolina soil could not be supported initially by the monetary returns derived solely from deer hunting.

Theoretically, certain areas in South Carolina, if encompassed by a deer-proof fence, could produce trophy-class bucks sooner and in greater quantity than is currently being done in Texas. There are no areas in the state where management is being practiced with a deer-proof fence, but there may be in the future as the demand for this rather exclusive harvest method increases. Based on the observations of Al Brothers and several other Texas biologists during a tour of South Carolina's lowcountry in 1982, there are regions of our state that produce bucks superior to those of the same age on many Texas ranches under trophy management. In addition, these bucks were harvested from deer populations with relatively high densities (for example, 1 deer/10 acres).

Before discussing the application of trophy management practices in South Carolina, I feel it is worthwhile to mention some of the existing conditions that pose a dilemma for wildlife biologists and managers. Intensive management for trophy bucks is currently not practical for the majority of hunt clubs in South Carolina. Also, such a management plan is not well suited for public hunting. Therefore, this discussion will not apply to public lands in the Game Management Area program under the direction of the South Carolina Wildlife and Marine Resources Department.

In the lowcountry, hunting traditions are deeply ingrained. Dog hunting for deer has been a "way of life" for most private hunt clubs, although interest in still hunting is growing. Hunters are accustomed to a three-to-4½ month deer season with no limit on bucks on most private lands. This is the most liberal season length and bag limit of any state.

A doe quota program for private lands has been in effect since 1967 and the number of tags issued has increased annually. During the 1982 hunting season, 16,223 tags were issued to 1,200 doe quota cooperators in 25 counties.

There are, however, a number of hunt clubs that adhere to the buck-only harvest system. Harvest records of the typical club reflect a classic herd composition: a high deer density and an imbalanced adult sex ratio resulting from the protection of does and a young age structure in the buck segment of the population caused by years of extreme hunting pressure.

Supply and demand have become a problem for deer hunters on public and private lands alike. Each year hunting activity on public lands has increased. In the private sector there has been a trend toward the formation of new clubs and an increase in the average membership; changes due in part to rising costs of land leases. In many cases the carrying capacity for hunters is being exceeded. Large expanses of land have been laced with a network of roads to facilitate forestry operations, but this form of progress has increased the efficiency of hunters using four-wheel-drive vehicles, CB radios and dogs in pursuit of deer. Consequently, the cumulative effects of all these changes have put emphasis on "quantity" harvests rather than "quality" harvests.

My intentions certainly have not been to criticize methods of hunting deer in South Carolina or to discourage hunt clubs from attempting trophy management. Rather, I wanted to single out some of the reasons many hunt clubs are seeking advice to remedy their harvest problems. Our department's game biologists are becoming more involved each year with clubs that are opting for QUALITY deer management. We have learned through working with a select few hunt clubs during the past five years that a transition from traditional hunting methods to intensive management for trophy bucks is too great a step to take. The initial objective of an improved management plan should be to enhance the quality of the animals harvested. Thus, the term QUALITY management appeared appropriate for the situation. Basic guidelines for trophy management are followed in quality management, with the only difference being the harvest of bucks with well-developed antlers in the 2½- and 3½-year-old age classes.

When considering a change to quality management the members of a hunt club must first define their criteria for the quality of animals to be harvested, which will determine the intensity of management efforts. Factors to be considered are: acreage of the hunt club property, existing agricultural and forestry practices, deer herd composition (for example, sex ratio and age structure), habitat quality, types of habitat management to be employed (for example, food plots and prescribed burning), management practices on adjoining property, degree of isolation and access, possible poaching problems, number of club members, frequency and type of hunting (the use of dogs is not recommended), and, if the property is leased, the terms of the lease agreement are especially important for long-range planning.

What are the general harvest recommendations during the first couple of years for a club with classic herd composition problems? A heavy harvest of adult does ONLY will be the most expedient way to lower population density and balance the sex ratio, but this approach requires a great deal of commitment and is not readily accepted by most hunt clubs. A combined harvest of adult does and a quota of quality bucks with eight or more antler points is the next best method, followed by a combined harvest of adult does and a quota on spikes and quality bucks. The least intense management plan would be the harvest of adult does, spikes and quality bucks. This latter method should be the one used for quality management after the desired herd composition has been attained.

Bucks with small, branched antlers are excluded from the harvest at all levels of quality management. The recommendation for not harvesting spike bucks initially is designed to maximize the number of bucks passing into the older age classes at the expense of perpetuating undesirable genes in the population. Only after population density is being maintained below the carrying capacity can genetically inferior yearlings be identified.

Note: *This article was published in the Proceedings of the Third Annual Forestry Forum – Integrating Wildlife Considerations and Forest Management, Clemson University, Cooperative Extension Service, Department of Forestry, Clemson, South Carolina (March 15, 1983).*

Follow Up: It can be embarrassing to read something you wrote more than 30 years ago. This is one such occasion. To be fair though, how a writer interprets conditions or current practices at the time must be considered. One thing you can count on when dealing with wildlife and their habitat is change. When we stop learning we stop advancing.

One of the subsections in this manuscript was entitled Deer Census. This is absolutely wrong. A census involves counting each individual in a population. Whereas, a Deer Survey is an attempt to sample a population through a variety of measures including spotlight surveys, track counts, hunter observations, and more recently, camera surveys.

I referred to an unbalanced sex ratio of one buck to 10 does. Mathematically, this is not possible in early fall, pre-hunting conditions. Perhaps one of the reasons for someone thinking that the sex ratio is this out-of-balance is based on hunter observations well into the hunting season. In areas where the season opens early, as in most of the Southeast, the regulations allow for buck-only hunting. This is especially true in the eastern portion of South Carolina where the buck season opens as early as August 15, and there's no buck limit. When the season on antlerless deer opens a month or six weeks later, the adult sex ratio can be as out of whack as one adult buck per 10 adult does. Imagine how this form of traditional hunting can affect the breeding season. We've proven what can happen. The breeding season is protracted simply because there aren't enough bucks to breed all of the does that are in estrous simultaneously. Some does that are not bred on their initial heat period are forced to cycle again. But that's another month later and there is still a lot of hunting pressure on the bucks. Therefore, the adult sex ratio is more out of balance then. The saving grace is that white-tailed does are seasonally polyestrous, which means that they will cycle every 28-30 days until they are bred. In some situations, adult does can cycle up to five or six times before being bred. That's the way it can be with traditional deer management. Thank goodness, practicing quality deer management can rectify this problem.

I mentioned that it was common knowledge among wildlife biologists that an increase in deer density usually results in an increase in the percent of yearling bucks (1½ years old) with spike antlers. This happens because as the density increases without concomitant improvement in the habitat, the availability of quality browse diminishes as well. Nutritional stress begets the incidence of spike-antlered bucks. I also stated that spike-antlered yearlings on good range are considered genetically inferior, and should be harvested. What about a yearling buck that was a result of his mother breeding late in the fall or even early winter? The cards were stacked against him from the beginning, and he could have entered his first fall as a yearling several months behind his cohorts. His nutritional intake will be directed to muscle and bone development, not antler development. Yet, if allowed to progress into the older age classes he will have the opportunity to exhibit his genetic potential. Some research has shown that spike-antlered yearlings tend to have smaller racks in later years than their cohorts with branched antlers. Other researchers have stated that it was impossible to predict antler development in later years of a buck that began with spike antlers as a yearling. Who do you want to believe? Just don't worry about it. There are more pressing problems in deer management that need to be addressed. An adequate doe harvest and habitat improvements should take precedence.

With regard to wheat being more nutritious than oats, it has been stated recently that they are equal in nutritive value. For some reason I thought wheat was more nutritious because it was preferred over oats as late fall-early winter browse. I found that in some regions deer prefer oats. I also said that alfalfa provides a good year-round food for deer. This can be accomplished in south Texas only if it is irrigated, and that is an uncommon practice. Even in the best of conditions, alfalfa will be dormant in winter. There is no forage in any region of the country that can be promoted as having year-round availability to deer.

I used the term "cull" to describe bucks that had reached the older age classes and did not have the desired antler development for their age. I now find this distinction demeaning. In most instances, a mature buck, regardless of his antler development, remains a challenge for most hunters. Because he has not reached the desired antler development does not mean that he is less of a challenge. The term "management" buck has taken the place of "cull" and I agree with this distinction. A management buck is one that you can remove from the herd without measurably affecting the buck/doe ratio or diminishing the buck age structure.

Trophy Deer Management was said to be unsuitable for groups that hunted deer with dogs or for public hunting properties like state or federally owned or managed wildlife management areas or national refuges. Well, that statement continues to have validity, but quality deer management (QDM) has turned out to be quite suitable for some conscientious dog hunting clubs and for many public hunting areas.

A common complaint or alibi among dog hunters was that it is next to impossible to judge the size of a buck and its antlers as it passes quickly, darting in and out of thick cover. Having grown up as a dog hunter in southeastern North Carolina, I completely understood the frustrations. So we compromised by deciding on a buck quota without antler restrictions combined with an antlerless deer quota. In most cases, clubs were able to harvest more deer with the QDM program than with the traditional management approach of taking only bucks. In one familiar case the dog hunting club was mounting eight to 10 bucks a season by their fifth year of QDM. Prior to that they put one on the wall each year and it was usually a 2½-year-old with a 14-inch-wide, eight-point rack. That dog hunting club still holds the neighborhood record, a 5½-year-old buck that scored just over 146 Boone and Crockett points.

Dog hunting for deer remains a strong tradition in the Southeast and QDM is a viable option for some, especially on large-acreage tracts. In early 2015 the Florida Fish and Wildlife Conservation Commission enacted statewide antler restrictions, and dog hunters supported this monumental change in deer management regulations.

The South Carolina Quality Deer Management Association and the renowned ACE Basin Project were founded in the South Carolina lowcountry in 1988. A basic tenet of the ACE Basin Project was land conservation which fit hand-in-glove with the objectives of the new deer management organization. Why promote sound deer management if the habitat is being destroyed? The playing field must be protected, and that it was. By the QDMA's 25th anniversary there were 85,000 acres of public hunting lands under the guidelines of QDM in the Coastal Plain of South Carolina. And, hunter satisfaction has been overwhelmingly positive. This monumental feat is testament to land conservation, the tenacity and dedication of progressive-minded deer hunters, and the wisdom of the state and federal agencies to do what was right with regard to properly managing the white-tailed deer on lands under their purview.

During my initial visit to south Texas in 1981 I encountered high fences for the first time. It was obvious that the impetus for such barriers resulted from frustration in dealing with uncooperative neighbors. My early experiences were with properties upwards of 10,000 acres, and I understood the reasons for managing a deer herd at a lower density with a better buck/doe ratio, and allowing the bucks to reach older age classes. My thoughts have not changed since. Later, there were situations where the best buck on a property was captured by helicopter and transferred to a holding pen with 20 does, also captured in the same manner. Once the does had been bred by the prime buck they were released into the larger enclosure. That made sense to me then and it continues to. But now, the drive to produce genetically superior bucks involves artificially inseminated does, transporting "superior" bucks or semen straws of such bucks from elsewhere, often from other states, and that is where I draw the line.

The drive to produce what has been labeled "Frankenbucks" has reached epidemic proportions. There's no doubt that genetic engineering has produced young whitetail bucks with abnormally large antlers. In fact, some 2½-year-old bucks have grown antlers that exceed the normal measurements of a mature elk's rack. According to my mentor Aldo Leopold, "Very intensive management of game or fish lowers the unit value of the trophy by artificializing it."

Obviously, there is money to be made from the production of such animals. Somewhat akin to the chinchilla or ratite (emu) businesses of the past, the availability of whitetail breeding stock fuels establishment of additional captive deer facilities. Will this relatively new business, like similar ones before it, reach a saturation point and ultimately dwindle? Probably so, but political intervention in some states will supersede biological concerns and prolong the situation.

The incidence of disease transmission increases as deer are transported across county and state borders. Some diseases of major concern are brucellosis, tuberculosis, chronic wasting disease (CWD), and some parasitic diseases. Proponents of the captive deer industry have commented that "armchair" wildlife biologists have sensationalized the significance of CWD and some have postulated that CWD is more of a "condition" than a disease. Really? If a sickness has 100 percent mortality, don't you think it deserves the title of disease?

There are numerous negative spinoffs from this genetic engineering which should arouse concern among wildlife biologists, the general public, and particularly those who prefer to hunt wild, free-ranging deer. There is a market for those substandard bucks produced in deer breeding facilities to be used in canned hunting operations. These bucks are infinitely larger than bucks of the same age in the wild. It is disappointing that there are patrons of such a business.

Genetic engineering is focused on dramatically increasing antler development, but what about the possibility of promoting skeletal disorders, organ dysfunction, or behavioral aberrations? Could genetic tampering render animals more susceptible to some diseases or affect their ability to interact naturally with others of their species? Who knows, but we will find out eventually.

Other negative spinoffs related to the captive deer industry are financial with regard to taxpayer responsibilities. Millions of taxpayers' dollars are being used to subsidize the captive deer industry. This is a prime example of how lobbyists can steer politicians at the state and federal levels to favor small, special-interest groups at the expense of the majority. The general public is providing a financial safety net for those in the captive deer breeding business.

Chronic Wasting Disease (CWD) was first identified at Colorado State University's Foothills Wildlife Research Facility in 1967. The disease has been found either in captive or free-ranging herds or both in 23 states, two Canadian provinces and Korea. Its potential impacts on the nation's deer herds are a serious concern over the long-term. The prions that cause this dreadful disease in deer are impervious to heat and cold and can persist in the soil for extended periods — perhaps even decades. Currently there is no proof that captive deer have ever spread CWD to wild deer, and disease experts agree there is no "smoking gun" case. However, there is compounding circumstantial evidence from Missouri and Wisconsin.

CWD was first detected east of the Mississippi River in Wisconsin in 2002. Since then the disease has cost that state 49.3 million dollars — primarily in surveillance and monitoring. CWD continues to spread in regions of Wisconsin despite efforts to contain it.

CWD has not been detected in samples from wild or captive deer in North Carolina. Since 2002, surveillance has been continued and is being increased because discovery of the disease in North Carolina would have significant biological, economical, and sociological ramifications. CWD surveillance in wild deer from July 1, 2012 to April 2014 resulted in a total cost of $125,535 whereas the cost for surveillance for captive deer was approximately $72,000 during the same timeframe. Personnel with the North Carolina Wildlife Resources Commission (NCWRC) have made a concerted effort to collect samples from throughout the state, but the low deer density and rough terrain in the mountain region prevented a representative sample. The NCWRC's Division of Wildlife Management established a Chronic Wasting Disease Response Plan in February 2006. Response plans were developed regarding the source of CWD, whether in free-ranging deer or in captive facilities.

There were over 100 deer pens in North Carolina in early 2,000. The NCWRC spent $247,850.00 on a buy-out program from May 2002 until June 2004 that reduced the number of captive deer facilities by 15. Later, a number of the smaller facilities closed voluntarily and now there are only 37. Twenty-four of the existing facilities contain less than 10 deer and only two have in excess of 50 captive deer.

Unfortunately, there is another chapter in this saga. Fueled by campaign donations from an individual proponent of the captive deer industry, the political wheels began turning. For nearly two years hundreds of emails, letters, and personal telephone calls and visits were directed to politicians expressing concerns over the captive deer industry. Public hearings conducted by the NCWRC across the state in 2014 produced a landslide of opposition to the practice of raising captive deer for profit. Yet in the spring of 2015 two senators introduced Senate Bill 513 to transfer the responsibility of the captive deer industry from the NCWRC to the Department of Agriculture and Consumer Services. Warnings were not heeded by elected officials, and the stage has been set for history to repeat itself. There is no reason to think that North Carolina will be immune to the problems other states have experienced with the captive deer industry.

Several years ago the state of Mississippi had about the same number of captive deer facilities as currently exist in North Carolina. There are now 112 permitted white-tailed deer enclosures in Mississippi and at least nine new ones are under construction. A white-tailed deer biologist serves as the Enclosure Program Coordinator and oversees permitting of enclosures containing white-tailed deer. In addition, the wildlife agency has trained 39 law enforcement officers for surveillance and monitoring of the existing deer enclosures. Enclosure permit fees were implemented to fund the permitting, inspection, and regulation of white-tailed deer enclosures, but expenses currently exceed permit revenue.

In late fall of 2014 the owner of a captive deer facility in Iowa had a deer that died and was diagnosed with CWD. The entire herd of 356 captive deer was euthanized and checked for CWD. The infection rate was over 79% — the highest infection rate ever detected in a captive herd. The USDA provided the owner of the operation with a check for $917,100 for indemnification, the value of the deer that were "destroyed" because of CWD. This money that came from the USDA was taxpayers' money.

In states where responsibility for captive deer has been transferred from the wildlife agency to the department of agriculture and the deer have been classified as domestic livestock, deer "farmers" have been compensated by the Farm Bill for captive deer that have been lost to epizootic hemorrhagic disease (EHD). EHD, identified in the 1950s, is a common viral disease among wild, free-ranging whitetails in North America. Furthermore, the Farm Bill has paid deer "farmers" for fencing, shelters, and concrete slabs (in situations with poorly-drained soils). Where does this money come from? The answer is governmental programs, or more precisely, taxes paid by the general public.

In 2014 the state of Florida passed legislation to close the borders to deer trafficking into or out of the state. This was a noteworthy accomplishment since there were over 400 deer pen facilities in Florida at the time. Such a bold action is an admission that the captive deer industry has inherent problems, and the Florida Fish and Wildlife Conservation Commission is to be commended for their stand on the issue.

The QDMA held the 2014 North American Whitetail Summit near Branson, Missouri. More than 200 people attended this inaugural meeting to discuss the pressing challenges related to deer issues. Attendees represented 19 companies in the hunting industry; 18 state wildlife agencies and one provincial agency; 10 leading institutes of deer research; 17 major landowner groups; 15 hunting or conservation organizations; and deer hunters from more than 20 states and one Canadian province. The Top 10 issues impacting deer hunting and management were identified and ranked on a scale of 0 (not an issue) to 5 (big issue). Number 5 on the list was the captive deer industry and the ranking was 3.99. Deer diseases followed with a score of 3.94.

Sadly, the lucrative nature of the captive deer breeding business fosters illicit behavior and the federal Lacey Act is neglected and violated on a regular basis. A friend who has an inside track with deer "farmers" told me several years ago that I wouldn't sleep if I knew how many deer were being transported across state borders illegally every night! And, he said, "... don't expect to see them in stock trailers with plywood over the windows — they're traveling in comfort nowadays in climate-controlled motor homes."

So, after reading my ranting about activities behind high fences, there should be no doubt of my position on the captive deer industry. If deer movement occurs between high-fenced operations, I'm wholeheartedly against it. A business as lucrative as the captive deer breeding industry also breeds illicit activities among some of its participants. Frequent violations of the Federal Lacey Act provide testimony to this fact, and the health of native, free-ranging whitetail populations is compromised.

What is Quality Deer Management?

Emily Stewart, a seven-year-old of Jacksonville, Florida, with her first deer taken on Millaree Hunt Club in South Carolina. Her parents, younger brother, and Marion Burnside (huntmaster) were there for the celebration.

In the most liberal sense of the definition, quality deer management is the use of restraint in harvesting bucks combined with an adequate harvest of antlerless deer to maintain a healthy population that is in balance with existing habitat conditions. This level of deer management involves the production of quality deer (bucks, does, and fawns), quality deer habitat, and quality deer hunting.

Today's hunters are much better informed about the biology and management of their quarry than ever before. The natural progression from education to awareness to enlightenment to understanding and finally to respect explains a change in hunter attitudes and the desire for quality hunting experiences. Voluntary participation in quality deer management has increased markedly within the past five years and South Carolina currently has nearly 175 hunting clubs representing in excess of 500,000 acres under such guidelines.

Involvement in quality deer management extends the role of hunters from mere consumers to that of managers. Again, the progression from education to respect for the quarry bestows an obligation upon the hunter to practice sound management simply because it is the right thing to do. Management guidelines are formulated according to particular desires, goals, and limitations. Participating hunters enjoy the benefits (both tangible and intangible) of following those guidelines. Pleasures can be derived from each hunting experience whether or not a shot is fired. What is important is the CHANCE. When a quality buck is taken, the pride is shared by all club members because it was THEY who produced it by allowing the animal to progress into an age class represented by individuals with larger bodies and antlers.

The harvest of antlerless deer, particularly adult does, is an integral part of quality deer management. Removing a specified number of adult does from the population helps to balance the buck/doe ratio, serves as a means of controlling population growth, and ensures that the remaining deer produce better antlers, attain higher body weights and have more success in producing and raising fawns.

Note: *This article appeared in Volume 1, Issue 1 (Summer 1989) of The Signpost – Official Newsletter of the South Carolina Quality Deer Management Association.*

QDMA Deer Barometer

There was a time in the not too distant past that hunters sat around campfires and spoke with reverence and mystique about the deer woods – remote pockets of deer populations. Now, almost any woodlot can be labeled deer woods. Whereas managers a decade or so ago were concerned primarily with biological factors, we are faced with economic and social considerations as well.

Burgeoning deer populations throughout the whitetail's range have spawned changes in management strategies. The need to control numbers combined with hunters' desires for deer like those produced in "the good old days" have brought us light years away from our traditional BUCKS ONLY beginning.

There is a list of generalities or "rules of thumb" dealing with most deer herds. If the herd is healthy and the habitat conditions are optimal you can expect the following: body weights are good (based on neighborhood standards), a high percentage of yearling bucks have branched antlers, the litter size among adult (2½ and older) does favors twins over singles, antler mass among adult bucks is respectable, lactation in yearling does may approach or exceed 20 percent (evidence of breeding as fawns), fat accumulation is obvious, and parasite levels are low. As population density grows, some of these characteristics exhibit an increase whereas others will decline. For example, the number of yearling bucks with spike antlers will increase, antler mass among the adult bucks will decline, body weights will decline, twin fawns will become less frequent, the incidence of doe fawn breeding will decline, fat accumulation will be less obvious, and parasite levels and associated diseases will be on the incline. Deer barometers will vary depending upon the type of management regime, traditional versus QDM, to which the deer herd has been subjected. With traditional deer management (TDM), a majority of bucks harvested are yearlings (1½ years old). Therefore, this age class of bucks is a good barometer of herd health. Managers look closely at changes in body weight and antler development among yearlings as a measure of success or failure in herd management. Yearlings have become the proverbial "sacred cow" in most QDM strategies. Self-imposed restrictions on harvesting young, small-antlered bucks over time produce a much larger sample size of 2½-year-old bucks. This age class of bucks has become our barometer with increased involvement in QDM.

Deer store fat in obvious locations, and in some that are rather obscure. The degree to which a deer's kidneys are covered with fat provides a clue as to that individual's condition: no fat, poor; 1/3 covered, fair; 1/2 is good and 3/4 to totally covered is excellent. Fat levels in bone marrow determine the color and consistency of the marrow. Crack open the femur (largest leg bone) of a deer that has died of malnutrition and the marrow is red and gelatinous. Have a look at the femur marrow of a deer in good flesh and it will be white and flaky. Someone even used the fat content of a deer's mandible (jawbone) as an indicator of health. This became known as the mandibular cavity fat index, an innovative measurement, but not a widely used barometer.

A simple method for determining a deer's fat storage is to pinch the tail where it joins the rump. If you can feel the projections of the tail vertebrae, there is little or no fat accumulation. Conversely, the base of the tail of a healthy deer is round and smooth or tight, and no bones can be felt. This barometer can cause confusion in that a healthy yearling buck grows muscle and bone and is not prone to build fat reserves like adult deer.

The number and abundance of external and internal parasites serve as a barometer of health. A deer's true stomach, the abomasum, is the fourth compartment of storage in the digestive tract. It is in the abomasum that several common parasites reside. Their numbers, referred to as the abomasal parasite count (APC), have become a measure of a deer population's relation to habitat conditions. These parasites, collectively, have become an accurate barometer of herd health because they are density dependent. As a deer population reaches or exceeds the habitat's carrying capacity the APC will elevate and reflect this relationship. This barometer is a tool of professional wildlife managers.

A recent trend in our society is to move into the countryside — into deer habitat. The escape from city life is traded for more commuting mileage, thus increasing deer/human encounters. In such situations the deer population can be within the habitat's carrying capacity, but it has reached a density that is economically and socially out of balance. Another deer barometer has been created. This barometer is a measure of attitude toward deer. Deer density can elevate to a level that changes their "place" in the ecosystem from an asset to a liability. With this change the status of the whitetail

Carrying Capacity
Deer Population Density
Herd Health
Optimum Low Good Poor High Low

QDMA Deer Barometer

as a game animal diminishes. In some suburban situations deer have been referred to as "hoofed rats." This dilemma is sure to be repeated as human and deer populations share common ground.

One factor that can be assured in dealing with deer populations is change. Often the actions of managers and the attitudes of hunters do not keep pace with the changes inherent in deer populations. These changes must be monitored — with barometers.

Standard biological entries on a harvest data sheet should include: accurate body weight (live or field-dressed), sex, number of antler points, antler spread (inside or outside, be consistent), main beam length, antler diameter or circumference one inch above the burr, and lactation (yes or no). Advanced managers record the reproductive condition of females, including age of the fetus(es) and the conception and birth dates (breeding and fawning seasons).

Harvest information collected on private and public hunting lands throughout the whitetail's range has been subjected to various analyses ranging from simple tabulation of males and females in the harvest to complex computer-generated models of population characteristics. The primary objective of harvest data collection over time is to identify trends in population characteristics from which to base management recommendations. The desired result — healthy deer populations and satisfied hunters.

Consider what goes through a biologist's mind when he/she receives a phone call from someone requesting deer management recommendations. Without the proper information you would be starting "cold." The list of necessary information includes: acreage of the hunting property, number of hunters (including visitors), herd health history, management objectives, land use patterns throughout the neighborhood, regional and state regulations (bag limit and seasons).

Sounds easy enough doesn't it? It is if all of the necessary ingredients — deer barometers — are available for the initial management recommendations to be made. Also, it is important to visit the property with the landowner to discuss the management objectives and to determine if they are realistic with regard to potential. Management goals should be made with neighborhood deer population standards in mind.

Note: *This article appeared initially in Quality Whitetails (V 2, I 2 - 1995) and was revised, with better graphics, for Quality Whitetails (V 10, I 3 - 2003).*

A doe with twin fawns.

The Dynamic Nature of Antlerless Harvests

W hite-tailed deer populations were brought to their lowest ebb during the late 1800s and early 1900s, an era of extensive deforestation, market hunting, and year-round harvesting to feed the growing populations of European settlers. Recovery from their near extirpation throughout North America was slow, but protective laws and the establishment of state wildlife agencies in the 1930s and '40s provided a turning point for the whitetail. Buck-only hunting seasons and restocking, which began in the late 1940s, were the impetus for deer populations to spread into habitats that had been devoid of deer for nearly a half century.

Within a matter of 20 to 30 years, the whitetail had "recolonized" so successfully that populations in some regions had become overabundant. A late-arriving management technique, the novel approach of harvesting female (antlerless) deer, was met with a range of emotions from uncertainty to disdain among hunters. Even today, the era of overabundant whitetail populations, there is an element of reluctance in the hunting fraternity to harvest antlerless deer aggressively.

Quality deer management (QDM) appeared on the scene in a timely fashion just when deer populations were in need of change. Years of overzealous harvesting of bucks had severely diminished their age structure, while the antlerless segment of the population had prospered from overprotection. One of the most common challenges facing those QDM practitioners is harvesting enough antlerless deer on their hunting property each year. In fact, it appears that no matter how many antlerless deer are harvested in some areas, little, if any, population impact is achieved. Many properties under QDM guidelines begin to achieve their initial antlerless harvest goal during the same period they establish food plots and improve the native habitat. This combination of factors improves deer herd productivity and the antlerless harvest must be increased.

Although rare, there are still some areas where aggressive doe harvests are not warranted. The possible reasons can be numerous, therefore a qualified wildlife biologist should be contacted to assess the problem and provide a solution. Poor quality habitats, resulting in many cases from highly acid soils with low mineral content, have a negative effect on a deer herd's reproductive capacity. We have already witnessed through historical accounts that periods of excessive harvests can lower deer populations. There are even situations today where too many antlerless deer have been removed from certain habitats or regions. The QDMA currently is involved in the management of a 2,000-acre property in middle Georgia where the initial recommendation was to harvest NO does for a year or two in response to extremely high doe harvests throughout the area. Extensive habitat improvements are being applied to the property in an effort to provide optimum conditions favoring increased productivity, more fawns per doe and better survival rates. We have taken our management approach a step further by inviting neighboring groups/clubs to participate. Thus, the Bear Creek QDM Cooperative was formed just prior to the 2007 hunting season, quadrupling the acreage receiving intensive management attention. Our first season as a cooperative was a learning experience for most. There were a few bumps in the road, but when the dust had settled our loose-knit group appeared to be heading in the right direction.

Last year's outbreak of epizootic hemorrhagic disease (EHD) resulted in extremely high mortality in some areas or even states. Reducing the prescriptions for antlerless harvests in these unexpected and infrequent situations has obvious merit.

There is possibly an emerging situation that could warrant a more conservative approach toward antlerless harvests. Predation, primarily from expanding populations of coyotes, could be a factor throughout the Southeast, Midwest, and Northeast like it has long been in the Southwest, especially in south Texas. The annual influence of predation on whitetail fawns in south Texas has been tied directly to rainfall. When rainfall is normal the vegetative cover abounds and fawn survival is relatively high. But, in drought times there is scant cover for newborn fawns and the loss to coyote predation dramatically increases, to as high as 90 percent of the annual fawn crop.

How do you limit coyote predation on your deer population? Consider your habitat first. Create cover and the production of buffer foods including berries and fruits. This activity also will increase the number of small mammals (e.g., rats, mice, and rabbits) which serve as buffer foods for coyotes. Controlling predator numbers should be the last consideration and it should be based on hunter observation data of fawns and does, and certain harvest data like a decrease in lactation rates. If it is determined that predation is taking a measurable toll on the deer population, another management response would be the relaxing of antlerless deer harvests.

The primary purpose of this article is to discuss selective antlerless harvests. The category of "antlerless" deer includes all females, and six-month-old males, commonly called "button" or "nubbin" bucks. Some hunters still refer to these button buck fawns and their female counterparts as yearlings, however in technical terms, a yearling deer is in the 1½-year age class. In some states bucks with antlers less than two inches long are also grouped into the antlerless category. Regulations vary among states, so become familiar with the situation in your locality.

When your management goal is to produce quality deer (bucks, does, and fawns), selectively harvesting antlerless deer goes hand-in-hand with letting young bucks walk. Antler characteristics (i.e., number and length of points, main beam length, spread and mass) and body characteristics provide the necessary clues as to which bucks should be harvested. Considerations for harvesting antlerless deer are based on size, shape, and behavior of deer and also upon actual hunting conditions.

What are the management implications of selective antlerless harvests? One of the primary objectives of QDM is to improve your herd's sex ratio. The combination of harvesting adult does and passing up small-antlered bucks and button bucks provides the most direct path to that goal. Moving more bucks into the older age classes produces animals with better antler development and larger bodies. Also, as the sex ratio becomes better balanced, the breeding season may be shortened and shifted to earlier in the fall. Based on research conducted nearly 20 years ago, orphaned button bucks have a greater chance of survival and are more likely to remain in your hunting area as they are less likely to disperse and face all of the associated dangers with establishing a new home range one to five miles away.

What should the deer hunter/manager look for when selecting the correct antlerless deer? The following list of harvest recommendations was formulated over many years of living with deer. Not all scenarios are steadfast — there are exceptions to every rule when dealing with the wily whitetail. Nevertheless, the intention is to add to the conscientious deer hunter's arsenal of knowledge in hopes of enhancing the quality of deer and deer hunting.

- Don't shoot "lone" antlerless deer — wait until other deer arrive to provide a size comparison.
- Don't shoot in poor light during the early morning or late afternoon.
- Don't take long distance shots.
- Avoid a moving target, especially when other deer are nearby.
- Begin harvesting antlerless deer as early in the season as legally permitted. Late in the season there is less of a size difference between adult does and button bucks. Button bucks are more adventuresome as they get older, but they are still careless, inexperienced, and vulnerable.
- When deer are traveling in single file between feeding and bedding areas, their positions often are determined by social rank and thus age. Take the lead doe and more often than not you will have the correct one.
- When spooked by sight or sound, deer frequently will return to satisfy their curiosity. They will circle the "problem" to get downwind for their noses to confirm if danger exists. With few exceptions, the dominant doe will initiate the investigation.

Luggage simulating a doe (suitcase) with twins (brief cases).

- When watching a group of antlerless deer, possibly including several small bucks, pay particular attention to the antlerless deer that holds its ears back and rushes other deer. Often the front feet are used to strike or "flail" subordinate deer. The aggressor is the one to remove. Also, fawns are likely to be involved in bucking and frolicking. Watch for aggressive body postures and adolescent "play" behavior.
- During the peak of the rut, it is common to encounter small groups of temporarily abandoned fawns. Their mothers are away courting. If the deer appear unusually small, just wait for a behavioral hint. Also, a somewhat less reliable clue is the color difference between buck and doe fawns, particularly late in the fall. Buck fawns often appear darker, colored with a hint of gray or charcoal compared with the lighter brown or reddish coloration of doe fawns.
- Size and shape are important clues to identifying adults and youngsters. An adult doe has a long face and neck and is basically rectangular in shape. Fawns have short faces and necks and appear more square in shape. Compare these two descriptions with luggage — a suitcase is rectangular and the smaller brief case is square. The head of an adult doe could compare with a 12-ounce drink bottle and a fawn would match a 6-ounce bottle. Taking time to think about these size and shape comparisons before shooting will increase your chances of making the correct decision.
- In most cases adult does should be harvested because they are the most productive antlerless deer in the herd, generally yielding twins annually.
- In areas with low to moderate deer densities, a balanced harvest of all age classes, focused primarily on yearling and fawn does, is generally more appropriate.
- Use the best ocular equipment (scopes and binoculars) available.
- Use a gun rest whenever possible and avoid off-hand shots.
- The bottom line to harvesting deer selectively is to follow this golden rule — when in doubt, give your quarry the benefit.

In most states, hunter numbers are decreasing and antlerless deer bag limits are increasing. Together, these trends suggest that the deer hunter/manager of tomorrow will have to become far more efficient at harvesting antlerless deer than those of the past.

Remember, antlerless deer harvests are the primary method of maintaining deer populations at levels compatible with habitat conditions. Hone your skills and allow this management tool to provide a quality experience.

Note: *This article appeared in Quality Whitetails (V 3, I 3 - 1996).*

Follow Up: When this article was written deer populations were experiencing an all-time high in many states and regions. For example, the statewide deer population in South Carolina peaked in the mid- to late-1990s at an estimated one million animals. To control continued annual herd increments and the associated elevated levels of crop damage and automobile/deer collisions, an aggressive harvest strategy for antlerless deer was necessary. Now, the statewide deer population is estimated at 750,000 and the annual harvest has decreased by 25-30 percent.

Conditions have changed since then, and wildlife biologists have had to adjust their management/harvest recommendations accordingly. The dynamics are not consistent across the whitetail's distribution; therefore, recommendations for antlerless harvests also vary in different locations. Listed below are various conditions that have changed over the past 10 to 20 years:

Record outbreaks of epizootic hemorrhagic disease (EHD) occurred in 2007 and again in 2012. This viral disease is common among eastern whitetail populations, and annual mortality is usually minimal (<5% of the population). However, a new strain of the virus was particularly deadly in the Northeast and Midwest in populations with little or no experience with this viral disease. In some areas the mortality exceeded 50 percent of the population.

There have been below-average winter temperatures for extended periods in the upper Midwest.

The conservation reserve program (CRP) suffered reductions, mostly in the Midwest, as vast acreages of marginal agricultural lands reverted to crop production, driven primarily by an increased demand for ethanol production. The decrease in CRP resulted in a dramatic loss (>25%) of critical fawn rearing cover and early succession browse.

Changes in land use and increased human development continue to rob the whitetail of habitat. As expected, these changes have a negative effect on hunter access and recruitment.

Predators — including bobcats, black bears, and coyotes — are increasing in numbers and/or extending their distribution throughout the United States. Of course, rates of predation and the effect on a prey population vary without regard to longitude or latitude. To complicate matters, predation by coyotes can be experienced in extremes of high and low within a state or even within a county or township. My home county in South Carolina is a prime example. Agriculture, primarily the production of corn and soybeans, is prevalent in the western end of the county where farmers welcome the coyote as a controller of deer density and crop damage. Landowners in the eastern portion of the county manage their large-acreage properties for hunting deer and wild turkeys. And, it is here that predation by coyotes has caused a dramatic reduction in fawn recruitment. In response to the continued decrease in annual deer harvests and the report that approximately 30,000 coyotes were shot or trapped in 2014, the South Carolina Department of Natural Resources is promoting the control of coyote numbers throughout the state. Turkey numbers have declined also, but it is thought that a reduction in trapping and hunting furbearers has resulted in a dramatic increase in nest predators such as raccoons, opossums, and skunks. However, there are some veteran turkey hunters who believe that harassment by coyotes has changed turkey behavior, such that gobblers are less vocal during the breeding season. Fortunately, there are exceptions, and the zest for matching wits with cagy gobblers remains strong.

So, what is the collective effect of these conditions on the whitetail resource, and how have management/harvest recommendations changed? From 2010-2014, the national deer harvest declined from nearly seven million to about 5.5 million. During a longer period, 1998-2015, national fawn recruitment declined from 0.9 percent to 0.55 percent. There are regions in the Midwest where fawn breeding, at one time the highest in the nation, has dropped considerably in recent years. Lower deer densities and recruitment rates have prompted wildlife biologists to revise their recommendations, exactly what they should do. This is an example of adaptive management. A reduction in the female harvest is relatively common across much of the whitetail's distribution. Also, rather than harvesting the older and more productive females, hunters are encouraged to focus harvest pressure on younger, less productive females. Deer managers/hunters in the upper Midwest are encouraged to concentrate more of their antlerless harvests on fawns. This focus is biologically correct in that fawns in this region experience the highest winter mortality because of low fat reserves, and it is sensible to harvest a portion of this age class to provide meat for the table and decrease post-season mortality.

Continued research on the eastern coyote is important. In particular, the effect of extensive cooperative trapping programs and the effect of improving fawning cover at an appropriate scale are warranted.

The bottom line is that dealing with white-tailed deer is an ever-changing situation. Learn to identify the limiting factors and adjust your management practices accordingly. The QDMA has a good track record of "keeping its ear to the ground" to identify problems, and an education agenda to help hunters/managers solve those problems. Expect change and be prepared to handle it.

Fetal Aging Article – Applied Research

Initial studies of fetal development in white-tailed deer began in the 1940s in New York and involved the northern subspecies (*Odocoileus virginianus borealis*). The development of a fetal scale in West Virginia during the 1950s was based on information from New York. Additional efforts to determine the fetal development pattern continued with a Michigan study in 1970. These studies dealt with small sample sizes of known-age fetuses (21 or less) collected at irregular intervals of pregnancy.

The South Carolina Wildlife and Marine Resources Department (SCWMRD — now the S.C. Department of Natural Resources or SCDNR) began a long-term white-tailed deer research project in 1979 and among the primary goals were the development of fetal aging criteria for southeastern whitetails and the identification of differences between data from the Northeastern subspecies.

Methods

The deer research facility located at the Dennis Wildlife Center, Bonneau, S.C., covered approximately one acre and contained a large breeding pen (6,600 sq. ft.) with 26 adjacent, smaller pens for separating various deer groups by sex and age class.

Each spring and summer from 1979-83, fawns were obtained from the wild. Approximately 15 female fawns, including those born to captive does, were reared annually. Research animals were ear-tagged and freeze-branded for individual identification. All fawns were bottle fed until reaching weaning age at 12 weeks and were then maintained on a diet containing 16 percent crude protein and essential vitamins and nutrients.

Beginning August 15 and proceeding through March each year, bucks were paired with does once or twice daily for five to 30 minutes. Otherwise, bucks and does remained segregated. Detailed records of breeding behavior were maintained. When a doe bred she was then paired with a vasectomized buck several times within the following 48-72 hours to determine the period of receptivity of estrous does. Bucks used for breeding ranged from 1½ to 4½ years old, whereas does were in the 1½ to 3½ year age classes.

Following each breeding season selected does were euthanized at various stages of gestation to provide fetuses of known age. Precise measurements were made on each fetus and each was weighed to the nearest one-tenth gram. The relationships between fetal weights and age and fetal measurements and age were subjected to rigorous statistical analyses. Each year some pregnant does, ranging in age from 1½ to 3½ years old, progressed to term, yielding information on gestation length.

Results and Discussion

Sixty-four known-age fetuses, including 25 sets of twins, were obtained from 39 does. Fetuses were obtained at weekly intervals from five to 27 weeks. Forehead-rump length had the best predictive value of measurements used during this study. For management purposes, separate prediction equations for sex and litter size were not needed due to the relatively insignificant differences determined. Forehead-rump measurements were plotted against fetal age in days, and development was linear from the late-embryo stage (35 days) through the entire fetal period.

When known-age fetuses from this study were aged by the techniques of the New York and Michigan studies, estimated ages generally were within seven days of actual age.

Estrous does were found to be receptive to bucks during a 24-hour period. Does that bred and did not conceive or does that entered into estrous and did not breed cycled again in 28-30 days. The length of gestation was determined to be 198 days with a range of four or five days either side of the average.

Conclusions and Management Implications

Forehead-rump length has been used widely to age fetuses in field studies because it is an objective measurement and is easily obtained. Most importantly, the forehead-rump length (crown-rump or neck-rump length for embryos) is the only measurement that can be applied to small fetuses, the size frequently encountered during late-fall hunting seasons.

Although other fetal aging techniques have been relatively accurate in estimating ages of southeastern whitetail fetuses, the prediction equation (using forehead-rump length) developed from the South Carolina study provided valuable additional information to be used in the development of a revised fetal-aging scale.

The principal investigators of this study were Joe Hamilton, Melvin Tobin, and Gerald Moore, deer research biologists with the South Carolina Wildlife and Marine Resources Department. Information presented herein was published in the *Proceedings of the Thirty-Ninth Annual Conference of the Southeastern Association of Fish and Wildlife Agencies.* The technical paper was presented in October, 1985, in Lexington, Kentucky.

Development of the Fetal-Aging Scale

Soon after the South Carolina research was completed, fellow wildlife biologist, Tim Ivey, assisted Joe Hamilton and Melvin Tobin with the development of the fetal-aging scale. Since fetal development was determined to be linear throughout gestation, the task was to convert fetal age in days to calibrations on a plastic scale. The final product was completed in 1986 and its use and application are discussed in detail below.

The scale for aging fetuses is applicable throughout much of the whitetail's range, although there are exceptions. Portions of Alabama and Texas, for example, have breeding seasons occurring very late in the hunting season and the collection of fetuses from hunter-harvested deer may not be possible.

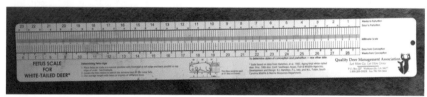

A plastic scale for aging whitetail fetuses.

Collecting Fetuses from Harvested Does

Interested hunters can collect reproductive data from their own hunting area or hunt club. The most efficient method for removing the reproductive tract is with the doe hanging from its hind legs. This removes pressure from the abdominal region beneath the udder. Make an incision (photo on page 205) and remove the entire reproductive tract. Once removed place the tract on a flat surface, make an incision in the tract, and remove the fetus or fetuses. Cut the umbilical cord flush with the abdominal surface.

Determining Fetus Age

1. Place fetus on scale in a natural position with forehead at left edge and back parallel to top edge of scale. See example top of page 206.
2. Locate the line closest to which the extreme end of the rump falls.
3. Use average length with twins or triplets of different sizes.

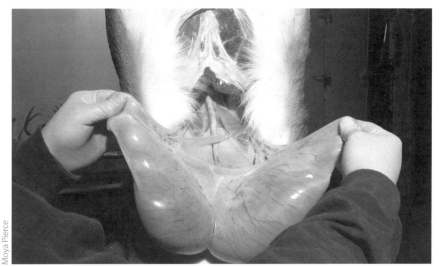

Removal of a pregnant doe's reproductive tract.

4. There are five sets of measurements on the fetus scale. These include a millimeter scale, days from conception, weeks from conception, days to parturition (birth), and weeks to parturition.

Determining Dates of Conception and Parturition

1. Locate within a calendar the date the doe was harvested (see other side of scale). Note Julian date (which runs from one to 365 days on one calendar and from 366-730 days on the other calendar).
2. Subtract the age of the fetus in days (days from conception as measured on scale) from the Julian date noted in 1.
3. Locate the date block with the Julian date found in 2. This is the date of conception.
4. The procedure for determining date of parturition is similar except days to parturition (as measured on scale) are added to the Julian date noted in 1. Two calendars are provided. Select the calendar that allows you to subtract the days from conception from the Julian date and also allows adding the days to parturition to the Julian date.

Example: A doe was harvested on December 15 and the age of the fetus was 51 days. The Julian date of December 15 is 349. This number minus the fetal age in days (51) is 298. The Julian date of 298 occurs on October 25. This is the date of conception.

The number of days to parturition was 147. This number, added to the Julian date of the harvest (349) is 496. The Julian date of 496 occurs on May 11. That is the date of parturition. See diagram on bottom of page 206.

Application of the Data

Your data can be viewed easily by constructing a simple bar graph as (page 207). Plot the number of pregnant does (sample size) on the vertical axis. Begin numbering

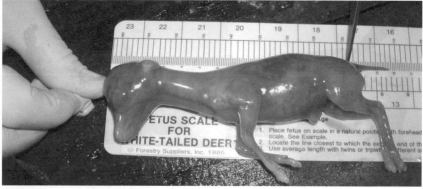
Determining the age of a fetus in days and weeks.

with zero at the bottom and number upward to 10. The conception dates will be on the horizontal axis and should be grouped on a weekly basis (due to small sample sizes) from September through December or January, depending on the closing date of your hunting season. Plotting all of your samples will reveal the range of breeding dates and the peak of the breeding season.

Analysis of the Data

Generally, the onset of breeding activity in a whitetail population is triggered by a response to photoperiod. Thus, as daylength shortens in early fall, a deer's pituitary gland begins the process of hormone production. There are other influencing factors as well. The sex ratio, age structure, and health of individual deer also have been shown to affect the timing of breeding. With a well-tuned QDM program there should be an

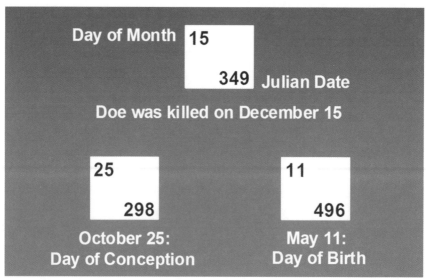
Determining conception and birth dates.

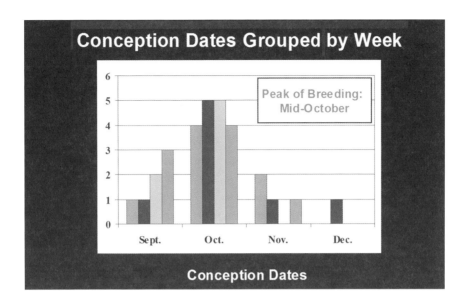

Conception Dates Grouped by Week

Peak of Breeding: Mid-October

Conception Dates

ample number of older bucks (3½ years and older) in the population and overall health will be improved due to density reduction through an increased harvest of females.

The "chemistry" of older-age bucks is thought to act in two ways: Pheromones, or olfactory signals, deposited by older bucks at rubs and scrapes throughout their range as well as being worn by individuals, stimulate does to come into estrous (heat) earlier and more synchronously while they may also suppress the libido (sexual drive) of younger bucks. Therefore, the range of breeding dates and the timing of peak breeding provide a barometer for how well your deer population's sex ratio and age structure may have been managed. In contrast, a deer population subjected to an extended period of traditional harvest management (a very young age structure among bucks and a heavily skewed sex ratio with more does than bucks) usually will exhibit a longer breeding season with a poorly defined peak.

A deer population subjected to QDM guidelines over time should mimic a natural, or unhunted, population regarding sex ratio and age structure and have a concise, well-defined breeding season. Add a fetus scale to your collection of management tools and you will create yet another barometer for measuring your success.

Note: *This article appeared in Quality Whitetails (V 10, I 4 - 2003)*

These 5½-year-old bucks (left to right) weighed 186, 175, and 198 pounds. Their Boone and Crockett scores are 145, 137⅛, and 146⅜. All three racks were over 20 inches wide and carried 11, 8, and 10 points, respectively. The successful hunters requested that their names not be mentioned in lieu of the pride expressed by all participants who produced these fine specimens — the best of our neighborhood.

A Quality Cooperative

If each of these bucks had been taken in one afternoon it would have appeared as though the rifle shots came from the same property. Actually, the three successful hunters were neighbors — participants in an extensive Quality Deer Management Cooperative.

All three bucks were 5½ years old. Before the cooperative management effort was launched in the mid-1980s, bucks in this age class were unheard of in the neighborhood. While barn scenes like this are common now, this is only the tangible aspect derived from concerted efforts to manage the deer population. The list of intangible values seems to grow every year.

What is a QDM Cooperative, and how does it function? Members of adjoining clubs worked in conjunction with their local wildlife biologist to formulate management guidelines that were tailored to the respective properties that suited the goals of participants, and were designed to produce quality animals according to neighborhood standards. It must be emphasized that a group's expectations not exceed the habitat's ability to produce deer of a particular size and number.

How much acreage is necessary to have a viable cooperative management program? A group hunting a 100-acre tract would have little chance of affecting the quality of their deer. But, if they are patient, dedicated, and committed, they should have a positive influence on their neighbors. Every hunting community needs a pioneer group to set the standard. Once two adjoining clubs or groups adopt common guidelines, others usually will follow suit and the cooperative is up and running. Actually, instead of stating a minimum acreage for successful cooperatives, I would rather share an attitude that seems to work. If you are more pleased with the change in deer quality than you are distressed over what you may be losing to your non-participating neighbors, then you have a large enough property.

One observation is that there appears to be no jealousy among the members of these adjoining clubs. Rather, there is an air of community pride in the accomplishments of the cooperative. Also, participants are more protective of what they have produced. The popular Neighborhood Watch program of residential areas has spread, at least in concept, to our countryside. Participants in our cooperative are ever vigilant, particularly regarding the actions of "strangers" driving through our neighborhood on public highways. Anyone observed driving slowly during peak deer activity, especially during the rut, will have their automobile tag number recorded and reported. Furthermore, several "scouts" are positioned within view of the highway to monitor illegal activities like shooting from the highway or putting someone out to hunt on our leased property. We have had the support of our DNR's law enforcement officers, and during the past several years four cases have been made involving the illegal shooting of deer on private land from a public highway. In one instance, a road-hunter shot a "dummy" deer…four times! His intent was unquestionable. A local newspaper article disclosed this culprit's actions countywide.

Deer hunters are quite mobile these days and traveling to an area known for its big bucks is common. For us homebodies, reliance on neighborhood standards is our yardstick for deer quality. The three bucks in the photograph are very nice, no doubt, even though they don't hold a candle to those famed monarchs up north. However, they have redefined the term "quality bucks" for our neighborhood. All of us are satisfied with the size of our deer now, but what is most important is the improvement in quality since our cooperative originated.

Our community firepot is just that — it knows no boundaries. It is here, at fireside, that we solve our problems, share our success stories, and discuss management strategies. Occasionally, when the fire subsides, we will place a grill over the glowing coals and prepare venison for all to enjoy.

Whatever happened to the "good old days" of deer hunting? Because of quality cooperatives like this one those days are here now!

Note: *This article appeared in Quality Whitetails (V 3, I 2 - 1996).*

American jointvetch or Aeschynomene.

Deer Peas: A Perfect Summer/Fall Food

When you read the title, you obviously wondered what deer peas must be. Now that I have your attention, you might know this plant as American jointvetch or Aeschynomene, its Latin name. This plant also has been called deer vetch, although it is not a vetch at all. It is a legume that resembles partridge pea, a naturally occurring quail food throughout the Southeast. Legumes are plants having seeds growing in pods, including peas, beans, etc., and root nodules that produce nitrogen.

A native legume from the southeastern U.S., jointvetch was recognized first as an important food for cattle in Florida, and later as a favorite deer food. When properly managed, this plant will provide a high level of protein (20+ percent) for deer through summer and until the first frost. Jointvetch grows best in moist soils with a pH of 6.0. Conduct a soil test in your chosen sites and add enough lime to adjust for the desired pH. Since jointvetch is a legume and "fixes" its own nitrogen, a fertilizer low in nitrogen is required (e.g., 3-9-18 or 0-10-20). Your soil tests usually will call for 300-400 pounds of fertilizer per acre and at least one to two tons of lime per acre.

Seeds can be purchased at a price of about $3 per pound from most wildlife food suppliers and the seeds will be either hulled or unhulled. We have had best results with seeds that have the hulls removed, thus hulled seeds.

Prepare the seedbed by liming, fertilizing, and disking. Seeds must be mixed with an inoculant immediately prior to planting. The inoculant, a black, dusty material, enhances the germination rate. Make certain the proper inoculant is purchased and applied — one for peas and beans is suitable. Broadcast the seeds (by hand) with a

George Grossek, a visitor from Australia, stands beside an excluder cage that demonstrates the head-high jointvetch growing without deer browse pressure. The plants outside of the cage are less than knee high. The tallest plant in the cage is sesbania.

cyclone seeder or use a grain drill. Seeds should be planted at a rate of 10-15 pounds per acre. Cover the seeds by disking lightly, or by dragging a section of chain-link fence over them, or by using a cultipacker. These small seeds should not be planted more than ½ inch deep. Optimum planting time throughout the Southeast (from east Texas to Florida and northward through North Carolina) is late-April to early-May. In Northern states, plant immediately after the threat of a late frost has passed. Wildlife openings of one to three acres are ideal. Openings spaced throughout your property should prevent concentrating deer, thus minimizing disease and parasite problems.

The leaves of young plants have a feathery appearance and they "close" when touched and at night. It is during the early stage of growth that jointvetch is easily confused with other moist soil plants. Mature plants resemble partridge peas, but are usually much taller.

Competition from other plants is to be expected, but not necessarily feared. The one advantage of the competitors which outgrow jointvetch is that they provide protection from scalding sunlight during early summer. As rains increase during summer the competitors can be mowed to "release" the jointvetch. In fact, periodic mowing of jointvetch will enhance growth of succulent, nutritious, and palatable browse for deer.

American jointvetch is a reseeding annual, although heavy browsing by deer will prevent adequate seed production for maintaining a patch for several years. It is best to start new each spring or early summer by planting your patches.

As with any kind of habitat management, you must be innovative and vigilant. Constant surveillance of your jointvetch patches will help you determine how and when to modify your management. Habitat management (food plots) still involves the "art" of decision making. You will learn through experience when to mow your patches and how much should be mowed. Perhaps the best barometer for measuring the degree of deer browse is to place several circular wire exclosures (three to four feet in diameter, and at least six feet high) in your patch. You shouldn't be surprised to see the jointvetch reaching out of the six-foot-tall enclosures in late summer, while the "stand" of jointvetch is only ankle to half-knee high on the outside. Furthermore, if you are keeping accurate data on deer weights, antler development, and reproduction, there should be a noticeable difference if only minimal habitat management preceded your culture of American jointvetch.

I consider American jointvetch an excellent choice for summer food plots because:

- It is easy to plant and maintain by periodic mowing.
- It is economical (10-15 pounds/acre at a cost of $35-$45/acre for seeds).
- It can utilize moist soils where other plants will not do well.
- It produces high-protein forage that is available for four to six months.
- It is somewhat drought tolerant, especially in conjunction with naturally occurring competitors.
- It is relatively shade tolerant and can be planted in thinned pine plantations or under mature hardwoods.

Note: *This article appeared in Quality Whitetails (V 2, I 1 – 1995).*

Follow Up: This article was written before I had any knowledge of the use of herbicides in food plot preparation and maintenance. As noted in this article, competing weeds were a problem in American jointvetch patches. Weed control, a common practice now, is critical to food plot success. Preemergence and postemergence applications of herbicides are necessary for maximum production in many areas.

I stated in the original article that the inoculant, a black, dusty material, enhances the germination rate. This is not the case. Rather, the inoculant contains the proper bacteria to colonize the roots and manufacture nitrogen that the plant can use. Make sure to use inoculant from the Cowpea Group (code EL) for proper inoculation.

I said to cover broadcast seeds by disking lightly. This should not be done because disking, even lightly, will bury the seeds too deep. The use of a cultipacker is the best way to ensure proper soil-to-seed contact when seeds have been broadcast.

The price of American jointvetch seed has nearly doubled since this article was published. You can expect to pay at least $5 to $6 per pound for seed these days.

In his book entitled *Guide to Wildlife Food Plots and Early Successional Plants,* Dr. Craig Harper, Extension Wildlife Specialist at the University of Tennessee, recommends the "Lowcountry mixture":

10 pounds of American jointvetch (Aeschynomene)

10 pounds of alyceclover

5 pounds of buckwheat

Buckwheat provides quick green-up for available forage and soil stabilization, and also provides an umbrella effect for American jointvetch and alyceclover, which are relatively slow to establish. If buckwheat is not added, a preemergence application of Pursuit (4 oz/ac) may be used to control various broadleaf and grass weeds. Of course, a grass-selective herbicide can be used to control grass weeds.

Deer crossing sign and road-killed deer.

Driving Defensively in Deer Country

Throughout the Southeast deer and human populations are on the increase. There has been a trend recently for more people to move to the "country" to escape the hustle-and-bustle of city life. Deer populations are spreading into suitable habitat in regions once devoid of deer.

These factors are bringing deer and people closer together. Hunters and those who simply enjoy observing deer are happy with these changes. However, motorists are among those who pay the price for an increase in deer-human encounters. Last year in South Carolina there were nearly 3,000 deer killed by automobiles. While that figure might seem high, other states report staggering numbers. In some Northeastern states the annual highway deer kill exceeds 30,000.

Sound deer management involving regulated annual harvests is the most effective measure of curtailing the highway kill, but there are some common-sense rules for driving defensively in deer country.

The white-tailed deer is well deserving of being called wily. These cunning animals are masters at evading predators, including hunters. Centuries of evolution prepared the whitetail for survival. Only recently, in an evolutionary time frame, a new "predator" has appeared — the automobile. Deer and vehicles have not coexisted long enough for these animals to have evolved the appropriate defense mechanisms to avoid encounters.

Keep this fact in mind when deer are seen crossing highways or standing on the roadside. Always anticipate ANOTHER deer if you see one or more crossing the highway.

Avoid actions to frighten or scare the animals. Changing headlights quickly from bright to dim and back or blowing your horn will only confuse deer and increase the chance of a collision. If deer are seen at night, dim your lights and reduce your speed. Do not slam on brakes as this will confuse the deer and increase your chances of losing control of the automobile. Swerving to miss an animal is also dangerous.

A study conducted by wildlife students at The University of Georgia's School of Forest Resources revealed that deer "whistles" attached to automobile bumpers are NOT effective in preventing deer-vehicle collisions. A variety of sound detecting equipment was used to test the performance of the whistles. At normal driving speeds the whistles did not emit a sound — at least not a sound audible to deer. Furthermore, if such a device could produce a sound, I would consider it a liability rather than an asset. Again, unnatural sounds or noises could frighten nearby deer onto the highway rather than away from it.

Deer are creatures of habit. They have favorite "crossings" along highways. Those observant motorists who travel familiar roads will recognize these high-risk areas as have the highway departments. Many such crossings are clearly marked by a diamond-shaped sign bearing the silhouette of a deer.

Pay attention to changes in habitat types along the highway. The zone between habitat types is a likely place for deer to cross a road. Creek bottoms and agricultural fields are also prime choices for crossing.

Rural or secondary roads rank highest in deer-vehicle accidents. The reasons are obvious. With frequent curves and narrow shoulders characteristic of many secondary highways, motorists often have little warning and therefore limited reaction time when deer are seen during the day or night.

Regardless of how carefully one drives in deer country there are just some situations that are unavoidable and a deer will be hit by an automobile.

What is the motorist to do if a deer is hit? Report the incident to the State Highway Patrol and to your insurance company. If the deer is killed and you wish to take it, please contact the South Carolina Wildlife & Marine Resources Department at this 24-hour toll-free number (1-800-922-5431). Also, if the deer is injured, do not risk personal injury by handling the matter yourself. Call the number above and a wildlife conservation officer will be notified immediately.

It is strongly urged that in addition to practicing safe and defensive driving techniques, each motorist should carry adequate collision and comprehensive insurance. Neither the South Carolina Wildlife and Marine Resources Department nor any other state agency will compensate motorists for injuries or damages resulting from deer collisions.

Author's Note: *Methods of reporting a deer-vehicle collision and the ability to keep a road kill vary by state. Interestingly, deer-vehicle accidents have increased markedly since this article was written. An article in the QDMA's 2013 Whitetail Report revealed that Pennsylvania had the highest accident rate in 2011-12 of 115,571. The number of deer-vehicle accidents in South Carolina in 2011-12 was 26,408.*

Note: *This article appeared in The Signpost newsletter (V 2, I 3 – 1990).*

Antlers: Lost and Found

Back during those blissful years as a neophyte deer hunter when I was busy learning myths like: once a spike always a spike, flop-eared does are barren, deer breed year round, piebald or "calico" deer are actually deer/goat crosses, and you can't find shed (cast) deer antlers 'cause rats, mice, and squirrels gnawed them literally to nothing soon as they fell from a buck's head.

Now, after enjoying many sunrises and sunsets in the deer woods, enduring hours of "deer" talk in country stores, around campfires, in college classrooms and the like, I have been busy relearning nearly every tidbit of deer lore taught or imagined as the gospel.

When stressed physically by injury, disease, parasites, or poor nutrition, bucks often will lose their antlers before the end of hunting season. But those that remain healthy throughout fall and into winter may retain their antlers until mid-March.

Older bucks tend to follow subordinates in losing their antlers. Antler casting dates also can vary among age groups of bucks in the same population. To complicate matters, casting dates in a particular region can vary from year to year depending upon the availability and quality of food. For example, during a year with an abundant mast crop the antler casting dates will occur in late winter. Frequent field observations will yield dates of antler casting which collectively serve as a barometer of deer herd health as well as environmental conditions.

Shed antler being gnawed on by a mouse.

Let's go back a few years, into the 1960s and '70s, to determine the circumstances that prompted deer observers to adopt the notion that antlers are "eaten" by rodents. Year after year of heavy hunting pressure on bucks, often coupled with overprotection of females, can produce a deer population with an unbalanced sex ratio (more females than males), a young age structure of males and a herd density approaching or exceeding the habitat's carrying capacity. Thus, when the antler casting season rolls around there are few antlered male survivors, they are young, possibly malnourished and have small antlers. In addition to being scant in number, small antlers are difficult to find.

This aspect of deer lore began to change with the advent of quality deer management. Each year more 2½-year-old and older bucks live through the hunting season, and cast antlers on well-managed properties are becoming commonplace. Searching for cast antlers is developing into a favorite pastime for QDM participants. This is also a way of scouting for buck "haunts" and potential stand locations for the next hunting season.

J. Hamilton '93

My collection of Native American artifacts is testimony of many hours spent searching the rain-washed furrows of plowed fields. My annual collection of deer antlers reflects many hours of searching as well, but it also provides a measure of management success. There are other similarities in finding arrowheads and antlers. Seeing such a treasure lying on the ground, especially at a distance, immediately quickens your pace. You rush to claim your find as if someone were competing. The first touch of a newly found arrowhead is exhilarating. A gap of hundreds, perhaps thousands, of years has been bridged. Questions begin to flow. Who made this arrowhead? How did he live? Was the arrowhead lost during a hunt where I now pursue descendants of the same deer? If so, time has melted away the cultural differences and we have something in common.

When an antler is found, catalogue it. Mark on the beam with a permanent marker and include the date, exact location, and who found it. Each antler will serve as a page of information in your deer record book. Survey the dimensions and characteristics of each antler: main beam length, number of points, and the basal circumference. These characteristics will enable the seasoned hunter/manager to assign an age to each antler.

Collectively, the antlers found on a particular property each winter provide a store-house of information on physical condition, age structure, buck survival, and habitat preference.

Although much time has been spent searching for cast antlers along trails and in bedding areas, it is my experience that most antlers are found in food plots — wheat, rye, and oat patches.

Note: *This article originally appeared in The Signpost newsletter, Volume 5, Issue 1, 1993, and was edited recently.*

Aerial views along many coastal areas have remained unchanged since pre-Columbian times — a testament to land conservation.

South Carolina's ACE Basin

R outine was a fitting description for the chain of events that began this particular day. From the parking lot, through the security gate, to a line of sleepy-eyed travelers, and finally to my ringside seat for the brief air safety program presented by a well-dressed lady with wings over a breast pocket and a straight-forward stare. Thunk, thunk and the landing gear found its place in the belly of our Atlanta-bound jet with Charleston, South Carolina in the rear view mirror, so to speak. What can anyone accomplish in a 45-minute plane trip complete with the usual cabin activity, announcements, offers for coffee or orange juice, and too many people turning newspaper pages in unison?

A glance through my plexiglass porthole provided the necessary escape. The view was spellbinding. Flying along the coastline at sunrise presented a world of stark contrast as silvery waters meshed with the characteristic jagged outline of a blackened landmass. There were no lights or buildings in sight, nothing man-made, only silver and black, just as the landscape must have appeared in pre-Columbian times.

Turning inland revealed widening ribbons of rivers in their patient search for an ocean. My thoughts reeled as the rivers meandered westward toward their origin. Increasing sunlight erased the silver hue, allowing individual rivers to show their true color. Some were red or yellow while others were as black as freshly brewed coffee.

Rivers inherit their color from the soils that give birth to them. Those with the greatest foothold on mother earth transect rich clay soils of the highcountry. Rivers originating in the flatlands are stained by the tannic acid of swamp-dwelling vegetation.

Rivers have played an integral role in the lives of our human race since time immemorial. They have served as avenues for travel and transport, and now provide boundaries between countries, states, counties, communities, and even neighbors. Countless children and many adults have never seen an ocean, but no one is untouched by a river.

Whether splashing over boulders in mountainous terrain or gliding quietly among ancient butt-swelled cypress trees in coastal swamps, the varied personalities of rivers have spawned songs, poetry, and volumes of folklore. Battles have been fought on their banks, and their waters have engulfed the victims.

Gazing down from 25,000 feet at a particular red river took me back to my boyhood days spent playing, fishing, and eventually hunting along the banks of the Cape Fear River in southeastern North Carolina. The streams and creeks forming its headwaters reach deeply into the piedmont near the Old North State's capitol. This river, too, is a muddy, reddish brown color. Once, during a freshet, an elderly gentleman from my hometown commented that the river was so muddy you could see coon tracks 10 feet out from the bank. Another person jokingly remarked that there was so much clay in the river that he believed you could plant corn from bank to bank.

A familiar bong…bong…bong rang over the cabin's intercom. We were preparing for an approach to the Atlanta airport. Through my window to the world, details of our spreading civilization grew sharper as we began our descent. Capillaries of red clay roads, soon to be paved, reached into fragmented hardwood forests. Large patches of bare soil marked the sites of future subdivisions, shopping malls, and other "necessities." The Atlanta metropolitan area appeared to be unfolding in every direction — the winds of change are constantly blowing.

The renowned father of wildlife management and author of *A Sand County Almanac*, Aldo Leopold, delivered a prophetic message that is as true today as it was when delivered in the 1940s. "Like winds and sunsets wild things were taken for granted until progress began to do away with them." We must be acutely aware of what we are doing to our environment, and to ourselves. Our quality of life will depend ultimately on how we treat this precious land that is being borrowed from future generations.

Checking newspaper and magazine headlines regularly will provide a barometer for our stewardship as individuals, a community, and a nation. Recent headlines in Columbia, South Carolina's newspaper *The State* read: "Wetlands continue to disappear despite best efforts of government." It was to be taken as good news that more than one million acres of United States' wetlands vanished from 1985 to 1995. It was good news by comparison, because wetland losses approached the three-million-acre mark in the previous decade (1975-1985).

Why all the fuss over losing those blank spots on the map that we can't even walk through? What good are they, anyway? Well, countless numbers of birds, fish, and other species of wildlife and plants depend on this habitat. Wetlands have obvious mechanical usefulness, too. Contaminants are filtered from the waters that flow gently through these systems. And wetlands serve as natural reservoirs for water from heavy rains, thus diminishing the damaging effects of surging floodwaters. These vital wetlands are also the progenitors of our rivers.

The Southeast has been the hardest hit region of the United States regarding wetlands loss. Fifty-one percent of the wetlands were destroyed during the decade from 1985-1995. This computes to a loss of 60,500 acres each year. Most of the blame for wetlands loss can be attributed to agricultural encroachment, although development,

Botany Bay Island is representative of tens of thousands of acres in the ACE Basin that have been protected in perpetuity by conservation easements.

especially in some areas, is worthy of concern. Computer-enhanced satellite images of the Charleston metropolitan area's growth from 1973 to 1994 revealed an urban expansion of 255 percent — six times greater than population growth.

This magnitude of growth, or "progress," has an obvious direct effect on wetland habitat, but the ramifications are far-reaching and alarming. Sam Passmore of the South Carolina Coastal Conservation League, assessed the situation: "If we don't make some basic choices about what should be urban and what should be rural, we'll lose the countryside and bleed the urban areas of their vitality."

Trendy moves to the country are cumulatively destroying the "wild" nature of our rural areas. Habitats critical to neotropical migrating birds are being fragmented, causing noticeable decreases in numbers of certain species like many of the warblers, tanagers, and thrushes.

How do we measure the value of those natural resources and their associated traditions that are being displaced or threatened by residential, commercial, and recreational (golf course) development? Results from a recently published national survey of fishing, hunting, and wildlife-watching activities indicated that South Carolina received $1.4 billion in expenditures in 1996.

What is being done to protect those traditions associated with the enjoyment of our natural resources? Another quote from Aldo Leopold's *A Sand County Almanac* is appropriate for this topic: "Man always kills the thing he loves, and so we the pioneers have killed our wilderness. Some say we had to. Be that as it may, I am glad I shall never be young without wild country to be young in. Of what avail are forty freedoms without a blank spot on the map? … To those devoid of imagination, a blank place on the map is a useless waste; to others, the most valuable part."

SCDNR

A biologist and technicians of the SCDNR inspect a newly installed rice field trunk on the Bear Island Wildlife Management Area.

Concern for the destruction of wetland habitat and the effect on migrating waterfowl, wading birds and a myriad of other species that depend on these areas for life support spawned a concerted effort among Canada, the United States and Mexico in the mid-1980s. The North American Waterfowl Management Plan (NAWMP) was designed in 1986 to protect and enhance wetlands and their associated upland habitat. As part of the Atlantic Coast Joint Venture, focus areas were established to accomplish the mission of the NAWMP. Focus areas are local, grass-roots projects designed to concentrate conservation efforts regionally, and typically are comprised of major waterways and river systems or several counties within a geographical region.

South Carolina's flagship initiative, in cooperation with the Atlantic Coast Joint Venture, is the nationally acclaimed ACE Basin Project, established in 1988. The basin's boundary encompasses 350,000 acres of diverse habitat types including pine and upland hardwoods, forested wetlands, 117,000 acres of fresh, brackish, and saline tidal marshes, the largest estuary system in the state, numerous barrier islands (many uninhabited), and coastal beaches. The Basin derives its name from three undammed, pristine, blackwater rivers: Ashepoo, Combahee, and South Edisto.

The ACE Basin is the largest undeveloped wetland on the Atlantic Coast. Ironically, an unusual chain of events, beginning in the late-1600s, set the stage for this unparalleled opportunity 300 years later to protect entire ecosystems "now" and for future generations.

Early settlers in South Carolina's coastal region began hacking away at vast expanses of cypress/tupelo swamps. Their goal was to tame the wilderness and convert it to a productive state. Golden-grain rice from Madagascar was the new crop to be grown and slave labor rendered the venture possible. Cleared swamps were corralled by dikes, and fields with a network of shallow and deep canals were created. Wooden trunks (their design and function originated in the Scandinavian countries) placed in the dikes were used to control water levels within the rice fields. Shaped like a shoebox with a flapgate on each end, the rice field trunks could be adjusted to bring river water into the rice fields during a rising tide, or to reverse the process on a falling tide. Maintaining an optimum water level within the rice fields was crucial to the production of rice.

South Carolina reached its peak rice production in 1850 with nearly 160 million pounds of the golden grain harvested from over 100,000 acres of tidewater rice fields.

The Civil War had a profound effect on the South's rice culture. Abolition of slavery

As an example of the cooperative agreement among state and federal agencies, various conservation organizations, and private landowners, the U.S. Fish and Wildlife Service protected nearly 12,000 acres now known as the Ernest F. Hollings ACE Basin National Wildlife Refuge.

slashed the necessary work force and the era of Southern rice plantations dwindled by the early-1900s. The winds of change are constantly blowing.

Although some of these extensive properties were subdivided and resettled, most remained under the ownership of prominent South Carolina families. Other plantations were purchased by wealthy Northern industrialists to be used as sporting properties. A new era of land utilization had begun. Stewardship of large acreage is a key element in current conservation efforts.

The ACE Basin Habitat Protection and Enhancement Project was bold considering the scope of the venture. Objectives of the project were to: (1) maintain the natural character of the area by promoting wise natural-resource management on private lands and protection of strategic tracts by public conservation agencies; (2) encourage traditional natural resource uses, including hunting, commercial and recreational fishing, forestry and agriculture; (3) support land purchases at fair market value from willing sellers and encourage the establishment of perpetual conservation easements with willing participants; and (4) maintain and enhance access for public use and provide wildlife management assistance to improve habitat.

Such a venture needed a directing body to oversee conservation efforts. The ACE Basin Task Force answered the call. The coalition was comprised initially of partners from Ducks Unlimited, The Nature Conservancy, the South Carolina Department of Natural Resources, the U.S. Fish and Wildlife Service, and most important, private landowners. Currently, over 60 other groups and organizations endorse the ACE Basin initiative.

Following through with such a plan would be complex, expensive and time consuming. A prediction was that it might take 25 years to fulfill the plans proposed by the Task Force. Only a decade from its inception, the ACE Basin Project is a resounding success. Protected property exceeds 128,000 acres with conservation easements in perpetuity on more than 45,000 acres of private lands. Without a doubt, there is reason for celebration. Plans are underway for a 10th anniversary commemoration of conservation in the ACE Basin.

The adage "success breeds success" certainly pertains to the influence of the ACE Basin Project beyond its boundaries. Four additional coastal focus areas have been established and each has a directing task force. Collectively, nearly a half-million acres of blank spots on the map, including over 100,000 acres under conservation easements, have been protected for their outstanding ecological value. Aldo Leopold would applaud these accomplishments.

It has been particularly gratifying to those involved with the project to witness the evolution of land protection efforts originating from a concern over wetlands loss and culminating with broad-scale application involving entire ecosystems, including rivers. The winds of change are constantly blowing, but alas they are blowing favorably for those who cannot live without wild things and blank spots on the map.

Those haunting conclusions from a television documentary on the human animal several years ago would lead one to believe that initiatives like the ACE Basin Project were impossible because we, as a species, are innately shortsighted. However, viewing the expanse of ACE's blank spots from 25,000 feet above the ground offers hope for the future.

According to Aldo Leopold, "Conservation is a state of harmony between men and land." We, the stewards of our precious natural resources, must remain ever vigilant of our demands on the environment. A critical balance must be maintained through continued support of educational efforts, partnerships, and stewardship. Otherwise, those attributes of the natural world that draw us in increasing numbers will be compromised in the process. Our deep-rooted traditions will become only a footnote to history. We will become modernized and miserably unfulfilled. Our health, the health of our economy, and the health of our environment are inseparable.

Note: *This article appeared in the August 1998 issue of River – The Magazine of Moving Water.*

Follow Up: Having been involved in this monumental land conservation process since its inception nearly three decades ago, it is rewarding to restate this adage from the article: "…success breeds success."

The ACE Basin Project's success spawned similar land conservation efforts upward along the coast to North Carolina, southward to Georgia, and inland along the expansive plantations bordering the many winding Coastal Plain rivers.

Only a decade later, 20 local and three national organizations were involved in land conservation from the coast to the mountains. In 1998 the South Carolina Land Trust Network was formed. This association of land conservation groups was designed to function as a unified entity to promote land conservation throughout the state.

And now, the footprints of land conservation in the Palmetto State are visible to astronauts. Over a half million acres of private lands are protected statewide. And, in the Coastal Plain of the state alone, the total protected acreage of state, federal, and private lands has reached 1.2 million acres. Aldo Leopold would be proud indeed. Our children will inherit a gift etched indelibly by the caring hands of land stewards. Let's hope their descendants can maintain this "…state of harmony between men and land."

Protecting the Playing Field

Local, state, and federal officials have been setting aside monuments, parks, and refuges since the late-1800s. The first national park, Wyoming's Yellowstone, was established by Congress in 1872; the National Park Service was established in 1916. The U.S. Fish and Wildlife Service's National Wildlife Refuge System recently celebrated its 100th anniversary. These publicly owned acreages, numbering in the hundreds of millions, were set aside from development and they have played an integral role in providing habitat for a myriad of species of flora and fauna. They also have served as the playing fields of countless outdoor enthusiasts.

The success of these various means of conserving nature for public enjoyment is noteworthy, although something was long missing in the equation since a vast majority of undeveloped land is under private ownership. There was a dire need to compensate the private landowner for his or her stewardship of the land. One such "tool", the conservation easement, was redesigned in the 1980s to accomplish this task and has gained popularity and acceptance since. The federal government used the original document in the 1930s for scenic easements on the Blue Ridge Parkway.

Numerous private properties have been protected by conservation easements, thus ensuring continued involvement in agriculture, silviculture, and wildlife management.

A conservation easement is a written legal agreement between a landowner and a qualified conservation organization or public agency that contains a series of voluntary restrictions relating to present and future uses of the land.

Conservation easement restrictions are tailored to the conservation values and characteristics of a particular property and to the owner's personal financial needs and conservation goals. A landowner's incentive for protecting his/her property through the donation of a conservation easement is usually tied to a love of the land and a desire to keep it in its natural state for future generations.

A conservation easement is designed to protect the natural integrity of a property and to prevent industrial or commercial development in perpetuity while allowing the owner's continued involvement in traditional uses of the property including hunting, fishing, wildlife observation, agriculture, and silviculture.

When a landowner "donates" a conservation easement on his/her property, it is the development rights that are donated to an appropriate grantee. There can be significant financial benefits derived from personal income taxes, estate taxes, and in a limited number of states, tax credits applied toward state income taxes. Obviously, these tax implications involve the Internal Revenue Service (IRS). Therefore, it is imperative to involve one's legal counsel, accountant, and estate planner if available.

Conservation organizations qualified by the IRS to serve as the grantee of the conservation easement include The Nature Conservancy and Ducks Unlimited on a nationwide basis and nearly 1,500 land trusts throughout the United States that serve local communities or regions. In South Carolina, for example, there are approximately 16 local land trusts with groups like the Lowcountry Open Land Trust focusing their attention along the coast while others are concerned with land conservation in their immediate neighborhood.

An appropriate example of this tool at work is the nationally acclaimed project that began in coastal South Carolina in the late-1980s. The ACE Basin Project was the flagship venture of The North American Waterfowl Management Plan (NAWMP), designed to protect and enhance wetlands and their associated upland habitats. The ACE Basin, largest undeveloped wetland on the Atlantic Coast, derived its name from three undammed, pristine, blackwater rivers: Ashepoo, Combahee, and South Edisto. The Basin's initial boundary encompassed 350,000 acres of diverse habitats including pine and hardwood uplands, forested wetlands, marshes, estuaries, barrier islands, and coastal beaches. Success in land conservation for 15 years and identification of additional priority tracts resulted in the recent extension of project boundaries into Dorchester, Orangeburg, and Bamberg counties to include a total of 1.6 million acres.

The ACE Basin Project celebrated its 15th anniversary in March, 2003. The Project's land conservation accomplishments have received national acclaim. The concerted efforts of conservation organizations, state and federal agencies, and private landowners have resulted in the protection of over 150,000 acres through land gifts, fee-simple land acquisitions and conservation easements. As part of the project's plan, a state wildlife management area and a national wildlife refuge were established for public enjoyment. Most of the total protected acreage has been protected in perpetuity with conservation easements on private properties.

Private properties with conservation easements will remain undeveloped regardless of future ownership. The importance of conservation easements to hunters, fishermen, wildlife observers, and land managers is that key properties are being secured while vast acreages of natural lands are being converted to retirement homes, golf courses, schools, hospitals, highways, and shopping malls — results of increasing and shifting human populations.

The bottom line is that traditional uses of the land will become historical uses in the long term if the playing fields are not protected. Those of us who depend on natural resources for our enjoyment and livelihood must rally in support of conservation efforts. In South Carolina, this playing field for hunters, fishermen, and wildlife observers yielded over $1.4 billion to the economy in 2003. Yet many of the acres of these playing fields are managed primarily for agriculture and silviculture, also extremely important factors in South Carolina's economy.

Author's Note: *Due to the complexity of conservation easements, it is advisable that interested landowners contact representatives of conservation organizations for guidance.*

Note: *This article appeared in Quality Whitetails (V 10, I 2 - 2003).*

The old "mossy oak" tree stand is typical of wooden structures used for hunting deer during the early days throughout the Southeast.

Odocoileus dynamicus [The Ever-Changing Whitetail]

F our million years in the making, the Virginia whitetail (*Odocoileus virginianus*) has 38 subspecies ranging from South America into southern Canada. This adaptable animal inhabits the driest deserts, the wettest swamps, the highest Appalachian Mountains, and the near sea-level coastal islands from the Pacific to the Atlantic. What has been dynamic (thus, the fictitious Latin name in the title) is not so much the animal, but the myriad of regulations and hunting techniques associated with its pursuit and management.

Last winter (2008), Tunica, Mississippi was the site of the 31st annual meeting of the Southeast Deer Study Group (SEDSG). The theme for this year's Monday evening Shooting-From-The-Hip session at the SEDSG meeting was: "Is Huntin' Still Huntin'?" The title suggests that something may have gone awry, but has it? First, we must define the term hunt (huntin'). According to Webster, hunt means to chase game for food or sport; to search eagerly or carefully for; to go through a tract of country in pursuit of game; and among other definitions, to use dogs or horses in chasing game.

As one of the panelists in this year's session I want to elaborate on my impression of the topic. Having hunted the wily whitetail for a half century (sounds longer than 50 years) I have occupied a ringside seat in an arena of change. Since I grew up in North Carolina and have lived in Georgia and now in South Carolina, my observations will be limited to this portion of the Southeast with no intention of slighting the Northeast, Midwest, or the Gulf Coast states. It is obvious, at least to me, that changes in regulations and management of the whitetail and in particular hunting traditions have been more varied and dramatic here than in these other regions mentioned.

My introduction to deer hunting occurred in the late-1950s when my age was still a single digit. The ONLY method of hunting deer was with hounds and loosely knit groups of hunters. There were no four-wheel-drive trucks, no CB radios, no camouflage, no hunter's orange clothing, no lease fees, a buck-only season with a limit of two (coastal South Carolina was the exception even in those days with no limit on bucks), and virtually no hunting club dues except a shared responsibility to assist the houndsmen with dog food expenses. Deer were not plentiful and when a buck was harvested it was divided usually among 10 to 15 hunters, thus the individual hunter's share provided one meal for his family. The neighboring hunting group was across the Cape Fear River, and our hounds often swam the river in pursuit of deer — so did theirs. There were no other hunters on our other three borders. When a chase left our hunting property no one was bothered. Often, the deer would lead the hounds back onto our property, back home, within a few hours.

I remember vividly the seasoned houndsmen speaking vehemently against those who sat in a tree to ambush a deer that was totally unaware of the hunter's presence. Those hunters were referred to abashedly as "buzzard" hunters and accused of taking deer in an unsporting (non-traditional) fashion. Even rifles were spoken of with disdain; called highpowereddeerrifles (one word) and considered unfair for the game and unsafe for fellow hunters. The winds of change are constantly blowing. Today's norm is written as outdated in tomorrow's history book.

Nearly a decade later, as deer moved into new terrain, a handful of young hunters from my hometown were inspired by articles in sporting magazines about hunting deer from tree stands. The first stands I remember consisted of wooden or nail steps and a small wooden platform on which the hunter stood. This novel approach to deer hunting spread quickly throughout the Southeast.

Beginning in the 1950s and carrying through the next 20 or more years, southeastern state wildlife agencies were involved in restocking deer. National forests and state wildlife management areas became the deer hot spots, primarily in the 1960s and '70s. Since hunters were not allowed to build stands on public lands, the use of portable stands became the norm. The first portable, climbing stand I can remember was a Baker, made in Valdosta, Georgia. At first, hunters using these stands had to hug the tree and pull the stand up with their feet. Later, a hand bracket replaced the traditional hug, and safety belts or harnesses appeared on the scene.

With buck-only laws still in effect in many areas, extreme hunting pressure suppressed the age structure, resulting in annual harvests comprised mainly of young bucks with

Patches of the S.C. Quality Deer Management Association and later the Quality Deer Management Association.

small antlers. Many southeastern states initiated antlerless harvests in the 1970s and early '80s to control the burgeoning deer populations.

During this time, paper companies were acquiring extensive tracts of forested habitat in an effort to feed their mills. Groups of hunters, disgruntled with the prospects of deer hunting on public lands, gravitated to these newly available hunting opportunities and began leasing. This marked the beginning of a new era in deer hunting — one that would involve private lands as well as the industrial forests. Hunting groups organized into clubs, complete with a slate of officers and a budget. For the first time they had a vested interest in taking care of their hunting property to ensure access from year to year.

As deer populations continued to increase throughout the Southeast so did the interest in hunting with primitive weapons, including archery equipment and muzzleloaders. Deer densities had reached levels that made hunting with primitive weapons a success-ful venture. When I began using a recurve bow in the late-1960s we had to attach the broadheads onto the arrow shafts with heated glue. Threaded inserts make that job very easy now and eliminate that characteristic "wobble" of an improperly glued broadhead. By the end of the 1970s the compound bow with its sophisticated sights and string releases had all but replaced the recurve. Increasing deer densities and the continuous spread of deer populations into unoccupied habitats, primarily along major drainage systems, prompted many state wildlife agencies to increase buck quotas and develop additional programs to facilitate an adequate harvest of antlerless deer.

A combination of high deer density, skewed sex ratio, and a young buck age structure provided the necessary stimulus for change in the early-1980s. Progressive-minded hunt-ers throughout the Southeast embarked on a mission to put a proven Texas program to work. Quality deer management (QDM) guidelines were embraced by one group after another, and a new paradigm for nationwide deer management had found its place in the history book. To serve this growing number of QDM managers, an organization was founded in 1988. Known originally as the South Carolina Quality Deer Management Association, interests beyond the state borders resulted in a name change to reflect the widespread acceptance of a change in deer management philosophy and a need for a supporting organization. These first steps of the Quality Deer Management Association (QDMA) turned out to be giant steps in the annals of wildlife management.

As the 20th century gave way to a new millennium, the need for changes in deer management followed. A recent trend among many southeastern states has been the reduction of the buck limit while continuing to embrace adequate antlerless harvests. These actions are biologically sound, but more important, they have come about at the request of hunters. Today's hunters are more educated about deer management than ever before, and many have made the transition from mere consumers to that of managers.

Many changes have taken place with regard to regulations (bag limits, season lengths, etc.) and hunting techniques (even though dog hunting remains in the Southeast, this traditional technique has given way to still hunting). Yet, there are still many differences in regulations and hunting techniques not only among states, but between neighboring states and even within states. In some areas Sunday hunting and baiting are not allowed and in others they are allowed. Rifles are forbidden in some areas while legal in most. Firearm seasons are long (4½ months) in some states and shorter in others (seven to nine days).

Venison is readily available now instead of a commodity to be shared with family and friends only at holidays. In Virginia, for example, deer hunters donated more deer to the Hunters for the Hungry Program in 2007 than were harvested in that state in 1951. Deer-processing businesses are commonplace throughout the Southeast now. Hunters harvest a deer, deliver it to a processor, and return later to pick up neatly wrapped, labeled, and dated packages of venison.

Land ownership patterns are changing. Many of the major paper companies are divesting of their extensive acreages. While some of these properties are being bought by timber investment management companies, known as TIMOs, others are being purchased by individuals or groups to ensure their future as hunters. For example, nearly 70 percent of the QDMA members are landowners, and collectively they own and manage over 13 million acres. This trend is likely to continue as more hunting lands are lost to development.

In general, deer hunters have become overwhelmed by the array of gadgets advertised to maximize harvest success. Probably the most ridiculous of them all is a device that emits the sound of an automatic corn dispenser. Boy, you don't have to pay the fiddler much for this dance! The problem as I see it is that in some cases the use of lime, fertilizer, seeds, and natural vegetation management are taking a back seat to high fences, supplemental feeding, and baiting. It's difficult to defend that these practices are not setting the stage for an increasing number of hunters to shoot deer rather than to hunt deer.

Considering all of the changes that have occurred in the last 20 or 30 years, how do we respond to the question: "Is huntin' still huntin'?" Well, first let's revisit the basic definition of hunting: The pursuit of game for food or sport. Next, we must realize that hunters progress through a series of developmental stages before reaching the destination of sportsmanship/stewardship. Along this path each category of hunters is actively involved in pursuit. I know firsthand, and I suppose most seasoned hunters will agree, that an introduction to hunting is wrought with a desire to shoot a lot, shortsighted enthusiasm, and a less-than-necessary respect for the quarry. Only through educational efforts and establishing a culture with the animal can these factors be remedied. But hunter numbers are waning; therefore we must support a concerted effort among natural resource management organizations to curb this trend — to encourage youngsters and other potential hunters to join our ranks. We must realize, though, that a "shooting" mindset among new hunters will prevail initially over a "hunting" mindset. The QDMA's Mentored Hunting Program is designed to take young and other first-time hunters through this transition from shooting to hunting by providing an experienced hunter, a mentor, to lead this long-term educational process (it can be completed in less than a year).

In many areas throughout the whitetail's range, involvement in a quality deer management (QDM) program will require a lot of shooting of antlerless deer in high-density areas to control deer numbers and create a better balanced sex ratio. Allowing more bucks to reach the older, mature age classes will present a challenge with regard to maintaining hunter success. Participants in a QDM program quickly learn that encountering mature bucks requires patience, persistence, woodsmanship, cunning, and a bit of luck. In essence, this level of management involves shooting does (antlerless deer) and hunting mature bucks. There is a clear distinction between these two methods of harvest, due primarily to a higher availability of antlerless deer and the elusiveness of the mature bucks, but it is of paramount importance that individual hunters foster the attitude of a true steward whenever pursuing the wily whitetail.

It is the responsibility of wildlife professionals and the hunting fraternity to ensure that the pursuit of game animals is biologically, socially, and ethically sound. Education will be the key to unlock our future. Considering the rampant growth of the QDMA and QDM, I think it is safe to say that huntin' is still huntin'! The winds of change will only enhance our hunting tradition if we remain on our present course.

Note: *This article appeared in Quality Whitetails (V 15, I 3 - 2008).*

42 Years of Experience as Deer Hunter and Manager

Beginnings

My life as a deer hunter began in 1956 at the ripe old age of nine. A neighbor and close friend of my family in North Carolina invited me to spend a weekend with her relatives in South Carolina. Her brother had quite a reputation as a hunter and I was enthralled by all the stories that were told of his conquests, especially involving deer since there were very few in my home county of Bladen.

To say that I was primed for the chance to hunt deer would have been an understatement. We made the trip to the community of Williams, deep in the South Carolina lowcountry. It seemed to take forever — there were no Interstate Highways then. When we arrived, my friend's brother said he had something to show us. We piled into his truck and drove to a nearby farm. There, a walk-in cooler concealed his prize. When the door swung wide, I stood face-to-face with the first whitetail I had ever seen. It was a monster of a buck with eight points. "That's what we're hunting for tomorrow, boy." I didn't sleep much that night.

We left way before daylight the next morning because there were no deer around Williams either. A plantation 30 miles south was said to be loaded with deer, and that was our destination. Several truckloads of hunters and their dogs gathered at the hunting spot. I was issued a single-shot 16 gauge shotgun and ushered to my "stand." It was just a place in the woods with no structure to be seen. My host informed me that a stand was simply a likely crossing for deer. "When you hear the dogs barking in unison and heading in your direction, get ready, and be on the lookout for a big buck!"

I stepped up onto a large tree stump to get a better view of my surroundings. My stomach was already tied in knots for two reasons. The expectation of a buck coming my way was one reason, and the thought of having to cock the hammer on that shotgun was the other. It took both thumbs and all the strength I could muster to accomplish the task. There was another concern. What if the deer came toward me, I cocked the hammer, and the deer passed out of range? Then I'd be faced with having to let the hammer down without firing the gun. These thoughts kept me occupied until I realized that the dogs were barking and they seemed very excited. Sure enough, they were getting louder by the second and heading straight toward me.

Sooner than I had expected the buck was

This sketch was done as I attended church one Sunday in the early-1960s. It was my vision of a trophy whitetail. As luck or fate would have it, my first buck looked a lot like this.

in view, and the dogs were not. I had assumed that it would be a sight chase, but there was a lot to learn. Adrenaline rushed into my thumbs and the hammer was readied with ease. The stock was too long, so I placed it under my arm and snugged it down to sight along the barrel. As the buck passed I pulled the trigger — what an explosion! The gun reared against my loose grip and bumped me squarely in the nose. Through blurred eyes I saw a white flag disappearing through thick timber. I had missed, but I was hooked for life. I told my host that when I grew up I wanted to live in the deer-rich lowcountry of South Carolina. There's a lot more to that story, but I'll save it for later.

Deer numbers slowly increased in my home county, and by the time I was in the eighth grade there were several scattered groups of deer hunters. In those days hunting with dogs was the only approach. In fact, I didn't know anyone who owned what was referred to as a highpowereddeerrifle (spoken as one word). Hunting had evolved with the growing deer herd, thus the age structure of bucks remained rather young. Also, deer hunting during the '50s, '60s, and into the early '70s was restricted to bucks only. Not only was it illegal to kill a doe, it was considered unethical to remove the very animals that produced bucks. All of us had a lot to learn.

Due to the circumstances, our expectations of connecting with a wallhanger were slim at best. An eighth-grade classmate and next-door neighbor called late one October afternoon with the news that he had killed a cowhorn (a long-antlered spike), his first buck, on the morning's deer drive. That same season another friend got his first buck — a peghorn (a short-antlered spike). On January 1, 1961, the last day of the following season, I got my first buck. It, too, was a spike. A deer hunter's first buck is a trophy regardless of its size. Each of us was pleased with our buck primarily because that's what we expected to get — something young with small antlers. While in church one Sunday morning I decided to sketch my idea of a nice buck. Naturally, it was only a spike, but a nice one!

Persistence paid off though, and each of us had a mounted buck on the wall by the late-1960s. These bucks all came by happenstance. There was no management plan. Our only expectation was to get a chance to take that one buck-of-a-lifetime. We still had much to learn.

The Georgia Years

Bowhunting was gaining popularity throughout the Southeast during the late-1960s. Several classmates at The University of Georgia had taken up the bow and encouraged me to join them. Being short of cash, I traded my Ruger .44 magnum carbine to a friend for a recurve bow and a handful of arrows. We practiced regularly and became somewhat proficient. Rumors had it that Blackbeard Island National Wildlife Refuge (between Savannah and Brunswick, Georgia) was THE place to go. We applied for the October hunt in 1967 and were drawn. It was the 20th anniversary of bowhunting on Blackbeard Island.

We arrived at the island after a long boat ride through winding marsh creeks and across Sapelo Sound. All hunters were required to camp in one designated area and to arrive the day before the three-day hunt began. That first night the refuge manager assembled everyone (about 100 archers) around a roaring fire and explained the hunt rules. He also called the names of three gentlemen who had hunted Blackbeard Island each year since 1947. I was shocked that one of those fellows was still alive. He appeared to be well into his 70s and a bit feeble. I didn't expect him to be able to climb a tree. His name was Ben Franklin! How could you forget a name like that? I haven't.

Blackbeard Island is seven miles long and all hunters must walk to their hunting spots. The extreme north end of the island is five miles from the campground, so we decided to trek to the south end for our first morning's hunt. Our expectations were high. We had heard stories of hunters shooting all of their arrows, climbing down from their stands, gathering the arrows and climbing back into position for another foray. Most of the ones in our group saw deer, but no shots were taken. Hunting hours were over at 9 a.m. and we met to walk back to camp together. Along the way we happened upon a buck that had been pulled to the roadside for refuge personnel to haul to the skinning shed. The buck's rack was impressive for the Blackbeard Island subspecies of whitetail; animals known for their small size and narrow antlers — anatomical features that matched fluctuating food availability and the extremely dense understory of palmettos.

Although the outside spread was probably less than 14 inches, there were 15 total points, including three brow points on each antler. Branched brow points are not uncommon among mature bucks from Blackbeard and neighboring Sapelo Island. While

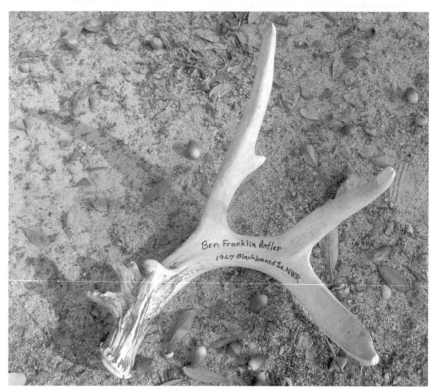
My treasured Ben Franklin Antler from Blackbeard Island in Georgia.

marveling at this fine specimen someone unfolded the paper tag attached to one antler and read the hunter's name. It was Ben Franklin! My expectations missed their mark and I had a newfound respect for the elderly archer. Our paths never crossed after that October hunt. I'm sure he sits in his climbing tree stand in the big sky and has a twinkle in his eye knowing that I hunted those diminutive Blackbeard whitetails for 10 years and never connected with a buck the caliber of his. A decade of expectations produced only a shed antler, which I affectionately and respectfully call my Ben Franklin antler. Until now it has been a secret treasure from the haunts of Edward Teach, alias Blackbeard.

Expectations go with the territory. The deer woods east of Athens (The University of Georgia) were turning out exceptional bucks like an assembly line during the late-1960s and early '70s. A "wave" of deer was flowing westward along major waterways and into a wealth of pine/hardwood forests and croplands. Higher deer densities elsewhere drew hunters' interests, allowing numerous bucks in the pioneering herd to reach their potential. All conditions were optimal: genetic stock from the whitetail's largest subspecies (in the Midwest), abundant and highly nutritious foods, and minimal hunting pressure.

Forestry and wildlife students and professors had access to a walk-in cooler in the School of Forest Resources. Although classroom obligations limited my hunting in those "good old days," I did find time to check the cooler on a regular basis during hunting season. To my surprise, there were no spike bucks. And, even the young bucks were huge by home-county (N.C.) standards. When doe days rolled around later in the season, I was impressed with the nonchalant attitudes of successful hunters. There was no stigma attached to the harvesting of does — they were deer, too. Obviously, a short-lived tradition of buck-only hunting yielded more flexibility than that of my boyhood.

Farther east, in Putnam County, the Central Georgia Branch Station, better known as the B.F. Grant Wildlife Management Area, was producing some fine specimens of "northern" bucks. In the winter of 1974 I visited a graduate school classmate who was living in one of the big-game check stations while conducting his master's research project on 'possums. There were two shed antlers in the check station that caught my eye. One was found by a quail hunter the previous winter. It was massive, with eight major points and several smaller points around the base. The other antler had just been brought in by the area manager, another of my classmates. This antler came from the same area as the first, and it looked like a carbon copy, except there were more points. The antlers weighed 6¼ and 6½ pounds, respectively.

Again my expectations of hunting such an exceptional animal were clouded by academic responsibilities. That spring I began my master's project on black bears in southeastern North Carolina. The quest for this particular buck was passed to those with a more suitable hunting schedule.

In the predawn hours one November morning a hunter approached the check station on B.F. Grant WMA as asked the area manager for directions to a likely spot to get a deer. He was told that a large buck was known to be frequenting Area 2, and he was given a map with that location marked. About mid-morning Tom Cooper and a Boone and Crockett buck met. The buck sported a non-typical rack with 26 points, the obvious owner of those famed shed antlers at the check station. It scored 215 7/8 and was the most outstanding whitetail taken by a NRA member throughout North America in 1974. Mr. Cooper received NRA's prestigious Silver Bullet Award for that buck and Putnam County added another claim to fame. Its county seat, Eatonton, is the home of the Uncle Remus Museum.

Return visits to the Athens area deer woods during graduate school were laced with problems common to established deer herds. Hunting pressure on the buck segment of the population and a high deer density had diminished my expectations of finding that buck-of-a-lifetime. I had learned to trust a prime barometer — young bucks resembled those of my boyhood days, and many had spike antlers.

The South Carolina Years

My first job following graduate school kept me confined in a one-acre chain-link pen. For seven years my position as deer research biologist with the South Carolina Department of Natural Resources (SCDNR) literally thrust me into a life with deer. In addition to conducting projects within the research facility, I assisted regional wildlife biologists with spotlight surveys of deer populations on private and public lands, and performed necropsies (animal autopsies) on deer from throughout the coastal counties to determine the cause of death. There were times when I had to pinch myself to realize that this was a profession and not an extended holiday, but there was still a lot to learn.

Several events occurred during the late-1970s and early-'80s that really started the wheels turning. Robert Folk, the biologist in the deer-rich lowcountry, asked me to join him in conducting a spotlight survey on a 10,000-acre plantation owned by Mr. Gene duPont. The deer population had been managed for six or seven years in a very unique manner. Mr. duPont allowed only does and spike bucks to be harvested. Rarely did he make an exception, and that was to allow a special family member or friend to take a "nice" buck. The plantation manager drove while Robert and I tallied deer from the bed of the truck. We were accompanied by Mr. and Mrs. duPont. What a night it was! We saw approximately 130 deer, and at least 25 of them were bucks with large racks. My wildest expectations had been stretched to the limit. By contrast, for the next 20 years of spotlighting, the number of mature bucks observed in one survey was never equaled. That night marked my introduction to the notion of letting bucks get older, and therefore larger, before harvesting them.

A trip to Texas in 1981 for the annual meeting of the Southeast Deer Study Group brought me in contact with a stalwart in deer management. His name was Al Brothers, the co-author of a recently published book entitled *Producing Quality Whitetails*.

The next year the SCDNR hosted the meeting in Charleston, and Al Brothers was invited to attend as the keynote speaker. His challenge was straightforward. "Isn't it time to afford young bucks the protection traditionally given the female segment of the population, while reducing doe numbers to have a herd in better balance with habitat conditions?"

Al's message was delivered to 300 attendees and half were deer hunters from the surrounding area. Biologists were cautioned for educating each other and encouraged to meet the hunters on their turf to discuss the merits of this novel approach to deer management. In 1981 the portion of does in the harvest of the 28 coastal counties in South Carolina was approximately 25 percent. Within 12 years that percentage increased to 51 and 52 percent for the last four years. Primary reasons for this change include: Hunters desired the transition from traditional deer management, the educational process was effective, and the establishment of quality deer management guidelines on more than two million acres of private land.

In the wake of this excitement there was a need for communication among hunters and a defined path to follow. It seems appropriate that the deer-rich lowcountry of South Carolina which provided direction to my life also gave birth to an organization, the Quality Deer Management Association that would ultimately chart a course for deer hunters universally.

Where do I stand in the midst of this revolution in deer management? I am savoring our accomplishments as managers and hunters. Each passing deer season seems to give way to a more promising one. Last fall I was fortunate to catch a glimpse of a monstrous buck while hunting. That glimpse and the occasional sighting of a huge track in my favorite hunting area gave me a season to remember. My thoughts of next season are filled with expectations. After all, isn't that what affirms our desire to hunt?

Note: *This article appeared in Quality Whitetails (V 5, I 1 - 1998).*

What is a Wildlife Biologist?

I am a stranger to most of you, but we have something in common. Three classmates and I were on The University of Georgia team that competed in the first student wildlife conclave in 1972. We won that year and again in 1973.

I must set the stage with what I gleaned from readings and personal interviews in preparation for this keynote address.

The winds of change are blowing. These winds are having a profound effect on the wildlife profession and the academic systems designed to feed the profession with a continual supply of young wildlife biologists.

Dr. Steve Williams, President of the Wildlife Management Institute, has a column in the Boone and Crockett Club's quarterly publication, *Fair Chase*. In the winter issue of 2006, Dr. Williams' column was entitled: For Everything There is a Season. He is a professed older baby boomer and his concerns and those of retirement-age professionals are presented in the context of changing seasons. "Just as fall turns to winter, so does one generation of biologists turn to another, and the practice of wildlife management has turned dramatically."

The Wildlife Society

INCORPORATED IN WASHINGTON, D.C.

grants the designation

Certified Wildlife Biologist

Dr. Williams harkened to the days of our profession 30 years ago. He said, "We managed wildlife as we knew best and would decide what resources and opportunity the public needed and deserved. We practiced 'command and control' management and it was relatively simple."

Our society has changed. Now, 80 percent of the U.S. population resides in urban areas. Despite this fact, wildlife agencies spend most of their efforts in rural neighborhoods with people and issues associated with a rural lifestyle. Dr. Williams stated that "Expecting staff from an urban upbringing to effectively interact with and understand rural lifestyles may prove ill-advised." Most agencies are adjusting to an increased complexity in wildlife-human interactions, management of species at risk, declining revenue and budgets, increased training requirements, and integrating new employees into a veteran workforce. According to Dr. Williams, "The future of wildlife management will depend on how we weather this storm."

Some universities continue to provide practical experience training like operating a tractor, chainsaw, boat, or 4 x 4 vehicles, but their numbers are declining. Recent surveys reveal that more than half of today's wildlife students have never hunted or fished.

The lack of these traditional skills and lifestyles will challenge the future practice of wildlife management.

On a positive note, today's universities are providing students with a sound scientific background steeped in theory. And in contrast to yesteryear, they teach communication, analytical, and conflict-resolution skills. The human dimensions' influence on our profession is only going to escalate. Wildlife biologists of the 21st century must be well grounded in the science of wildlife management. But more than ever before in our profession, communication skills are of vital importance. The success you have in managing fish and wildlife will hinge on how well you manage people.

Dr. Williams views the changes in our profession like those of the seasons — with an attitude of hope. "Let us anticipate that as agencies transition from one generation to the next, time will be available to teach and train new staff, institutional knowledge will be passed on, practical knowledge will be learned, and the transition will be smooth."

He closed with a challenge to universities and agencies to engage retired professionals as mentors for aspiring wildlife biologists. As an older baby boomer wildlife biologist, I share Dr. Williams' opinion. My presence with you tonight is testimony of my convictions.

Several weeks ago at the Southeast Deer Study Group meeting in Maryland, a fellow biologist and I were discussing my opportunity, my privilege, of being your keynote speaker. To get a professor's opinion of what was happening in the academic arena, he suggested a brief publication in the *Wildlifer's Log* in 2006. The article, entitled Dinosaur Ramblings, was written by Dr. Chuck Scalet, a professor with 35 years of experience and the head of Wildlife and Fisheries Education and Research at South Dakota State University.

Dr. Scalet stated: "There has been and continues to be a shift in university academic programs and faculty directions away from traditional wildlife and fisheries management" to what he categorized as an ecology/conservation ethos. "This shift has occurred in research and also in course and program content." One indication of this shift is that many academic programs have modified their department, program, and degree titles to reflect the change from management to ecology/conservation.

I have condensed and paraphrased some of the reasons Dr. Scalet listed for this shift in direction.

As research expansion occurred over the last 35 years it was more often in areas directed toward ecology/conservation and away from management because that was where the new money was located.

Management research is now generally viewed by many universities and faculty members as being less prestigious than ecology/conservation research. Greater numbers of faculty are avoiding their association with the "hook and bullet crowd," the hunters and fishermen who benefit most from management research. I must emphasize at this point that all of society benefits from management research.

More faculties are taking what they perceive to be a more holistic approach to natural resource management and conservation. There has been a shift in thinking from the population level to the community or landscape level. Therefore, as faculty shift, programs shift.

As more faculty move and have moved toward ecology/conservation they produce students in their own image and that is affected by research fund sources. Once a faculty member moves away from management research the likelihood of their going back is reduced.

Student demographics have changed appreciably, especially in such areas as male/female, urban/rural, and consumptive/nonconsumptive user student ratios. Overall, students come to universities with less "background" information in natural resources.

Student priorities concerning for whom they would like to work and the type of work they would like to do have shifted. That shift has been away from management, and money is a prime issue in this area.

This shift in emphasis within the academic world has had an effect on state and federal agencies. The winds of change are creating agencies unlike those in the days of us baby boomers.

Allow me to digress a bit by presenting an evolutionary review of our profession. Aldo Leopold stated that, "Conservation is a state of harmony between men and land." I'm sure he must have been thinking of the Native Americans when he coined the definition of conservation. Early settlers, followed by market hunters, brought about the era of exploitation. The renaissance was a period of reconstruction and restoration following in the wake of the Pittman-Robertson and Dingle-Johnson Acts. State wildlife agencies began with law enforcement personnel directed to uphold game laws to protect the remaining wildlife. The conservation era arose with the need for management, and wildlife biologists appeared on the scene to grow wildlife populations and to later manage their numbers.

We are now in the stewardship phase of conservation. It is here that public opinion has a greater influence on wildlife management than ever before in history.

So, what is a wildlife biologist and what can you do to become an effective wildlife biologist in the 21st century?

I was raised by a deer-hunting club in a time when there were few deer and storytelling before and following hunts filled the void of time afield. A proper story has two purposes. It must be entertaining and it must contain an element of education.

Research for my master's degree from The University of Georgia's School of Forest Resources was conducted on black bears in southeastern North Carolina from the early summer of 1974 through the fall of 1976.

I used radio telemetry to determine daily, seasonal and annual home range and habitat use by radio-collared bears. Collection of scats and stomach contents of hunter-harvested bears was used to determine food habits and therefore habitat preferences of bears. Hunters were skeptical of my reasons for studying black bears, and the feeling was that I was on a mission to close bear-hunting season. This couldn't have been farther from the truth, but I was persistent in harvest data collection. Successful bear hunters would take the animals to their camp, process the carcass, place the entrails in a large metal barrel, and then give me a call — usually late at night. I would drive to the camp, extract a small premolar for determining age, and proceed to dig through the gut barrel to collect the stomach from each bear and the reproductive tract from females. I never got a chance to weigh the bears or get body measurements. This situation continued throughout the study. Eventually, after my thesis was completed, the bear hunters realized that I was determined to protect the status of the black bear as a game animal and we established a long-overdue friendship.

My first seven years as a deer research biologist with the South Carolina Wildlife ans Marine Resources Department (now the S.C. Department of Natural Resources, or SCDNR) were spent in the pen — a research facility. During this time I was isolated from the public and from wildlife management. However, I wrote several articles on deer management for the department's wildlife magazine, participated in deer spotlight surveys with fellow wildlife biologists, and performed necropsies on white-tailed deer throughout eastern South Carolina.

In 1985 I moved to southeastern South Carolina as an assistant district wildlife biologist. My supervisor and I covered seven counties and shared 1,500 deer hunting clubs. We were also committed to working with private landowners on dove, quail, turkey, and waterfowl management — the whole gamut of wildlife management.

The author tracking a radio-collared black bear during a 1970s research project in southeastern North Carolina.

Idealism was still my number-one enemy. I assumed that diplomas on my office wall would afford me the respect of my constituents — hunters and the public in general.

My first identity crisis occurred late one night at a local gas station. As I was pumping gas into my state-owned vehicle the attendant approached curiously. He was wearing a plaid shirt and striped pants and both of his tennis shoes were untied. He looked disheveled at best, so I wasn't surprised by his question when he saw the logo on my vehicle. "Is you de new game warden?" No, I replied courteously, I'm the new wildlife biologist. He began walking away, but returned with this revelation: "You're one of those fellows that just drives around checking on stuff, aint you?" Without belaboring the point, I simply agreed. Completely puzzled at this point, he asked, "Well, that don't take much

A marbled salamander.

time do it?" Believe it or not, some mornings I start at 9 and am finished before lunch. Some conversations are better off ending as this one did. Always consider your audience when defending your position.

One of my biological duties involved working with private landowners and hunt club officials in the department's Antlerless Deer Quota Program. New applicants required a site visit and a discussion about the harvest history and management objectives. The dilemma that I faced when moving to this county was the circulation of a petition to end the harvest of antlerless deer. So, at the end of my first summer of working on this program, I was asked by my supervisor to visit our senator, a local attorney, to explain my activities. This meeting marked my second identity crisis. He began by mentioning the petition and then told me that my predecessor, a former classmate from UGA, had been overly aggressive in issuing antlerless tags. In his Charlestonian brogue he exclaimed, "They were ready to send him out of town on a rail — tarred and feathered! You seem like an astute young gentleman, so I presume that you considered the situation and did what was necessary." I assured the senator that I did what I was required to do, what was biologically sound. "Well, did you cut last year's quota by 25 percent?" No sir. "Did you cut it by 50 percent?" No sir. "Well, hell son, did you cut it by more than that?" No sir, I doubled the quota for this upcoming deer season. He grabbed the edge of his desk with both hands and shouted, "Great gawd, you're going to get both of us sent out of town on a rail — tarred and feathered!" I told the senator that his job was to serve as a heat shield and deflect any skeptics my way. I agreed to meet with the originators of the petition and explain my approach toward proper deer management.

To be effective I had a lot of homework to do, including a weekly, 15-minute spot at the local radio station and a no-holes-barred public relations program. I became a prolific writer and published articles in numerous newspapers and magazines. I spoke on wildlife management to any group that would sit still. Within the next four years that county harvested more does than bucks and in another year or so, our seven-county district harvested more does than bucks. Furthermore, the percent of yearling bucks in the annual harvest decreased appreciably, allowing more bucks to reach the older age classes before being harvested. These events led to the founding of the South Carolina Quality Deer Management Association in 1988. Interest in this fledgling organization spread quickly and the name was changed to the Quality Deer Management Association to reflect its universal scope.

And in conclusion, always remember the human dimension aspect of your profession. Try to provide your constituents what they need by tactfully influencing or guiding them in the right direction if they are off base, if their perceived needs and wants aren't compatible with proper management objectives. Your commitment to our natural resources and those who utilize them will serve you well in the long run. Remember, resource policy is a public debate, and no one ever won a public policy debate by keeping their mouth shut or ink in their pen.

You don't have to be a hunter to be a wildlife biologist, but to be an effective biologist you must embrace the use of hunting as a viable tool in wildlife management.

You will soon be embarking on a new journey in your life, and the job market is diverse for someone with your academic training. Here are some options for employment: state and federal agencies, consulting firms, timber companies, military installations, universities, managing private properties (25 percent increase in lands purchased for outdoor recreation) , and non-government organizations like Ducks Unlimited, The Nature Conservancy, Quality Deer Management Association, National Wild Turkey Federation, Rocky Mountain Elk Foundation, Pheasants Forever, Ruffed Grouse Society, and the Audubon Society.

Continue being a student. Nearly 65 years ago Aldo Leopold wrote: "The interdependence of the forest and its constituent tree species, ground flora, and fauna is taken for granted." So, strive to know your surroundings (trees, shrubs, wild flowers, birds, frogs, salamanders, snakes, and mammals large and small) because all things are inextricably linked. The more you know, the easier it will be to read nature's barometers. Write and speak often. Find a mentor and use them as a sounding board during trying times. Follow these simple steps to become a successful wildlife biologist and an asset to the profession.

Your primary challenges will include (1) protection of lands from development to ensure continued access by your constituents; (2) encouraging hunter recruitment, especially among our youth; (3) working cooperatively with agencies and resource/management organizations to perpetuate our hunting heritage; and (4) optimizing your relationship with your constituents (hunters and fishermen), the general public, and elected officials.

As always, I will close with a favorite Aldo Leopold quote. "An understanding of ecology does not necessarily originate in courses bearing ecological labels; it is quite as likely to be labeled geography, botany, agronomy, history, or economics. This is as it

Keep your outdoor bible in hand — *A Sand County Almanac.* Read it often and live it.

should be, but whatever the label, ecological training is scarce.

"The 'key-log' that must be moved to release the evolutionary process for a land ethic is simply this: Quit thinking about decent land-use as solely an economic problem. Examine each question in terms of what is ethically and esthetically right, as well as what is economically expedient. A thing is right when it tends to preserve the integrity, stability, and beauty of the biotic community. It is wrong when it tends otherwise."

Note: This keynote address was delivered at the banquet during the Southeastern Wildlife Conclave in 2007 at Rock Eagle State Park in Eatonton, Georgia. Approximately 450 students from 23 eastern colleges and universities attended the event.

The Hunting Spirit

We sat quietly on the pond's edge waiting and watching for something to stir. My Father was of a lineage of hunters, and I, perched on his knee at the age of three, was destined to follow. He pointed toward a new arrival to the pond. "It's a wood duck," he whispered. My first encounter with a wild animal is etched indelibly in my memory.

The colors of a drake woodie, unequaled in the avian world, permanently captured the attention of that youngster. But the most lasting impression was that my Father announced the duck with a whisper. Years, even decades would lapse before I understood the importance of reverence in nature's theater.

Drake Wood Duck.

As fate would have it, our times together on hunting and fishing trips were limited. My mentor slipped away to the happy hunting grounds only three years after our first visit to the pond. During that brief period, my Father had not only instilled within me a burgeoning love of nature, but he had introduced me to his sporting companions — hunters and fishermen. It was they who took me under their wings and served as surrogate mentors. In retrospect, my misfortune was overshadowed quickly by fortune.

Mom fueled my quest for nature lore by providing field guides on all sorts of "critters." In addition, she gave me free rein to spend countless hours in the woods with my Daisy BB gun acting the part of my boyhood idols, Daniel Boone and Davy Crockett.

Experiences as a Boy Scout further enforced my quest for nature. Fortunately, my scoutmaster, Mr. Doug Waller, was a hunter and fisherman, too. He unselfishly devoted a weekend each month, year-round, to take our troop camping. Through his guidance we learned to be at home in the out-of-doors. Tents were arranged in a large circle, and the centerpiece was named, appropriately, "the council fire." We had smaller campfires for cooking, but the council fire was for bonding, storytelling, and occasionally where the scoutmaster prepared his famous squirrel-and-rice stew — in a giant cast iron pot, enough for the entire troop. It was here that I was introduced to the "celebration of the hunt." During the meal our scoutmaster would spare no details in telling how he hunted the river lowlands and shot squirrels from tall hardwoods using a .22 rifle. Since most squirrel hunters in those days used shotguns, we were impressed with his woodsmanship and his marksmanship. The difficulty of the hunt, dictated by the choice of a challenging weapon, somehow compensated for a quarry not known for its cunning. Thus we celebrated the spoils of the hunt.

Before I reached the age to get a driver's license, I was adopted by a deer hunting club. Someone would provide transportation every Saturday morning throughout the season for me to participate in the traditional deer drive on a tract of land along the Cape Fear River only a mile from the outskirts of my hometown. Deer were scarce in those days.

We were fortunate to harvest eight or 10 each season with as many hunters. Our club had no name and there were no annual dues except for the occasional request from the hunt master following a successful hunt to "save a piece of meat for the landowner."

Perhaps my fondest and most vivid memories of hunting as a youngster in the late-1950s and early '60s were of prehunt and posthunt gatherings around a fire of sticks and twigs. We didn't have, or take, enough time to build a full-fledged log fire. Nevertheless, the fire served its age-old purpose. It was a focal point that forced hunters into a circle to hear tales of encounters with "old mossy-horned bucks" and favorite hunting hounds of bygone days. This circular arrangement appeared to erase barriers, namely age, so I felt as grown up as the rest and was more at ease when telling my stories. I was a teammate, an equal, and that was important to a young man.

I must confess that throughout these early years I did not progress beyond the shooting stage as a hunter. Although I had acquired an ability to identify a fair number

of wild animals, especially birds, I knew next to nothing about their daily habits, their movement patterns, or their biology. This was especially true with regard to my knowledge of the white-tailed deer, primarily due to their elusive nature and low numbers. To me, deer were an enigma. Their mere presence had mystical qualities, and that alone fueled my desire or, more precisely, my primal need to hunt.

Bronze medallion designed by Arthur Bentley. It is presented to each new member of the Keepers of the Hunting Spirit.

Our forefathers hunted out of necessity, to provide food and clothing for themselves and their families. The surplus of their pursuits was used for trade. Those who flourished I suspect were driven by an inner force probably unknown or unrecognized at the time, but it was present — the hunting spirit. The pace at which one experiences the steps of hunting is an individual process, suffice it to say that time, tempered by experience, is the measure. Passing from one plateau to the next as a hunter is quite subtle. Often, only hindsight will reveal the path to the present, with the future direction remaining vague. It has been said that some people live and learn while others just live. So it is with hunters — some attain the hunting spirit while others simply continue to hunt. The quest for knowledge of one's quarry appears to me to be a mark of potential to progress to another plateau as a hunter.

It was the members of my hunt club, my mentors, who encouraged me to continue my education beyond high school. Driven by hardships of the day, most had become farmers or loggers as young men. They bemoaned the fact that they did not get a better education. I was a neophyte with much to learn and I heeded their advice.

My college years came, lasted an eternity, and finally passed. I entered the academic world as a deer enthusiast and emerged as a deer enthusiast with degrees in forestry and wildlife biology. Psychologists have revealed that students suffering from agoraphobia, a fear of the unknown, an uncertain future, often turn to drugs, alcohol, and social cliques for security. My greatest fear then and now is living without hunting and seeing myself as a non-hunter. Security for me came from the educational process – a path from awareness to enlightenment, to understanding, and finally to respect for the animals of my studies and the quests of my hunting endeavors. This path was blazed by numerous top-notch professors, but there was one with distinction. Dr. Larry Marchinton was a hunter, too, and obviously one with the hunting spirit. Among his many contributions to my education was an introduction to the renowned father of wildlife management and author of *A Sand County Almanac*, Aldo Leopold.

One day in class Dr. Marchinton drew our attention to Leopold's Almanac chapter entitled "Thinking Like A Mountain." Having shot a wolf, Leopold recounted, "We reached the old wolf in time to watch a fierce green fire dying in her eyes. I realized then, and have known ever since, that there was something new to me in those eyes – something known only to her and to the mountain. I was young then, and full of trigger-itch; I thought that because fewer wolves meant more deer, that no wolves would mean hunter's paradise. But after seeing the green fire die, I sensed that neither the wolf nor the mountain agreed with such a view."

The lesson found its mark. I had been elevated from a shooter, one with trigger-itch, to the next plateau as a hunter with reverence toward my quarry and its environment, our environment. Through education, I now understood my functional role in nature's scheme rather than being a despoiler of it.

My college experience was a renaissance. Perhaps the greatest gift resulting from that grueling academic period of my life was that our professor/student relationship evolved into one of friendship, yet I remain a student of Dr. Larry Marchinton to this day.

Two decades as a professional wildlife biologist filled my life with deer people – hunters. In a 4-county area of southeastern South Carolina's deer-rich lowcountry there were more than 700 deer hunting clubs that commanded my attention. These clubs produced about 8,000 deer jawbones to be aged each year and required hundreds of annual harvest reports. In the beginning, I was dealing with deer densities and harvest levels beyond my wildest dreams of the 1960s, and reached the conclusion that as a commodity increases in number and/or availability, there is a corresponding decrease in the respect toward individuals. Thus, the whitetail's ability to procreate had reduced its status from a highly prized denizen of the deep forest to a common target of suburban woodlots. As a hunter and biologist I wanted to nurture a relationship with the whitetail as the noble game animal epitomized in my youth.

The task would not be an easy one. Still fraught with idealism that often comes from a formal education without experience, I found myself at odds with my constituents, the hunters. There was an obvious chasm between their knowledge of and attitude toward the whitetail and mine. Deer hunters had become disgruntled with the outcome of a traditional management approach designed to provide maximum recreation through liberal bag limits and seasons. What resulted from the limited understanding among hunters, the ultimate managers, was a young age structure of bucks, increasing densities from overprotection of females, and a decrease in deer quality related to deteriorating habitat conditions.

Aldo Leopold's teachings, as so often has been the case for me, provided the solution to this dilemma. To be effective, according to Leopold, wildlife professionals had to share their knowledge through the media, radio and newspapers at the time, and through personal contacts. All the while, wildlife professionals should remain students themselves, continually learning.

A trip to Texas in the early 1980s yielded the necessary message for me to deliver to deer hunters in South Carolina. Al Brothers was the source of that message involving a novel approach to improve deer herds and hunting. It was to become popularized as quality deer management, or QDM.

Select hunting clubs were introduced to quality deer management. Within a few years results were encouraging, and the word spread quickly through the deer hunting fraternity. There was something missing, though. We had no effective method for keeping in touch with this growing faction of hunters/managers. Other game animals had their support groups including Ducks Unlimited, the National Wild Turkey Federation, and Quail Unlimited, but the whitetail had no such backing. Those of us who worked with deer were told time and again by fellow professionals that deer hunters could not be organized.

Lessons learned from my initial visit to Australia in 1987 dispelled this notion. The Australian Deer Association (ADA) was founded in 1969 in an effort to unite deer hunters toward deer conservation. This organization would become the voice of deer hunters and the silent ones as well, the deer. In time, it would influence deer hunters half way around the world.

My experiences in the land down under were akin to those of a young, impressionable Aldo Leopold in the Southwest. I, like Leopold, was anxious to return home and begin putting my newfound principles to work. In the aftermath of my visit to Australia the South Carolina Quality Deer Management Association was born. Interest soon spread to neighboring states and beyond, necessitating a name change reflecting the geographical scope of this fledgling organization. Now (in 2004), the Quality Deer Management Association has international significance, with 30,000 members across the United States and in several foreign countries.

There would be return visits to Australia – a foreign exchange program of a sort. I shared information on quality deer management from the States while observing hunter attitudes and behaviors unique to me as a deer hunter. Was my intrigue influenced by common, yet distant ancestral roots? Perhaps to a degree, but I was impressed by the Australian deer hunters' knowledge of deer and their active involvement in all matters related to deer; matters ranging from poetry to politics. I was envious, and felt the need, or more precisely the necessity, to emulate these characteristics among American hunters. Without belaboring detail, I would like to take the opportunity to highlight only a few of my many Australian encounters that have had a profound impact on my life.

Deer hunting in Australia produced a pioneer, a man who would become respected as the "Father of the Deer." While still in his early 20s, Arthur Bentley became interested in deer in 1937. Except for the time spent serving his country in World War II, he has been actively involved in improving the status of deer in Australia ever since.

His book, *An Introduction to the Deer of Australia*, was published in 1967. This book remains the only comprehensive reference work on the deer of Australia. A primary driving force behind the founding of the Australian Deer Association (ADA) was none other than Arthur Bentley. The organization's logo bears this quote by Aldo Leopold: "Conservation is a state of harmony between men and land." Thanks to Arthur Bentley, the "Father" of wildlife management in the U.S. is shared by Australian deer hunters.

Arthur Bentley was awarded the British Empire Medal in 1975 for long and valuable services to deer conservation. No other Australian has been honored in this manner for services to deer. A man of many talents — author, artist, poet, sculptor, and conservationist — he became the first to be granted Life Membership in the ADA. This was a well-deserved honor for an individual with no formal biological training and one who has always served voluntarily. He is a man of conviction and dedication, a mentor of the first order. One of his many poems has particular relevance.

THE QUEST

In the soft soil of the log track
We've seen the sambar's mark,
From a silver wattle sapling
The gleam of antlered bark.

We've searched the tea-tree gullies
Where the blacktails thump and splash,
And climbed to the rocky basins
Above the mountain ash.

We've seen their strange wild bodies
Hang by the faller's hut,
Run fingers through the bristled hair
Soiled in October's rut.

But the sambar still is calling
As only the sambar can —
A haunting down the ages
In the questing heart of man.

Peter Stuart was my initial contact with Australia in 1984. We have traded visits several times since. In October 1989, this Life Member and former President of the ADA arrived in the South Carolina lowcountry to deer hunt with me. It was the fourth

Arthur Bentley

Pen and ink sketch of sambar stag.

year of quality deer management in my neighborhood and bucks were exhibiting signs of being in full rut.

He traveled 12,000 miles, purchased a non-resident hunting license, endured swarms of mosquitoes, watched the sun rise and set for six days, observed at least 25 bucks, and completed his visit without ever pulling a trigger. The intent was evident. He had taken game before and he has since, but he behaved as a true sportsman and always gave his quarry the benefit of the doubt. Peter returned to his native Australia with a storehouse of memories from our deer woods. I hope his life will continue to be enriched by those intangible values and I thank him for the treasure he imparted upon us — a prime example of patience and respect.

Incidentally, Peter passed up a particularly large buck one afternoon and the following morning because shooting conditions were not optimal. That buck was harvested by another friend of mine only two weeks after Peter's departure. That one remains among the top five bucks produced by the neighborhood deer population.

In the early years the ADA rested on the shoulders of Arthur Bentley, Geoff Moore, Peter Stuart, and Mike Harrison; all Life Members. These four, supported by their dedicated wives, were on the leadership front of every ADA function. Mike Harrison's scope of talents explains his reputation in negotiating successfully with government officials and politicians in an urban setting one day, and being "at home" in the bush the next. His fly rod and Lee-Enfield rifle are as much an extension of his right hand as is his ink pen. He can put meat on the table, a poem on paper, a provocative thought in your mind, and a smile in your heart. Mike is professorial — he is an educator. I remember regrouping after a deer hunt in the infamous mongrel country near Walhalla. Mike removed the wool daypack from his back, began fossicking around amongst its contents and exclaimed, "We have deer here, I know we have deer! How do I know?" He extracted a plant from his pack, held it high for all to see, and shouted, "BANYALLA!!! It's one of their favorite browse species." Mike's enthusiasm and inquisitiveness are admirable traits of a deer hunter.

Arthur Bentley has provided the inspiration for many of his "students" to put their thoughts on paper for all to read, and they have written books. I have selected poignant quotes from five books by Australian deer hunters and published by the Australian Deer Research Foundation.

Geoff Moore, teamed up with Ron Mayze to produce the world's most complete study of hog deer followed by a book of equal quality. In their book, *The Hog Deer*, they stated that hunting "…can be an exacting recreation, physically demanding and one which requires endurance, patience, persistence, a certain amount of individuality, an ability to observe and understand, and above all, a love of solitude and the wild things of the forest."

In his book, *Sambar Hunter*, Lu Cervi penned these thoughts. "Aldo Leopold wrote, '…a day afield will replete the soul.' Unfortunately there are those amongst us without souls who give more consideration to their own egos and successes than they ever do to the game they play, let alone the game they hunt. To my way of thinking, the attitude, ethics, morals — call them what you will — should be the main thing that guides all hunters. We should all 'play the game' so that there is something left to hunt."

Peter Burke's *Quiet Footsteps* contains this message. "The moment of truth (for hunters) is in what is seen and what is felt. If he has come for no other reason than to kill, he has lost. But he has come for more than venison and antler; he has come to hunt, to walk in time with the rhythm of the forest."

Cunning As A Fox was written by the fifth and most recent of ADA's Life Members, Jack Clark of South Australia. He wrote, "As each of the Clark boys reaches the age where they start to become interested in hunting, they are taught the fundamentals of safe gun handling. With age, skills increase and today the Clark family can field three generations of hunters. If I can get them to appreciate the environment we live in, and impart the high standard of ethics which all users of the bush should have and abide by, then I will have achieved an ambition which to me is of paramount importance."

Ken Pearce, a devout sambar hunter, was ahead of his time with this statement in his 1987 publication, *Walking Them Up*. "A hunter who spots a 'teenage' stag looking at him from across the gully, sporting what appears to be a 20-inch head, will prove nothing if he kills that animal while he has a 24- or 26-inch head on his lounge room wall. If you only want to fill the freezer, take a young hind or spikey instead, if the chance arises, and let your subordinate grow up to provide future hunting trips."

From a collection of letters spanning 17 years since my first visit to Australia, I have selected one written recently by Max Craig, a staunch supporter of the ADA from Queensland. Max had just learned that the property where he hunted was to be sold and developed. "When I was driving out of my friend's property, I had, as you would imagine, many mixed feelings...without being conscious of much. But when I shut the gate and realized it was to be for the last time, and then it really got to me. I think I sat in the ute (truck) for about 20 minutes...I reckon I relived every hunt and every sighting of the deer that I had encountered over all the years. It was really amazing, as prior to that, I just had this awful empty feeling. That was replaced by a feeling of satisfaction, pleasure, and all the other words that remembering does for you. The one word I must not forget was gratitude. I will be forever grateful to have been able to see and do all the things that I did on that property over a period of nearly 20 years...a long time in hunting terms."

In his introduction to the book *Hunters' Verses from the High Country*, game biologist Max Downes wrote: "To the deer hunter, deer are the numenon, the inner meaning of the mountains. Their presence or absence does not affect the outward appearance of deer country, but it does mightily affect our reaction toward it. Without tracks on the trail and the potential presence of wildlife at each new dip and bend of the hillside, the forest is an empty shell, a spiritual vacuum."

These quotes, collectively, capture the very essence of the spirit of the hunt. My Australian acquaintances have had a profound influence on my personal and professional life. I hope that my writings, actions, and spoken words from home will be of some value to my fellow hunters 12,000 miles away in Australia and elsewhere.

I mentioned earlier that the development of a hunter involves passing through a series of plateaus, ideally toward an ultimate destination or goal. Also, the changes experienced are individualistic and often subtle. Somewhere along the way, with proper influence from mentors, a hunter will realize that he has acquired the hunting spirit. The degree to which this process can be spread universally among the masses of hunters will determine our future.

The winds of change are blowing. Mankind is extending its tentacles into the heart of vitally important wildlife habitats around the world. The hunter/gatherer societies of yesteryear that spawned the likes of us have been replaced by urban societies who view hunting with disdain. While human populations continue to increase, our hunter numbers are waning. Given these trends, an optimist, aware of the efforts of wildlife organizations and land conservationists, would offer hope for the future of hunting.

How do we ensure that this prediction has merit? We stay the course that has taken several generations to plot. We stand with pride before all for what we are, hunters, and we apologize to no one. We must strive to educate all those affected by deer and foster the principles of stewardship. We must protect those natural habitat types, crucial to the well-being of our quests, and ensure our continued access as hunters. There is no question whether this effort should have a united front. If one loses, we all lose. Furthermore, we must police our own ranks by providing guidance for those exhibiting unacceptable behavior, but we should not be held accountable for the actions of incorrigible individuals. They are a bane of society as well.

Hunting's future will rest firmly on the shoulders of stewards who will persevere regardless of social pressures or an uncertain future. The Australian Deer Association and the Quality Deer Management Association appear to me to be at the forefront of

Brian Murphy

Keepers of the Hunting Spirit members (left to right): Geoff Moore, Peter Stuart, Arthur Bentley, me, and Mike Harrison.

this movement. We must remain steadfast in our convictions. Above all else, the leaders, mentors, of any such movement have a responsibility to adequately prepare their counterparts of the next generation to carry the torch.

This is my creed: A seasoned hunter, one with the hunting spirit, pursues his quarry on each occasion with the enthusiasm of his first encounter and with the reverence as though it were his last. I, for one, do not want to know when I have had my last hunt!

How do I wish to be remembered? Simply this: In his chest beat the heart of a hunter — a seasoned hunter who embraced the spirit of the hunt as he lived and how he lived so that those who follow will have a secure and well-defined path.

I want to be remembered as one of you — THE KEEPERS OF THE HUNTING SPIRIT!

Following my presentation, I joined Dr. Larry Marchinton as the only Americans to be inducted into the Keepers of the Hunting Spirit. Pictured with me from the left are: the late Geoff Moore, Peter Stuart (2011 recipient of the QDMA Ambassador Award), the late Arthur Bentley (2004 recipient of the Joe Hamilton Lifetime Achievement Award), and Mike Harrison (2016 recipient of the Joe Hamilton Lifetime Achievement Award).

Note: *This was my acceptance speech for induction into The Keepers of the Hunting Spirit in Melbourne, Australia in 2004.*

Calendar of venison meals.

Lead in Venison

Deer hunters provide venison through donation programs each year and make a substantial contribution to feeding the needy. In 2010, deer hunters from across North America donated over 2.6 million pounds of venison that was used to create nearly 10.5 million meals for the less fortunate. For a complete report on venison donation programs refer to the QDMA's 2011 Whitetail Report (pages 30-31) at www.qdma.com.

Only two years prior, this humanitarian effort was threatened by a movement beginning in Minnesota to remove hunter-donated venison from local soup kitchens due to concerns of contamination from lead fragments from hunters' bullets. The neighboring states of North Dakota and Wisconsin joined in knee-jerk reaction and tons of venison were sent to local landfills. A detailed report appears in the QDMA's 2009 Whitetail Report (pages 12-14) at www.qdma.com.

In May 2008, the North Dakota Department of Health and the U.S. Centers for Disease Control and Prevention (CDC) responded by conducting a study to measure the risk, if any, of eating wild game harvested with lead bullets. The study involved testing 738 North Dakotans who volunteered to have their blood tested for the presence of lead.

The CDC report indicated that the average lead level of the hunters tested was lower than among average Americans. The mean blood lead level in Americans is less than 3.0 parts per billion, and hunters in the study had a mean of 1.27 — far below 10 parts per billion, which the CDC considers to be a level of concern in children.

QDMA's Recommendations

Venison donation programs are a substantial benefit to society by providing high-protein, low-fat venison to needy families. However, these programs also play a key role in sound deer population management because hunters attempting to reduce deer densities where necessary often need to harvest more does than their families can consume. Considering that the CDC study found no evidence of health concerns related to consumption of venison harvested with lead ammunition, venison donation programs should be continued, and hunters and their families should continue to consume and enjoy venison. The QDMA recommended further study to confirm the CDC findings and to highlight methods for harvesting, field-dressing, and processing deer that can reduce lead fragments in venison.

Personal Study

Having been an above-average consumer of venison for many years, I decided to conduct a personal study. Beginning on January 1, 2010, a red dot was put on my "venison" calendar each time a meal of venison was consumed.

Here are my study results:

1. Consumed venison on 225 days of the 365 days (62 percent of the days in 2010).
2. Consumed venison on 299 meals of a possible 1,095 meals (27 percent of the meals in 2010).
3. Consumed venison twice/day on 49 days.
4. Consumed venison three times/day on 12 days.
5. If ½ pound of venison was consumed per meal, that would total 150 pounds of venison consumed in 2010.
6. A blood test conducted early in January 2011 revealed that my blood lead level was 1.6 parts per billion — well below the level of concern by CDC.

Personal Advice

All of my deer were harvested with a high-powered, center-fire rifle. I was careful to clean the wound channel of "damaged" (bloodshot) meat, and I processed all deer after hanging them in a walk-in cooler (38 degrees F) for at least a week. For those of you who use a venison processor, I would recommend that you are emphatic about having the wound channel cleaned by the processor.

Quality Venison

Venison is good and good for you. Use a little common sense and caution when preparing your meat for the table and you'll complete the circle of respect by sharing quality venison with family and friends.

Note: This article appeared in Quality Whitetails (V 18, I 5 - 2011).

The Real Trophy

By R. Joseph Hamilton and Dr. R. Larry Marchinton

Prior to the advent of quality deer management (QDM), yearling bucks comprised 70-90 percent of annual harvests throughout much of the whitetail's range. In those days of traditional deer management, most 2½-year-old bucks were considered trophies due to the fact that they were rare and usually larger than the yearlings. Early in QDM there was a need to rectify the young age structure of bucks and the unbalanced adult sex ratio of deer populations. Basically, this meant allowing bucks to reach older age classes and shifting more of the harvest to does. This was usually accomplished by restricting buck harvests to animals with a minimum number of antler points, spread, main beam length or mass. These larger antler characteristics, or combinations thereof, allowed the protection of young bucks. We have refrained from using the term "trophy" primarily because QDM's purpose was biologically motivated, but also due to the general public's dismal view of trophy hunting. QDM has been around for over 30 years, and is practiced on a broad enough geo-

Among bucks, AGE is the true measure of progress and success in a QDM program. When you display your achievement, include the real trophy — the JAWBONE.

graphical scale so that bucks 5½ years old and older have become much more common in many areas. Proof of this exists through the collection of cast antlers, trail camera photos, and annual harvests across North America.

In the animal world, white-tailed deer exhibit more physical diversity than most. Some of this diversity, especially body measurements and weights, is explained by two biological principles — Allen's and Bergmann's Rules. These generalizations state that warm-blooded animals in cold regions tend to be larger in size and have a lower body surface-to-weight ratio than related animals in warmer climates. Early biologists described over 30 subspecies of whitetails, as classified by body measurements and other characteristics. The idea of subspeciation, however, has been clouded by years of restocking programs where deer have been moved around the country.

Habitat quality can also affect physical characteristics of deer. For example, forage quality and availability will vary across a region that has a variety of soil types and land-use practices. Bucks within the region may display a variety of antler characteristics, reflecting the variability in habitat quality. In South Carolina, a state which did its restocking with resident animals, there exists a broad range of antler development within age classes.

Although this phenomenon has been shown to be related to forage quality, soil type, and habitat management, bucks inherently produce antlers of varying size and shape within age classes regardless of environmental conditions. No degree of habitat management or supplemental feeding will change this. Look around the next time you attend a class reunion or gathering of folks in general. Differences in size and shape are all too obvious, even among the adults.

A common theme in many QDM programs is that the hunter passes up bucks until they're about 3½ years old, and from that time on the bucks pass up the hunter. A buck that has reached at least 5½ years old is a survivor — A jawbone can be added to any type of mount to help tell the full story of the hunting and QDM achievement.

he's crafty, sly, elusive, and cunning. There's no guarantee though that he will have the greatest headgear. Long-term QDM has given rise to a new category — "management bucks" — that didn't exist under traditional deer management. Although some hunters call these "cull bucks," we strongly discourage use of this demeaning term for these older-age bucks with relatively small antlers. These bucks didn't reach their ripe-old age simply by being lucky, although some may have slipped through the cracks by having undesirable antlers throughout their lives.

According to population genetics theory, it is not best for the long-term maintenance of herd antler quality to only remove the mature bucks with the largest antlers. Why? Some professionals have expressed a concern that prolonged high grading could negatively affect body and antler characteristics or even alter behavior. For this reason, aging bucks on the hoof based on body characteristics and NOT antler development has become important. We also know that this approach is growing in popularity because so many QDMA members turn first to the "Age This" section of each new issue of our *Quality Whitetails* journal. Our five panelists state emphatically that bucks estimated to be 5½-plus years old should be put on the "wish list" for the upcoming hunting season

Jawbone attaches with magnet.

Magnet on base.

Admirers can easily take down the jawbone to view evidence of the buck's maturity.

regardless of their antler development.

Maybe it's time for QDM practitioners to resurrect the term "trophy" but to use it to refer to a buck's age without regard to antler size, shape, symmetry, asymmetry, or Boone and Crockett score. The "trophy" for these older bucks is in their mouth — it's the jawbone. This, and not the antlers, is the true measure of their ability to avoid hunters — it's their measure of survivability!

The hunter who can legally and ethically harvest old bucks deserves to be recognized accordingly. So, when you display the head or European skull mount of your mature buck be sure to include your "trophy" jawbone as well. This trophy provides a visual record of the buck's age and elusiveness and your hunting prowess.

Here's what we think. If you can consistently harvest bucks with trophy jawbones (5½ years old or older) you will have graduated to the next level as a deer hunter. More importantly, you will be properly managing your herd for the future!

Note: *This article appeared in Quality Whitetails (V 18, I 6 – 2011/'12).*

In Pursuit of Mature Six-Pointers

Henry Fair's monster six-pointer.

QDM has increased the occurrence of mature bucks with six points. A basic tenet of QDM involves moving more bucks into the older age classes. Benefits include creating a more balanced adult sex ratio, diversifying the buck age structure, and enhancing the hunting experience by increasing the availability of mature bucks with larger bodies and antlers.

One thing we didn't anticipate is that QDM could increase the number of mature bucks with six points. Before getting discouraged and thinking that your deer herd is riddled with inferior genes, consider the biology of the animal and the effects of your management. Even though a small percent of adult bucks produce racks with only six points, it stands to reason that as the number of adult bucks increases so does the number with six points. Also, antler point restrictions (APRs) using eight points as a minimum are designed to protect young bucks with fewer points, but mature bucks with less than eight points are protected as well. My concern is not directed toward herd genetics, rather the loss of opportunity to harvest a mature buck with an impressive six-point rack.

A fine six-point buck was "captured" last fall by a cell phone camera on a private property near Columbia, S.C. The hunter asked if I thought he should have taken this buck. My response was ABSOLUTELY! He is 4½ or 5½ years old and has a beautiful rack — the combination of body, rack and jawbone makes this quite a respectable trophy.

I have had an affinity for mature six-pointers for many years and hold them in high regard. A well-developed, symmetrical six-point rack can be beautiful — even regal. There are several six-point racks in my antler collection, but they were harvested by someone else. And the hunting stories featuring the harvest of mature six-pointers are all those of my hunting companions, not mine. Several years ago I stalked to the edge of an oak flat and encountered a six-point that would have gone on my wall. The crosshairs settled on his massive chest, but I thought about my two Australian friends who would be hunting with me the following week, and the trophy six-pointer walked away unscathed. Neither the Aussie hunters nor anyone else in the neighborhood crossed paths with that buck, that season.

Over time, voluntary participation in QDM usually takes experienced hunters beyond APRs to a suite of management/harvest options. A simple approach allowing the harvest of mature six-pointers, for example, is to ask these questions: If he does not have at least eight points is he 3½ years old or older? If he does not have eight points do his antlers have the mass of a mature buck? If he does not have eight points is the beam length that of a mature buck? I omitted antler spread from this list of questions because I have seen numerous mature bucks with a very narrow rack, less than 15 inches. In fact, I'll describe such a buck later in this story.

Dr. Larry Marchinton with a Texas "Slick Six" that had no brow tines and was 4½ years old.

The six-point vein

The deer woods of my neighborhood have served as a veritable classroom throughout my professional career. It is here that I hunted for the first time before my age was in the double digits, and it is here that as a lifelong student my identity has been molded by the noble whitetail. It has become obvious to me that veins of genetic characteristics or traits exist. In these isolated gene pools mature bucks commonly exhibit abnormal points, forked G-2s, and six-point racks. I chose the term "vein" because these genetic traits tend to occur in a long, linear pattern.

I have been monitoring two six-point veins for over 30 years. One exists along the border between the property that is the birthplace of the QDMA and the neighboring plantation. The featured photo for this story was taken of a buck from this vein. The buck, shot in 2008 by QDMA Charter Life Member Henry Fair, was 5½ years old and his rack scored 123⅛ Boone and Crockett points. Three others in my collection ranged in Boone and Crockett score from 112 to 120 points.

The other six-point vein exists on the northern portion of a large hunting club one county south. In October as I was compiling my notes and photos for this article I received a call from Melvin McQuaig, the club's president and a QDMA Life Member.

"Joe, the six-point gene pool is still alive and well on Log Haul. Nancy Jo Southwell shot a six-point late this afternoon that weighed 176 pounds, had an 18-inch outside spread, and was 4½ years old."

This portion of the property has produced several mature six-pointers each year for the last 30 years.

Here's a question for wildlife researchers to wrap their heads around: How do these unique antler traits continue to appear over time in localized areas? Is there a chance that females have more influence on antler characteristics, or at least certain antler traits, than we have recognized? It appears as simple as comparing the home ranges of females and males, with the smaller ranges and minimal dispersal of females limiting the expansion of these unique traits. Speculation breeds the need for further research.

Six-Pointers in Texas

Texas has been a home-away-from-home for me since my first visit there in 1981. What's the attraction for nearly 50 return trips? Well, it's a long list starting with Al Brothers and his family, the King Ranch, the Golden Triangle (a Mecca for mature whitetail bucks), Rio Grande turkeys and spring flowers, and many close friends, too numerous to mention here. When my wife Donna and I were married 20 years ago we headed to Texas to spend time with Al and Claudia Brothers on our "hunting moon" — it was turkey season and the countryside was awash with blooming bluebonnets.

The author photographed this mature Texas six-pointer moments before Jason Hart killed it with his bow.

Of all the Lone Star State visits, those involving encounters with six-point bucks remain high among my favorite hunting memories. Dr. Larry Marchinton and I visited our fellow QDMA Charter Life Member Al Brothers in the mid-1980s to get a first-hand account of just how QDM worked. We were on the very south Texas ranch where Al put these new principles to task. Al positioned me in a ground blind where a post-prime buck with a 5x3 point rack had been seen. Dr. Marchinton was directed to an oat patch frequented by a mature "Slick-Six" — an adult six-point buck without brow points. The scouting paid off. My buck had a 14-inch rack and was 8½ years old. Dr. Marchinton's Slick-Six was 4½ years old.

In 2002, I was with Jason Hart, who at the time was QDMA's director of branch development and now works for Mossy Oak, when he shot a mature six-pointer with his bow on the King Ranch. I shot first with my camera and "captured" Jason's buck both broadside and facing us.

During that visit I spent an exciting day with the late James Guthrie, editor of *Quality Whitetails,* as we pursued a fine six-pointer. According to our guide, Oscar Cortez, "You'll know it when you see him. His rack is narrow, very tall, and massive!"

The author and former *Quality Whitetails* editor James Guthrie stalked and shot this mature, high-racked Texas six-pointer in 2002. I was watching through binoculars when Guthrie shot.

Oscar was right. When we first laid eyes on him there was no doubt he was the one. Hours of playing cat-n-mouse with this elusive buck produced several slim chances to take him, but James commented to me that he had never missed a deer and he intended on keeping his record. As if following a script that we had written, the buck walked into a clearing 100 yards away with only 15 minutes of hunting time left. We stood there shoulder to shoulder, me with binoculars and James with his favorite rifle, for what seemed to me an eternity. The rifle reared and James's record remained untarnished. That narrow-antlered six-point rack had found a home in Georgia.

Several years ago I had the pleasure of hunting with fellow Charter Life Member Betty Marchinton on the King Ranch. Dr. Mick Hellickson, a QDMA Life Member, was our guide for the morning. He took us to an area where he had seen a sway-backed six-pointer, an old-timer. Within minutes Mickey uttered the words that sent a chill down my spine: "That's him!"

Betty was on point and on target. That buck's bleached skull and the trophy jaw-bone of 10½-plus years are displayed with pride among other hunting memorabilia in the Marchinton home.

This Texas six-pointer was estimated to be an amazing 10-plus years old. Betty Marchinton killed it on the King Ranch while guided by Dr. Mickey Hellickson.

The Big Six of Sugar Loaf

He walked in front of two brothers sitting together in a box blind, and the decision was reached to let him walk. Judged by body characteristics to be 3½ years old and carrying a tall, massive rack with only G-1s and G-2s, he was given a name — a title — The Big Six of Sugar Loaf. Throughout that fall and for the following two deer seasons, he traveled the haunts of my boyhood hunting days along the Cape Fear River in southeastern North Carolina, revealing himself often to the full-time scout, a trail camera, and only once more to a hunter who passed him up in hopes one of the kids would have a chance at him. The deer produced a larger six-point rack each year, and the timing of his movements could have given him a nickname — the Night Owl — because of his propensity for nocturnal activity. By the time he reached the age of 6½, there were two obvious changes. His rack sported an extra point — a short G-3 appeared on his left beam. Most important, he was showing up from time to time after sunrise, so he was huntable!

I was sitting in an elevated stand on a powerline right-of-way late one October afternoon in South Carolina. An hour into the hunt and my neck was beginning to pay the price of repeatedly turning left then right. It was like watching a windshield wiper. A vibrating cell phone in my pocket provided a respite from my vigil. Steve Guyton was on the other end, so I answered in anticipation of pending news about the Big Six of Sugar Loaf. An out-of-breath caller responded, "I got him! I got him!"

In the final, unwritten chapter of this legend, the hunter expressed a degree of sadness as he glanced in the rear view mirror at his quest with the Sugar Loaf tract in the background.

QDMA member Steve Guyton of North Carolina with the Big Six of Sugar Loaf.

This mature six-point buck was "captured" by a cell phone camera in South Carolina near Columbia. Within seconds, the hunter lamented that such a trophy passed by, unscathed.

"I felt as though I had robbed the property and my fellow hunters of something special, and suddenly realized that it was as it should be," Steve said. "The Big Six of Sugar Loaf had run his course and already there were other special bucks that had been named."

He has been granted a prominent position on the wall of the Chapter One cabin at Sugar Loaf.

My hunting future pales in comparison to the days I've hunted, but the quality experiences increase exponentially each year. If this trend continues, perhaps a mature six-pointer will come my way before the last sunset.

Note: *This article appeared in Quality Whitetails (V 21, I 1 - 2014).*

Anything But Typical

David Henderson has been a friend since he was in graduate school at The University of Georgia in the early-1990s. His master's research project was conducted on Hilton Head Island in South Carolina and I was fortunate to assist with his deer project when I served as a regional wildlife biologist for the S.C. Department of Natural Resources. David was hired as a wildlife biologist for Sea Pines Plantation on Hilton Head Island when he completed his degree. One of his primary duties involved sharp-shooting deer in areas where conventional hunting was not safe or practical. He has become quite proficient at harvesting deer — suffice it to say that his annual removal rates have been in the category of hundreds per year. He is a regular Cool Hand Luke when performing his job, but when it comes to hunting he has another side.

He called one day in 1995 as he was traveling to a tract on the mainland that he had gotten permission to hunt. The area was lightly hunted and had the reputation of harboring some adult bucks. I was on my way to a property that I had been involved with for 10 years. In the beginning, the deer herd there was overpopulated and the yearling bucks averaged less than 70 pounds live weight. A decade of QDM had brought about significant changes in the deer herd and the habitat. I was on a mission to assist with the doe harvest.

When leaving the property that night following my hunt, I called the manager to report that I had seen three bucks — a six-point, a young eight-point, and an absolute bruiser of a mature eight-point, probably a 4½-year-old, with a massive rack. I was still shaking from my encounter with the big buck, yet filled with pride to have had something to do with his presence. It was a great hunt! Within minutes of speaking with the property manager, my cell phone rang. An out-of-breath caller was on the other end.

"Joseph, its Davo (a nickname I had given David Henderson) and I have just had the hunt of my life!" Well, did you get a nice buck? "Almost — he walked within feet of the tree I was in, but I just couldn't get turned around for a shot. My heart was racing such that I'm not sure if I could have shot anyway." That was Davo's other side.

Fast forward to a phone call late in the hunting season of 2012. "Joseph, this is Davo and I have trail camera photos of a very unusual buck — one with an abnormally massive rack and he's still in velvet!" I could tell by the tone of his voice that he was on to something. This buck had remained a ghost to those who hunted the 100-acre, two-year-old clearcut tract in South Carolina's lowcountry. Other cameras were positioned

Cactus bucks are rare freaks of the whitetail world, and they may even be more challenging to kill than normal bucks because they don't take part in the rut.

throughout the property, but only one was successful in revealing this particular buck. Could it be that this buck was just passing through on a jaunt from his home range elsewhere? Or was that buck a homebody with a very small home range? Patience and vigilance would answer this question later.

I told Davo that it must be a "cactus" buck like one I shot in Texas back in the 1980s. My 5½ -year-old buck was in velvet in December and he had been seen in a relatively small area for at least three years — always in velvet. Examination of his south end revealed a tiny scrotum, so we cut into it and found the testicles to be about the size of kidney beans. Apparently, bucks with this condition don't have the testosterone levels necessary to control a normal cycle of velvet shedding, antler hardening, antler casting, and subsequent regrowth (more on this later). The antlers just continue to grow, and

David Henderson's young son and daughter named this buck "Prickles" after hearing that such deer are often called "cactus bucks." David caught Prickles in this trail camera photo on August 1. Two weeks later on August 15 — opening day of deer season in the South Carolina lowcountry — the author got a text from David exclaiming, "I got him!"

if the buck lives long enough his antlers will sprout points in all directions, thus the name "cactus" buck. Another interesting observation is that my buck had the slim neck of a doe and his tarsal glands were fluffy and nearly white. Reproductively speaking, he was in neutral. His only activities involved eating and sleeping. And, since he was never in the breeding mode, his home range was comparatively small but provided the necessary food and cover.

There was a message on my cell phone the following July. "Joseph, this is Davo with a report on that special buck. He's still here and his antlers are larger! My young son and daughter saw the photos and had heard it called a cactus buck, so they named the deer Prickles."

Davo's tone of voice was steeped in the same enthusiasm from the 1995 telephone message. His excitement and anticipation were obvious. "Our hunting season opens in just a few weeks on August 15, so how should I hunt him?" David asked. "Well, you've been putting corn in front of your trail camera and I would expect that your neighbors are beginning to establish their baiting sites with corn as well (Feeding and hunting deer over bait are legal in this area of South Carolina). You'll have to add something

"Prickles" on the afternoon he was harvested.

enticing — something different than your neighbors are providing. Perhaps you should add sweet potatoes and pears to your corn. That may encourage him to stay close by."

I was in east Tennessee for a QDMA Deer Steward I course on August 15 — a bittersweet assignment not because it was the opening day of deer season at home in South Carolina, but because it was my grandson's second birthday and I couldn't be there to help him celebrate. As we were sitting down for dinner my cell phone rang. "I got him, I got him!" My friend Davo and the cactus buck had crossed paths. A text message soon followed with a photo of this magnificent buck. I congratulated Davo on his patience and vigilance, and of course for harvesting the buck of a lifetime.

As sundown was signaling the end of a very special day, David Henderson reflected on this entire experience. "The anticipation I felt when checking the trail camera for the first time in July 2013 was unbearable," he said. "Prickles was the first deer captured by the camera, I couldn't believe it!" He viewed his experience as one that was against all odds.

The buck weighed 195 pounds and his rack was 22 inches wide. Davo stopped by on his way to the taxidermist for me to see his buck in person. He also brought the scrotum as I had requested. I measured the base of each antler and they were 11¼ inches and 10½ inches in circumference. The scrotum was filled with fat, something I had never witnessed before, and the testicles were about the size of black olives, which is to say abnormally small. Once the head was caped out by the taxidermist, the jawbones were removed and photographed. After a quick glance of the extreme wear on the teeth, I told Davo that this buck could be 10 years old. An incisor was removed and sent to Matson's Lab in Montana for aging. The report arrived several months later: 10 years

A rear view of "Prickles" with antlers in velvet, as they always had been.

old, with a high degree of confidence. Boy, it's nice when a guess — and that's all it can be on a deer that old — comes true.

Now, for the scientific discussion on cactus bucks.

Hypogonadism

Cactus bucks suffer from a condition called hypogonadism. A study conducted in Texas in 1964 reported that hypogonadal bucks exhibited the following characteristics:

- Affected testes are approximately one-third to one-sixth the size of normal male testes during the breeding season.
- Feminine facial and body conformation, especially the neck.
- Antlers, often with abnormal formation in older bucks, which retained the velvet to some extent throughout the life of the deer.

Mature hypogonadal bucks do not shed their antlers, which continue to grow from year to year. However, a study of young, ear-tagged, free-ranging hypogonadal bucks in Llano County, Texas, during the 1960s revealed a high degree of velvet antler breakage. Main beams were broken leaving a two- to three-inch cone from which antlers continued growth. As stated earlier, older bucks often adorn antlers with multiple abnormal points — resembling the growth of a cactus.

Hypogonadism has been prevalent in the Central Mineral Region in Texas. The earliest report occurred in 1916, but at least six scientific reports were recorded in the 1950s. From 1959-'65 the percent of hypogonadal bucks killed in Llano County ranged from 0.2 to 9.4 percent. Beyond this region the occurrence of hypogonadism in white-tailed deer is sporadic and rare.

The soils in the Central Mineral Region are granite based compared with the limestone soils of the nearby Edwards Plateau. In fact, a majority of hypogonadal bucks were killed on a particular soil type categorized as gravelly sandy loam and known locally as granite gravel. This soil type comprised 30 to 40 percent of the land in Llano County. The association of hypogonadism with a specific soil type and its cyclic behavior lend credence to the theory that the condition is caused by a gonadotoxic plant, yet to be identified. Furthermore, an increased occurrence of hypogonadal bucks appeared following a period of drought.

Cryptorchidism

Another condition in whitetail bucks that can affect antler development is cryptorchidism. This occurs when one or both testes remain in a buck's abdominal cavity. If only one testicle descends into the scrotum (unilateral cryptorchidism) the buck will produce enough testosterone to maintain a normal antler cycle. But when both testes remain in the body cavity (bilateral cryptorchidism), the testosterone production is minimal and the antlers usually remain in velvet and are not thought to be cast as normal. However, the results from a study of Sitka black-tailed deer on Kodiak Island in Alaska stated that bilateral and unilateral cryptorchids do shed their antlers. Surprisingly, in a particular region of Kodiak Island, the incidence of cryptorchid bucks approached 70 percent. This extreme occurrence has not been reported in whitetail populations and has not been explained in Kodiak's blacktails. With regard to Kodiak's situation, there may be a "culprit" plant involved as with hypogonadism in Llano County, Texas. Like hypogonadism, cryptorchidism in whitetails is sporadic and rare.

Bucks with bilateral cryptorchidism do share many of the same body conformations of those with hypogonadism. Both have feminine characteristics, especially thin necks, and the tarsal glands are not stained. The question of bilateral cryptorchids retaining their antlers through life is yet to be answered. Perhaps there are those that do not.

I concur with the statements that both conditions — hypogonadism and cryptorchidism — are extremely uncommon. Throughout my career as a wildlife biologist I have encountered thousands of deer and have only observed three hypogonadal bucks and one cryptorchid.

Regardless of the cause, mature bucks that retain their velvet well into deer season are capable of producing a quality hunting experience, and if harvested will deserve a prominent space in the memory of a successful hunter.

Note: *This article appeared in Quality Whitetails (V 21, I 4 - 2014).*

Heart Bones?!

Way back in the 1980s I read an article espousing the resiliency of the white-tailed deer. No doubt, whitetails possess an uncanny ability to ward off, or at least endure, many diseases and parasites. They also have a well-deserved reputation for rebounding from seemingly life-threatening injuries incurred during the hunting season or on our nation's highways.

The author of that article fancied himself somewhat of an expert on this popular big-game animal. I was soaking in the new information on my favorite quarry until the author cited an incident that had occurred on a hunting property in his neighborhood. Supposedly, a local hunter shot a deer that had overcome a traumatic injury in which a sliver of bone had become imbedded in the heart. Since the bone was surrounded by cartilage or "gristle," the author thought it was the deer's chronic or long-term response to an out-of-place bone fragment.

He was right about one thing — that bone had been there for quite a while. Would you believe for the life of the deer?

I was naive in those days. I thought that once something reached the stage of being printed it was the gospel. The article harkened me back to graduate school at The University of Georgia. One of my wildlife professors had a 3x5 notecard on his bulletin board that read: It's better to know nothing than to know what ain't so. The message on that notecard was beginning to ring true. I also remembered having to learn more

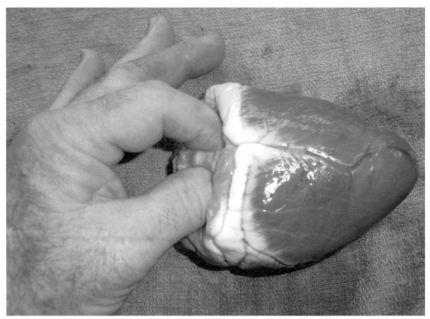

To locate the *os cordis* bone in a deer's heart, insert your forefinger and thumb into the two largest openings in the heart and pinch the divider. You'll feel a rigid, enlarged section in the divider and that's where the heart bone is located.

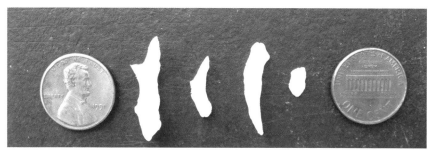

In preparation for this article I collected heart bones from four deer (left to right: 3½-year-old doe, 3½-year-old doe, 3½-year-old buck, and a 5½-year-old doe). I used the coins as a size reference and to make the point: You can't tell heads or tails about heart bones from deer. Like snowflakes — they're all different.

than I thought was necessary about the mammalian skeleton in a mammalogy course. I was already familiar with many of the bones, but it was the heterotopic bones, those in unusual places, that intrigued me. One, the rostral bone, occurs in the upper rim of a pig's snout. Another, also thought to provide strength or rigidity without connecting to another bone, is called the *os cordis*. It is found in the heart of ruminants including goats, sheep, cattle, and all species of the deer family. There are other heterotopic bones but I will not mention them now to avoid stealing thunder from the fact that white-tailed deer have a bone in their hearts.

As a young field biologist I encountered hundreds of hunter-harvested deer each year and also performed necropsies on scores of deer to determine the cause of death. With such a large sample size, I decided to conduct a study of *os cordis* bones in whitetails. My hypothesis (guess) was that these bones would increase in size as an animal grew older. I also thought, or at least hoped, there would be a difference in the size and/or shape of these bones in males and females. Throughout one deer season I collected the heart bones from both sexes of deer aged six months, 1½, 2½, and 3½-plus. A section of the heart called the aortic ring (see photo of location) was removed and boiled until the bone was free of meat and cartilage. The bone sample was placed in a small, plastic cup and labeled by sex and age.

Before I got too deeply involved in this project I could already see tremendous overlap in the size of the *os cordis* bones from fawns and mature deer. In fact, some bones from fawns were larger than those collected from adult animals three or four years older. Also, there was absolutely no correlation in bone size and or shape with the sex of the animal. Oh well, it was an honest attempt to learn more about the noble whitetail. We did learn something after all, even though it wasn't what was hypothesized. Such are the whims of scientific research. What we do know now is that a bone actually exists in a deer's heart! And we also know what ain't so.

Note: *This article appeared in Quality Whitetails (V 23, I 1 – 2016).*

CHAPTER 8

JONATHAN JENKINS — A TRILOGY

Jimmy Clark

Jonathan Jenkins accompanied our hunting group on my first successful deer hunt in 1961. My respect for this unique individual drove me to pay tribute by sharing three of my favorite stories about him.

Jonathan Jenkins was a real mountain man. Born just after the turn of the 20th century in North Carolina's rugged Appalachians, he spent his early years learning the ways of hunting from his elders. He later moved to eastern North Carolina and brought with him a unique ability to spin a yarn. His enthusiasm for hunting was infectious for young nimrods like me. I got my first deer, a spike, with Jonathan's hunting crowd in 1961. My love for deer hunting and, most importantly, for deer tales can be traced directly to Jonathan Jenkins, a man with a twinkle in his eyes and a splash of Cherokee blood in his veins. He "went on" to the happy hunting grounds in 1988 at the ripe old age of 83. A man of Jonathan's caliber should have lived to be a hundred 'cause he was a storehouse of untold tales. As a tribute to my mentor, I will share some of his favorite tales as accurately as I heard them. That was easy since I have those stories on tape. Well, it wasn't so easy after all — transcribing the tapes was a real chore. I did exercise my editorial privilege of "softening" the use of expletives.

His personal account of the "pert near albiner" buck is steeped with flavor — all of his stories were for that matter. Anyone who hunted with Jonathan will remember him best for his tale of the ghost deer. Jonathan was too young to have been a part of that story, but he told it like he heard it, as though he had witnessed it first hand.

Each of these "pieces" was printed in the Firepot Stories section of the *Quality Whitetails* magazine several years ago and they are presented here in their original form. There may be a bit of redundancy in the introductions, but each is meant to be read as a stand-alone story.

"Albiners" and Ghost Deer

"It weren't no true albiner, in other words, it 'uz spotted an' the white patches was big as both yer hands put together an' they 'uz all over the deer's body (It was a piebald deer). He lived on that property we hunted jest 'cross South River over in Sampson County (N.C.), an' you know well where that's at. We'd seen him fer two years, but nobody couldn't get a shot at him, least they couldn't hit him, 'cause several tried. One cold, windy morning in December 'tween Christmas an' New Year's I heared the dogs jump an' they 'uz circling the edge of the river swamp towards me. Three shots rang out, but the dogs never hushed. The next stander shot clean — five shots an' five misses. I knowed it 'uz a buck 'cause we didn't shoot does and I knowed exactly which buck it 'uz — the big spotted 'un. It didn't make no never mind how much the wind 'uz a'howlin', them dogs 'uz forever more puttin' it on that ol' buck. They 'uz cuttin' a beeline straight towards where I 'uz standin'. 'Bout that time he splashed through a shaller slough not more than 50 paces away. I couldn't believe my eyes! He looked all the world like a darned goat. Then I knowed exactly why everbody had been a missin' that spotted devil fer the last two years. They 'uz spending too much time a figurin' what it was and then shootin' too late. Hit never fooled me none from the second I first glimpsed him. When he jumped 'cross an old loggin' road I let a load of number one buckshot fly, an' he went on.

"Several minutes later the pickups started pullin' up to where I 'uz standin'." "Where's he at? Did you get him?" "I said, I shot didn't I? Anyway, the dogs had done hushed an'

272

The author with Jonathan Jenkins displaying his mounted "partial albiner" buck.

Walter McDuffie

'uz a millin' 'round like nothin' had happened. Anybody in his right mind that knows deer dogs should of knowed that I hadn't missed. I pointed the direction the buck left an' said, he'll be piled up less than 100 yards from here. Shore 'nuff we walked a short ways an' seen him stretched out on his left hand side, dead as a wedge. I rolled him over an' jest as I 'spected, they 'uz three buckshot holes you coulda covered with a biscuit right behind his front shoulder. That ole "Ethkins" (Ithaca) 12 gauge pump will throw three buckshot one time and two the next, then three an' then two again in a place that size all day long. I can't 'splain it. That's jest the way that gun throws buckshot.

"I had that buck's head stuffed 'cause he reminded me of one my daddy's huntin' crowd run into years ago up near the homeplace in the mountains.

"They went up to the head of Hazel Creek near Clingman's Dome fer a week's hunt. It 'uz my daddy, a couple of uncles an' my older brother that 'uz a huntin' deer. The first day they killed 60, an' they 'uz jest cuttin' the hams out. That evening, 'bout the edge of dark, they 'uz sittin' 'round the campfire eatin' venison an' havin' a good time when a big spotted 'un walked out. My daddy said he had the awfulest rack you ever wanted to see, an' he 'uz covered with white patches where the hair 'uz sposed to be brown. Anyway, he come into a clearing only 30 steps away and commenced walkin' backards an' firewards. My daddy an' uncles an' brother was all rifle experts. They could shoot a man's shirt buttons off at 50 paces. Well, they grabbed their rifles an' shot 'til they couldn't. Meanwhile, that spotted deer 'uz still out there walkin' this way an' that way only 30 steps from them rifle experts. He 'uz a deer all right, but he weren't makin' no sign — no tracks, in other words. My daddy said hit looked all the world like a deer, but hit 'uz only a image of one. Ye see, he weren't makin' no tracks. In…in other words, he 'uz a ghost deer!

"My daddy said the good Lord sent that deer down there to remind them that they 'uz doing wrong, jest cuttin' the hams out and leavin' the rest lay. They all realized what 'uz going on with that ghost deer they couldn't hit an' they left for home. I MEAN THEY DIDN'T WAIT FOR DAYLIGHT — THEY LEFT THEN!!!"

Jonathan's Bees

Jonathan Jenkins was a long-time friend and hunting companion. He will be remembered as the consummate storyteller by all of us who were fortunate to have spent time with him. As Jonathan would have put it, "We aint gotta be headin' fer a hunt or returnin' from one to be able to visit. We can do that year 'round." That's just what I did every time the opportunity arose.

Despite the difference in ages, everyone called him Jonathan…not Mr. Jenkins or "Old Man" Jenkins. The name Jonathan was always spoken with the respect due an elder. He was a mountain man — part Cherokee, and he was special.

I can't count the times his honey bees stung me while we sat in the shade of an oak during a hot summer day and talked about deer hunting. On one of those occasions I was rubbing a pinch of moist chewing tobacco on a fresh sting to kill the pain and keep it from swelling. At least that's what Jonathan said it would do. Well, I didn't admit to the lingering pain or draw attention to the fact that my left arm was getting noticeably larger by the minute. Fearful of a second "hit" from another of the honey makers and finding it difficult to concentrate on hunting tales, I glanced around at the hives scattered throughout the pine thicket in Jonathan's side yard. How many hives do you have? Boy, did that trip a switch! Jonathan's bees took second place only to deer hunting, and, of course, talking about it.

The following accounts about bees, the attributes of honey, and typhoid fever were transcribed verbatim from a taped conversation with Jonathan Jenkins in 1973. It may

Jonathan and one of his many beehives.

be of interest that this story was spoken with a strong Appalachian Mountain dialect, but I doubt the reading will be easy without a little practice. This is the kind of entertainment that kept our hunting group occupied before and after hunts. Without Jonathan's constant flow of stories, deer hunting in the distant past would have been a bit drab because there weren't many deer in those days.

"I had 120 some hives and I lost around 40 hives last summer. Ye see, I never took a drop of honey last year. They starved out! They wasn't no honey last year. Right durin' all the honey flow (pollen production) that's in this part of the country hit (it) rained ever day durin' that honey flow. Jest as shore as the days would come, hit poured ever day. An' I mean they starved out 'fore fall of the year.

"I don't feed bees, I aint never fed none, an' what honey I got is completely outa the darned woods. Aint no question about it. I did — I did — I got it this time. I got so darned sick and tired of workin' in honey — I got 'bout 20 cases I ain't even took off the bees yet.

"Down at my son-in-law's mother's and daddy's place they said a woman an' a man come in there an' said they had heared that someone had tested honey in a lavatory in Wilmington and said they 'us one germ that hit didn't kill on contact — ever other germ exceptin the one hit killed 'em absolutely on contact and said hit lived 15 seconds — the one did. They said hit 'uz the only thang that ever had proved out to prolong a person's life — 'uz honey. They said that if ye eat honey regular that there wouldn't be a germ left in you — of no description. Now, how true it is, I don't know. I didn't — I didn't hear 'em say that myself. I do know one thang, I've eat honey all my life, since I wasn't big enough to hardly go. My daddy and my granddaddy had bees, an' I've had bees 60 years myself. An' I've had one spell of sickness in my life — had typhoid fever in 1928.

"I 'uz workin' log jams in the river back when they 'uz a floatin' 'em down to the mill. I'd get there on them logs an' cut one or two of 'em loose an' hit would throw me tail-over-tin-cups into that darned river. They wasn't never a day that I wasn't jest as wet as water would make me for winter and summer, an' I took typhoid. I got real sick. I jest felt lifeless. I told my brother, I said, uh, I've got to go home. I told him, I said I can't walk. You'll have to go out there to my uncle's place about a mile or a mile an' a half an' get his mule for me to ride. An' I couldn't even sit on the darned mule when he got it there. He had to get the second mule to walk alongside the other jest to keep me on. An' when I got home, I — I remember when I went in momma said to me, 'What's the matter?' I said I believe I've got the fever. She said, 'I hope not!'

"I dragged in an' laid right down 'cross my daddy an' momma's bed, jest crossways

275

in the bed. I remember hittin' the bed. THREE WEEKS LATER the house 'uz full of people an' two doctors 'sittin' there when they broke the fever on me.

"It's the only sickness I've ever had. I 'uz poor as a whip-poor-will, an' couldn't even pick my hands up. I said, 'How long have I been asleep?' Momma said, 'You aint been asleep.' I said the devil I ain't. I said I see that I ain't where I laid down at. 'Well,' she said, 'you've been unconscience fer THREE WEEKS!' I ain't had a spell of sickness since, but that 'un danged near took me out.

"…in other words, I've owned bees 'bout 60 years, an' I can learn 'bout 'em today or, in other words, any summer. I can learn a heck of a lot ever day I mess with 'em. I've experimented with 'em ever way in the world that a man could experiment. Of course, I learnt to save bees by experimentin' with 'em, an' I lost a lot of 'em by experimentin' with 'em, too. A lot of people don't know a queen from a drone or a drone from a work bee or nothin' else.

"I'm — I'm gonna tell you somethin' or other that happened one time when I 'uz livin' in Calabass (Calabash, N.C.). I had some bees down there an' I 'uz down there at Ivey High's store in Calabass one day when a drummer (traveling salesman) come in. Ivey asked me, he said jest right outa the blue, he — he knew I had bees an' he knew hit 'uz time fer me to rob some — he said, 'Yer bees doin' any good this time?' I said, Yeah, they're doin' all right. They furnish me plenty of honey.

"That drummer set in to tell about one time him an' another feller was a passin' by a hive of a bunch of bees that 'uz near the side of the road. He said they come out an' come right 'cross the road, an' he said they stopped, an' as soon as they come out of that hive they were 'comin' out of, they got over there and pitched on the other side of the road on a leeumb (limb). He said him an' that feller went in there, and said, 'I've never saw so much honey in my life that 'uz in that hive they come out of.' He said them bees filled that hive plum full, then come out and went over there and pitched. I said, Wasn't there no bees left in that hive? He said, 'NAW, they all come out!' He said he got the awfulest mess of honey outa there that you've ever saw.

"I said, you're the gall darnedest biggest lying so-en-so I ever seen in my life. He looked at me right funny fer a minute. An' hit tickled Ivey High to death, 'cause he knowed darned well I knowed bees. That drummer said, 'What do you mean?' I said, yer the biggest liar I ever heared talk in my life. I asked him if they 'uz any bees in that hive when they went into it, an' he said, 'No, heck no, they wasn't no bees in it, they all come out an' went over there and pitched on that leeumb!' I said, Now yer — yer talkin' to somebody that knows somethin' 'bout bees an' that's the reason I told you that you were a gall darned lying so-en-so. I know — I know darned well that they 'uz more bees left in that hive than they 'uz over there on that leeumb that you 'uz talkin' 'bout. I said, What — WHAT GOOD does it do you to tell that darned lie? He said, 'I told the darned lie from the start.' He said, 'I heared that — I heared another feller tell that.' I said, Well, that's a heck of a note.

"Ivey High said to that drummer, he said, 'When yer a talkin' to a bee man, you better not put up them big tales, 'cause he knows what bees is — he's known 'em all his life.' That drummer said, 'Well, I 'uz only tellin' what I'd heared.' Well, I said, for gosh sakes don't tell a gall-darned lie like that no never no darned more! He said, 'I WON'T!'"

Memories

"Them bugs tells me a lot," were the words from an old sage I had the distinct privilege of hunting with and visiting frequently as a young man. Jonathan Jenkins and I sat quietly in the shade of a sprawling catalpa tree on a sultry August afternoon way back in the early-1970s. When I drove into his yard that day he motioned with a forefinger over his lips for me to approach with stealth. This had the makings of another memorable visit with a man that was full of outdoor lore. I approached as directed and noticed several dead "rain crows" (yellow-billed cuckoos) on the ground beneath the tree. "Them dang thangs is eatin' my pertawkah (catalpa) worms. In — in other words, if I don't keep 'em outa my worm supply, they're gonna ruin my bream fishing. You know quite well they ain't no better bream bait than a pertawkah worm turned inside out on a hook. Them big ol' copper-headed bream like 'em so good, you 'most have to hide behind a tree to put a worm on your hook. An' them thangs is tough, too. If yer careful you can catch five or six bream on one worm 'fore you have to fetch a fresh one."

Within a matter of a few minutes I had gotten a lesson in ornithology and fishing, but there was more, as usual. Silence lingered as we sat awaiting the arrival of another worm stealer. Out of the blue, Jonathan exclaimed, "We're gonna have a record snow this winter." What a statement when it's 100 degrees in the shade! Somewhat taken back by such a forecast, I quickly responded. How do you know? He hunkered over in his ladder-back chair, looked around as if to make sure no one else was listening, leaned toward me and said, "Them bugs tells me a lot." What bugs? He sat straight up in his chair and nearly shouted "CRICKETS," like I should have known. I didn't. "In other words, a cricket makes a chirping sound by rubbing his hind legs together. If ye count the number of chirps a cricket makes in a certain amount of time, ye can tell what the weather is gonna do."

As a humble visitor, I accepted Jonathan's prognostication as the gospel. He seemed confident, so why should I have any doubt? By the way, that very next winter southeastern North Carolina was blanketed with 14 inches of snow — a record since the 1940s.

When a cricket chirps I find myself counting, but I never bothered to find out what the "certain amount of time" was, and I have to be content with the abilities of our local weatherperson on TV. However accurate he or she is, something is missing in the message.

You can imagine that Jonathan's stories of his favorite subject, deer hunting, were steeped in the same enthusiasm and mystique as his "bug" story. Many a dog drive got off to a late start because Jonathan held us captive, or captivated, with a deer yarn. Deer were not abundant in those days and most hunts were unproductive. Nevertheless, Jonathan always emerged from the woods with an incredible story. Knowing that Jonathan would leave you with something to ponder for the rest of the week, filled the gap between our Saturday hunts.

We hunted nearly a dozen properties back then because deer populations were scattered and the competition for hunting lands was nothing like today.

Naturally, we hunted some properties only once or twice a season. An exception was a tract of land known as the Kemp Woods. Only a mile out of town, this was a favorite location for a quick hunt. It was relatively small, about 500 acres, but convenient. We

Jonathan Jenkins, my friend, hunting companion, and mentor was heading toward the sunset of life. His spirit will accompany me on excursions through the deer woods, henceforth.

always felt that we could "sew it up" with standers, but that was often not the case. On one such occasion we had positioned the standers in all likely escape routes and the dogs performed admirably, running in several wide circles before departing down through the river lowlands and out of hearing. When we gathered after the hunt everyone was asking what the dogs were running. Apparently, none of the standers had seen anything. Jonathan came ambling along. He made it a habit of being the last hunter to emerge from the woods. All eyes and ears were focused on the mountain man. One of the anxious hunters asked, "What was it?" Jonathan never hunted without seeing SOMETHING. "It 'uz a 10-snag and he came by me hardly 20 steps away literally flying, you might say, with Zorro, Yeller, Badeye, and Tuesday right on his heels." "If you saw all that why didn't you shoot?" "In — in other words, I didn't actually see the buck — only the dogs." "Then how did you know it had 10 points (or "snags" as Jonathan called them)?" "Well, the way them horns was a breakin' leeumbs and such I figured that ol' buck had at least 10 snags!" How could you question someone who predicted a record snow storm? We loaded up and headed for home with memories of a hunt that otherwise would have been forgotten if our mentor hadn't been along.

I visited Jonathan in July 1988. He had moved in with one of his daughters and her husband. New trousers, red plaid shirt and black hat couldn't hide the frail body. Eighty-three years of hard living had taken their toll, but that unforgettable twinkle was still in his eyes. Without uttering a word, Jonathan gestured simply by nodding. He wanted me to tag along to show me how near deer sign was to his new home, to share with me something we both realized. Times had changed. Respectfully, I followed as I had for a quarter of a century. His stride was altered by age, although his intention remained steadfast — to explore the mystery of deer. Our paths had crossed for the last time.

Note: *These three stories, the trilogy, appeared in Quality Whitetails. "Albiners" and Ghost Deer were in V 2, I 3 – Winter 1995, Jonathan's Bees appeared in V 5, I 2 - 1998, Memories appeared in V 3, I 3 - 1996.*

CHAPTER 9

AN'
STUFF

This book would not have been complete without a collection of stories that had nothing to do with hunting, but just had to be recorded. Now that they have been captured in print for the first time, they can be enjoyed by generations of readers.

While this book is laced with deer-related stories, there are other stories that must be told. This chapter is a compilation of accounts from my childhood days to the recent past. In the Southeast, folks often end a statement with "…an' stuff." For example, "We spent the entire weekend hunting, fishing, an' stuff." Or, "I stopped by the grocery store to get steaks, potatoes, an' stuff for dinner." So, I thought it was only appropriate to name this chapter An' Stuff just to capture the variety of stories that don't have anything to do with deer, but are nonetheless worthy of sharing.

Trash Johnson

My high school English teacher, Mrs. Katherine Inscoe, handed out an assignment to our junior class each Monday. We were given 25 vocabulary words to become familiar with during the week. And, on Friday, these new words were to be used in a theme or short story. Sounds easy enough, but the catch was that the title of our 55-minute writing exercise was posted on the blackboard as we entered the classroom. There was no way to prepare for the assignment except to know the definitions of all 25 new words.

As an introduction to the following story, I have selected 25 words that will somehow find their way into the piece. Looking over this list of words or phrases will have you guessing as to where the story will lead you. Perhaps in a twisted way this is a primer toward the art of storytelling. Here's my list of 25: ambidextrous, Alfredo Mendoza, jonboat, brambles, bobcats, Cypress Gardens, Heddon's Lucky 13 Red Head, Dick Pope Jr., thumb up, thumb down, beached, rat shootin', dump truck, outboard, inboard, mentor, rose-colored glasses, slalom, Johnson, shine yeah, red leather ball cap, cumbersome, Daisy Red Ryder BB gun, madness, and naw.

Trash Johnson was a real person, and he wore his name as a badge of honor of sorts. You see, he was the driver of the dump truck that was used to collect garbage or "trash" from households within the city limits of my hometown. Obviously, it was a small town, but Trash and his team of two helpers were as regular as clockwork twice a week. Trash was a seasonal friend. Since he made his rounds on weekdays I only saw him during the summer months when school was out. We became acquainted in the 1950s when my main mode of travel was a bicycle. Wherever I was in the neighborhood, when 9 a.m. rolled around on Mondays and Fridays, I tried to be home for Trash's arrival. Our house was at the end of a L-shaped, dead-end street and Trash had to maneuver the cumbersome dump truck up and back several times before turning around. I was impressed with his ability as a driver.

He was always the same. Regardless of the weather, hot or cold, he wore a red leather ball cap. His glasses had a reddish tint and I think of Trash every time I hear the phrase: Looking through rose-colored glasses. He drove one-handed, too. He had one of those knobs on the steering wheel that allowed control with his right hand. That impressed me as well. He must have held the steering wheel with his right knee while shifting gears because his left arm seemed to be a permanent fixture on the window ledge. While turning around in our driveway he cocked his head to the left and displayed a smirky or

Heddon's Lucky 13 Red Head.

even devious smile. Maybe he did that because he had an audience. I wouldn't know otherwise. Maybe that was his way of showing pride, with a slight degree of arrogance. But he was always the same and he was a friend. Even as a kid I was impressed by his work ethic — punctual, experienced and courteous. Trash was among my earliest mentors. I heard that he never took a vacation for fear that someone may take his job.

One day when he pulled up I was in the yard with my Daisy Red Ryder BB gun. He leaned out of the window and said, "Hey, when you get a little older you ought to come down to the dump and shoot some rats with a .22. They're running everywhere at times." It was probably deep into the 1950s or early '60s when I was introduced to the activity of shootin' rats at the city dump. News was coming from a group of older school boys, known hunters, that the nasty, cold, dreary weather of winter was losing its grip and spring was on the way — signaling the opening of rat season at the city dump. Even at that age I knew that rats didn't fall within the category of game animals, so I wondered why there was a season on them, especially a split season. It turned out that seasons were set by comfort levels of the shooters. The rats were always there, but spring and early fall weather provided the most comfortable shooting conditions — thus, the split season.

My neighbor, Bruce McCulloch, and I took this news to heart and decided the time had come to place our BB guns on the rack and go for bigger game. We would put our .22 rifles in canvas cases, strap them to our bicycles and head through town to the city dump, only two blocks from downtown. In those days Trash Johnson would back his dump truck to the edge of the hill, raise the bed of the truck and send the day's collection of trash careening downward. We learned to avoid huntin' rats on Mondays and Fridays 'cause the rats were more elusive due to the disturbance. We also determined that overcast, windy days were bad for rat activity. Clear days were the best for shooting. Although we didn't realize it at the time, our rat shootin' excursions were setting the stage for even bigger game — genuine game animals. We were honing our shooting skills and learning how to "read" the weather and its influence on animal activity.

There was a 1,000-acre, crystal-clear lake near home that was popular for water skiing. It was so popular that skiing conditions deteriorated as the crowds grew. Also, many folks had inboard boats, which put up a much larger wake than outboards. Several high school classmates wanted to escape the madness and rough water. We decided to put a boat in the Cape Fear River and travel about five miles downriver to a large sandbar known locally as Sugar Loaf. This was to be our staging area for skiing. The conditions were great — it was not crowded, and the water was always calm. There is one inherent difference in skiing on the river versus the lake — turning around due to the narrow water channel. With practice, we soon overcame that obstacle.

While pulled up to Sugar Loaf between skiing trips we were joined by two fishermen in a 12-foot jonboat powered by a three-horse Johnson. The fisherman in the bow was wearing a bathing suit and looked like a Heddon's Lucky 13 Red Head fishing lure. He had a red head and a chalk-white body. His left arm was tanned and the right was white. Although it had been years since we had crossed paths, and he was not wearing that tell-tale red leather ball cap or the rose-colored glasses, I said, Trash, is that you? "Yep, we heard all the commotion and thought we'd come around the bend to check it out." We told him that we had decided to ski in the river rather than in White Lake for a change. He asked, "Would y'all mind giving me a pull on the skis?" I couldn't believe it! I asked if he had ever skied before and he quickly replied, "Shine yeah!" Do you ski on two or can you use a slalom? "Two." We don't have a conventional pair of skis, but you can put on two slaloms. We have an Alfredo Mendoza and a Dick Pope Jr., and there's very little difference between the two. "That'll do." I asked him if he knew the signals for increasing or decreasing the speed with a thumb up or thumb down and he nodded affirmatively. I told Trash that I would hold one hand high and move it in circles to let him know it was time to turn around and head back to Sugar Loaf, and he nodded. There's one thing you have to be prepared for, when I'm turning, and it will be a sharp turn, you will have to cut back to the middle of the boat's wake' cause the river is rather narrow. Otherwise, you'll be overcome by momentum toward the bank. "I can handle that," he exclaimed with confidence.

Trash put on a ski belt and entered the river to put on his two, mis-matched slaloms. The ski rope was tossed to him and I eased off downriver. When the rope was tight I yelled, are you ready? He nodded. The boat lunged as I thrust the throttle forward and Trash emerged from the water in a squatting position, but eventually straightened. With that same smile of slight arrogance and tilted head I had seen many times in my driveway years ago, he dropped one hand from the rope handle and glanced down at the water. Moments later he brought his hand back to the handle and dropped the other, I guess to show us he was an ambidextrous skier, or he had seen the professional skiers doing that at Cypress Gardens, Florida.

Our turning around point had been selected earlier that day. The left bank of the river was clear of trees but covered with brambles, so there were no overhanging limbs to contend with. The moment of truth had arrived and I signaled to Trash that it was time to turn around. He nodded. I swung toward the right bank, turned sharply left, and was completely focused on making the turn without losing speed. At that point I couldn't be concerned about my man in tow. Once the turn was made I looked back only to see the ski rope bouncing in the boat's wake. Trash was nowhere to be seen. As warned, he had been overcome by momentum and catapulted straight to the bank. When we returned to the scene the two slaloms were beached firmly in the muddy shoreline. Trash emerged from the bramble thicket with the ski belt around his knees. He was scratched from head to toe and looked to all the world like he had been sorting bobcats in a barn fire. I politely asked if he wanted to ski back and he said, "Naw, I've had enough!" Edward "Trash" Johnson had two ski trips in one on the Cape Fear River — his first and last.

The Museum Specimen

While attending The University of Georgia and conducting the coursework for my master's degree in wildlife biology, I had a job as museum curator in the Biological Sciences Department. The renowned ecologist, Dr. Eugene P. Odum, was my supervisor. The job paid my school and living expenses, and my association with Dr. Odum was an education in itself — priceless. Due to the job, though, my coursework spanned a two-year period when it usually takes only one year on a full-time basis. With the required courses under my belt, it was time to move to my home county in southeastern North Carolina and begin a lengthy study of black bears.

Throughout my field work I was always on the look-out for museum specimens. The recipient of my searches was Mr. Bill Palmer, curator of the State Museum in Raleigh, N.C. I had met Bill several years earlier on a swamp trip to collect water moccasins and he asked that I be vigilant for anything worthy of being added to his collection in Raleigh. Not long after beginning the bear study I encountered a pigmy rattlesnake and

Copperhead.

it was sent to Bill. This was the first and only live snake of that species that I had seen.

I received a phone call one night from my boyhood neighbor, Jimmy Clark, who worked for a local forester at the time, and he said he had to deliver a check for several loads of pulpwood to a man in Kelly. Well, the 20-mile trip to Kelly was always an adventure, mainly because that small community was absolutely in the middle of nowhere and critters of all sorts could be seen along the remote highway. I jumped at the chance for an adventure through my black bear study area in hopes of seeing a bear that I could set a trap for later.

As we approached the Bladen Lakes State Forest, about 10 miles into the trip, we saw a large snake on the right shoulder of the highway. I shouted, go around him, it's a corn snake. Or, maybe it's a record copperhead! Turn around, that's definitely a potential museum specimen for Bill Palmer. We made the turn and the snake, sure enough a giant copperhead, had nearly crossed the highway. Jimmy stopped the car on the highway because there was no traffic at all. I grabbed a machete from the rear of the station wagon, held it flat, and smacked the snake's head firmly, but was careful not to disfigure it. The limp snake was taken to a headlight for a close-up look. I opened the snake's mouth and used a roadside weed to flip the fangs into full view. There we were, each of us on one knee, completely engrossed in examination mode with only the drone of the car engine as background noise. CHAOOOUSH!!! (How else can you describe the sudden sound of a passing automobile?) We didn't have a clue that a car was approaching from behind. It was just THERE! We screamed in unison and I nearly hooked my hand with the snake's fangs. That would have been a good story in itself, but this one isn't over yet.

I tossed the "dead" snake into the foot well of the back seat. We turned around and headed for Kelly. After traveling several miles, I asked Jimmy to turn on the interior light so I could have a look at the snake. He did and I did. I commented to Jimmy that the snake was not belly-up like he was initially. Turn that light back on. I leaned over the seat again only to see the snake's tail disappear under my seat! STOP!!! In response, Jimmy slammed on brakes. I think he had both heels on the brake pedal. Tires were squalling. The snake was thrust forward, ending up between my feet.

Thinking we had slowed enough, I opened the door and jumped out. We hadn't slowed enough! My first step was about 30 yards long, the second about 20 yards and so on until I began rolling head-over-heels on the sandy road shoulder. Somewhere through my long-distance fall I heard the "swish" of an object — I had narrowly missed someone's mailbox.

Once the sound of squalling tires subsided as the car slid sideways to a stop in the middle of the highway, I heard the desperate screams of the driver. I ran back to the car to find Jimmy partially out with his heels digging into the pavement. His screaming was incessant and LOUD. The snake had crossed to his side of the car and was striking wildly in every direction. Back then automobiles had seat belts — not the shoulder harnesses of today. Jimmy had tried to exit the car without unbuckling his seat belt. It was under his arms and he couldn't reach the buckle. Frantically, I reached past the striking snake and released Jimmy from his entrapment. Absolutely unnerved by the event, I grabbed a bush axe from the rear of the car, ran to the open door and chopped the snake into pieces about the size of a beanie-weenie.

The next time I encountered Bill Palmer I told him that I nearly had a world-record copperhead for his collection. "Where is it?" I'm sorry to report that it was lost in a horrible automobile accident. Bill, a man of few words, commented, "That's unfortunate!" I thought to myself, yes, but it could have been a lot worse.

Marbles and Golf Balls Don't Mix

The year was 1957 and I was in the fourth grade. Spring had arrived and with it came marble season. I always wondered who determined the opening of marble season, but in hindsight I guess it naturally followed the rigors of winter. It was a sport that began toward the end of the school year and carried well into summer. There were two methods of playing or "shooting" marbles. One involved drawing a circle on a section of clear ground and each player would cast his marbles into the circle. The objective was to prop your hand on the edge of the circle and use your "shooter" to knock your opponent's marbles out of the circle. If you missed or knocked one marble out of the circle and your shooter left the circle as well, it was your opponent's turn. Otherwise, you kept shooting. The key was to have your shooter "stick" — remaining in the circle. We always played "keepsies," which means that you kept your opponent's marbles that were knocked out of the circle

The other marble game was called "tracers." The leader would shoot his marble out across the ground and the opponent would attempt to hit your marble. This process continued until one hit the other's marble. Occasionally we would use larger marbles

Something in the circle is out of place!

287

called "log carts." Since many of my classmates lived on farms, ball bearings were readily available and were used in the place of marbles. We called them "steelies." Marbles came in assorted colors. Some were clear and we called them "clearies." There were cat eyes, solids (one color), and others were mottled. Regardless of the colors of the marbles, there was never any doubt about which ones belonged to a particular player.

When recess occurred each day during spring there was no question about our activities on the playground — we shot marbles. One day a fellow fourth-grader brought a golf ball to school during marble season. He was quite secretive about his prized possession. Many classmates, including me, had never held or much less even seen a golf ball. He tantalized us on trips to the restroom by removing the golf ball from his pocket and bouncing it on the wooden floor in the hallway. Each time he quickly returned the ball to his pocket, allowing no one to touch it. He told us to wait patiently until recess and he would demonstrate just how far this projectile would fly when cast against the back wall of the gymnasium.

Recess finally rolled around and we followed our pied piper to the playground beside the gym. By the time we arrived he had assembled quite an entourage of curious onlookers. As we stood in a semicircle he proclaimed that this golf ball was going to "pert near orbitize" after striking the gym's back wall. In unison we looked back across the football field and beyond to visualize the ball's proclaimed path.

The moment of truth had come. There was no turning back at this point. You could have heard a pin drop as the golf ball owner squared off against his target. His antics reminded me of the great Dodger's pitcher Sandy Koufax. He scratched the bare ground with his feet to get a firm stance. Then the windup came in slow motion and seemed to last forever. By gosh, is it ever going to happen? The windup continued and at last the ball left his hand. Silence was broken by a sudden BAP-BAP. That was the sound of the ball striking the gym wall and instantly hitting the "pitcher" right between his eyes. I had heard of levitation, but it was only then that I witnessed someone actually levitating. Time seemed to stop as the pitcher's body was hovering parallel to the ground. He landed in a puff of dust as the ball rolled toward the stunned crowd.

Anyone want to shoot a game of marbles? This ain't no place for a golf ball.

Dr. "B" and the Black Widow

Dr. "B" is our weekend neighbor. He is an orthopedic surgeon from Charleston, S.C. and he spends most of his "off" time at the family's plantation a quarter-mile from our home. Occasionally, to get a jump on the weekends, he arrives in the neighborhood on Thursday afternoons. His ritual is to put on his plantation shirt, a loose-fitting Hawaiian style garment, and piddle around the yard and garden, or take a ride through the property in his electric golf cart.

A couple of years ago he was in the "mode" — distancing himself from the hustle and bustle of city living. He slipped into his plantation shirt, grabbed a set of pruning shears, and began flat-topping shrubbery next to the main house. Only minutes into this escape activity he felt a sting near his belly button. As he said, "It felt like a fire ant bite, so I resumed my pruning." No drama. For those of us in the lowcountry, fire ant

Culprit and the victim.

bites are almost a daily occurrence. There was a difference this time, though. Within minutes there was severe muscle cramping along his spine and toward his neck. The cramping continued horizontally through the intercostal muscles between his ribs. He went inside and called an ER doctor at the hospital in Walterboro (10 miles away). The doctor said the cramping was indicative of a black widow bite and instructed him to come to the hospital's emergency room immediately. Before leaving for the hospital, the favorite plantation shirt was removed, hung in its usual place by the back door, and replaced by a more presentable shirt. He spent a miserable weekend in the hospital. Erratic blood pressure accompanied by bouts of chills and sweating soon succumbed to the constant drip of i.v. fluids.

He was nearly on the mend by the following Thursday and a trip to the plantation was to provide the final remedy. I called to check on him and he commented, "I'm tired of being cooped up inside, do you have anything in mind?" I was on the way to my hunting property to see how my food plots were doing without a recent rain, and asked if he felt like accompanying me. "I'll be ready in five minutes." That meant he had to don the appropriate attire — that darned plantation shirt. I swung by, picked him up, and we departed on our seven-mile trip to the hunting property. We stopped at the gate and as I was getting out of the car I heard a "YeeoOOW!" He exclaimed, "You know, that felt just like it did last Thursday." What do you mean? "Well, I just got stung again!" Get out of the car and take off your shirt. By the time I had walked to his side of the car, he was down to the last button. I looked into the gaping shirt and saw the culprit — a shiny black widow spider. Her egg case was "stitched" between the folds of his shirt at the juncture of the left sleeve. Apparently he shifted in his seat as I was heading to open the gate and pressed the spider against his chest. The spider was severely injured but not enough that it couldn't render its second bite in a week.

We had to take this ol' gal to the hospital with us for evidence. My arachnophobia was in full swing, but I managed to use a stick, a long one, to rake the specimen into a glass vial I found in the trunk of my car.

Our house is halfway between the hunting property and the hospital in Walterboro. As we were approaching the house at a breakneck speed, I called my wife, Donna, and said, You're not going to believe this. Dr. "B" has been bitten by a black widow AGAIN!!! I got exactly the response I expected. "I don't believe it!" That's how I began this conversation — listen to this. I held the car horn in full blast as we flew past the house at twice the speed limit. She said, "What was that?" It was us — we're heading to the hospital; call his wife and meet us there!

The remainder of our trip was a blur. I wheeled up to the door of the emergency room, extracted the patient from the car and walked in with him. As luck would have it, the doctor from the week before was on duty. He met us at the desk and asked, "Why are you here again?" Dr. "B" commented nonchalantly, "Oh, the usual."

Blackwater Treasures

Throughout the southeastern coastal plain there is an intricate capillary system of blackwater streams and creeks. Rainfall on a seasonal or even daily basis determines the life of these blackwaters, especially the small streams. The streams can be ephemeral and in some years nonexistent. Ardent blackwater fishermen know this and focus their piscatorial exploits toward spring and early summer — the best season for optimal water conditions. Fishing blackwater is the coastal plainer's equivalent of pursuing trout in mountain streams. One similarity is that neither requires a boat. But there are many differences. You'll never see a blackwater fisherman wearing waders because the water is warm and we don't mind getting wet. You'll never see a blackwater fisherman using a fly rod or wearing one of those fancy, short-waisted vests with tufts of sheep skin to hold the lures. Also, water moccasins don't live as far west as the mountains, therefore trout fishermen don't have to worry about foot placement, except for slippery rocks, and that's another difference.

Around every bend lies a stretch of blackwater treasures.

Years ago, local folks were known to go "pikeing" in the narrow, blackwater streams. Their quest was the red-finned pickerel (AKA pike), the smallest member of Esocidae — the pike family. They didn't use store-bought lures either. Instead, a strip of red flannel was used without a hook. When a pike hit this flannel its teeth got entangled and the fishermen would sling the prize toward the bank and then attempt to catch the fish with their hands before it was able to flop back into the water. Cane poles and braided line were used instead of rods and reels. That was before the days of monofilament line.

My introduction to blackwater fishing occurred in the 1960s when I decided to take my Zebco 33 and Mepps spinners to some of the larger creeks in my home county. These creeks were known haunts of jackfish (AKA: chain pickerel), the big game of the pike family, at least in my neighborhood. I would park at a bridge and trek along the bank downstream in search of deep water or eddies behind logs or butt-swelled cypress trees. I was "green" in those early days of blackwater fishing and had a lot to learn about the ways of my quarry. After catching two or three jackfish, enough for a meal, I returned home and cleaned my catch for a celebratory dinner. Those jackfish had a reputation of being bony, and not fit for eating. But I learned from an older fisherman that the fish could be filleted, placed skin down, and then "scored" with a filet knife every quarter of an inch along each filet. This technique cuts the bones into tiny pieces that are not detected when eating.

My discovery of this new-fangled blackwater fishing adventure was kept a secret for a number of years before I decided to share it with my long-time friend Walter McDuffie. We had fished blackwater rivers in the county for redbreast and bluegills, but always

Red-finned pickerel — AKA: pike.

from a boat. It took some coaxing to convince Walter that we should go for jackfish on foot. It is now an annual ritual. We use orange or red spinners — Worden's Rooster Tails are favorites, although I have found that the Panther Martin spinners tend to run smoother and are more durable because the spine of the lure passes through the spinner blade. Also, a preferred top-water lure that is irresistible to jackfish is the Smithwick Devil's Horse with spinners at each end and an orange belly.

Our favorite creek will remain unnamed to protect the blackwater treasures that abound. We practice catch and release on the jackfish nowadays except on rare occasions, but keep all of the yellow perch (AKA: raccoon perch, redfin perch) because they have the same food preferences, minnows, as the jackfish. And they're tasty.

Jackfish are cunning. They tend to lie near the water's surface and are easily spooked. Therefore, it is imperative that your fishing attire matches the colors of the swamp.

When asked to join us, John Moran, a friend from South Carolina, questioned the use of the "required" Zebco 33 reel. I told him that accuracy in casting was of utmost importance and using the Zebco 33 was akin to shooting a .22 rifle. You only have one chance at a basking jackfish and lure placement determines whether a fish is hooked or spooked. Approaching a likely spot to cast requires stealth much like stalking the wily whitetail. Due to overhanging limbs and vines, casting is often done underhanded or side-armed and the trusty Zebco 33 outperforms other reel designs. Hunting jackfish is addictive!

Another "required" tool is the hemostat. A jackfish is the freshwater version of a barracuda, and the use of a hemostat will spare your fingers of injury from the long, sharp teeth.

Soon after I moved to the lowcountry of South Carolina to assume the duties as an assistant regional wildlife biologist, I encountered several sportsmen who raved about pikeing. I confessed to being an avid fisherman of jackfish. They informed me that the streams they fished were too small for jackfish, and pikes were the only fish in those streams. I remarked on the methods used by folks in my home county in North Carolina: "Yep, we've heard about using strips of red flannel, but that's the way old timers caught pike — we use spinners and light tackle."

Well, that was all I had to hear. Expecting that they would be as tight-lipped about their favorite pikeing streams as I am about my jackfish spots in North Carolina, I didn't even bother to ask. My travels took me throughout a four-county area and I was always on the lookout for potential streams. They abound in the lowcountry. Once a likely spot was found, the next task was securing permission from the owners of land along the stream. So far, that's never been a problem, except some landowners informed me that fishing was not allowed during the spring turkey season. An avid turkey hunter as well, I understood their concerns and honored their requests. But there were many other opportunities and I quickly got "geared up" to go pikeing.

There was not a season or creel limit on pike since they are not classified as a game fish. I find that demeaning to such a sporty little fish. Only recently (2013) the creel limit for pike was established at 30 — the same for sunfish. I hold the pike in high regard for their choice of habitat — more on that later.

The ardent pike fisherman must learn to "read" the water. If the stream is spilling into the floodplain, pikes will be in the shallows and getting close enough for a cast is nearly impossible. On the other extreme, streams during times of drought, usually by mid-summer, tend to lose their flow and oxygen depletion stresses the fish to the point that they will not hit a lure. It's times like this that fishermen are replaced by all sorts of long-legged, wading birds — herons, egrets, and wood storks. I have even witnessed barred owls swooping down from a perch and grasping pikes as they skimmed the water's surface. As night falls the raccoons and otters have easy picking. This marks the end of the year's pike season.

Paul Warren runs a saw mill in the western end of my current home county and we've been friends since I was nine years old. He took me on my first deer hunt while I was visiting friends in his hometown of Williams. His office is a veritable museum. The walls are lined with racks of deer antlers — strings of turkey beards hang from the antlers. He even has a mounted pike! Once while visiting Paul, I commented that I had never seen a mounted pike, and the conversation launched immediately into pikeing. Paul said that his grandfather would walk to the edge of a bridge over a blackwater stream, take off his hat and wave it with his hand. If pikes were there they would scurry from the shallows into the safety of deeper water. "That's how he determined if pikeing that day would be worthwhile."

How do you know when the pikeing season has arrived? Roll your windows down while traversing hardwood swamps and listen for the sweet-sweet-sweet call of the prothonotary warbler as you cross a bridge over a blackwater stream. The presence of prothonotary warblers signals the beginning of pikeing season. Spring migration has

Paul Warren "swishing" his hat as his grandfather did on nearby bridges to determine if pike fishing would be worthwhile that day.

brought them from their winter havens in Central and South America to nest and raise their young in the insect-rich hardwood bottomlands along the eastern seaboard. Aldo Leopold was fond of this avian species. In his epic book, *A Sand County Almanac*, he wrote: "The real jewel of my disease-ridden woodlot is the prothonotary warbler. He nests in an old woodpecker hole, or other small cavity, in a dead snag overhanging water. The flash of his gold-and-blue plumage amid the dank decay of the June woods is in itself proof that dead trees are transmuted into living animals, and vice versa. When you doubt the wisdom of this arrangement, take a look at the prothonotary."

Trips into pike country are always flavored by the crisp, metallic calls of the prothonotary. The symphony of sweet-sweet-sweet rings continuously throughout a swamp and is truly a blackwater treasure.

Pikeing is well-suited for the buddy system among pike fishermen. We usually travel in pairs, but more than four anglers borders on crowding. One pair will fish up from a bridge while the other pair heads downstream. Rather than fishing across the narrow stream of each other or standing side-by-side, it is best to use the leap-frog approach. While one fisherman "works" a particular stretch of stream the other will walk quietly along the bank a hundred yards or so and begin casting. When the first fisherman encounters the tracks of his partner, he will go around and seek virgin water. This process is continued until our shoulder bags are filled with a limit of pikes. These fish are small, usually six to eight inches in length.

Occasionally, we'll hook into a trophy in the 12-inch category, like Paul Warren's mounted pike. The larger pikes tend to display a yellow color in contrast to the normal charcoal hue. Therefore, to recognize their trophy status, we have named them Amber Bulls.

Pikes are great table fare. Cleaning them is one less step than required for bass or panfish. Since they're small the head is not removed. We adorn them with Cajun seasoning, roll them in House-Autry "slightly hot" Seafood Breader, and deep fry them in peanut oil. They float to the surface when ready.

Pikes, like their larger cousins the jackfish, are bony. There is a technique for eating them. Remove the dorsal fin and hold the fish by the head and tail. Nibble along the back from one end to the other — this is the equivalent of a deer's backstrap. The sides, or flanks, can be eaten last. It's kind of like eating a home-style French fry with a backbone in it. By the way, they're also great broiled.

Combine the pike morsels with hushpuppies, cole slaw and grits for a meal fit for kings and queens. It's the ultimate tribute to your quest and a perfect opportunity to share one of the blackwater treasures with your family and friends.

My Heirloom Fishing Lure Goes to Canada

Dr. Larry Marchinton (retired wildlife professor from UGA) and I had been talking about fishing for northern pike in Canada for years. This trip was in the planning stage for over three years following visits with Tom Brooke at several QDMA National Conventions. Tom is a representative of the Shimano fishing equipment company and a member of the board of directors of QDMA Canada at the time. The trip finally came about in May 2012. Unfortunately, at the last minute, Larry had to cancel due to problems with his left knee. In fact, he had knee replacement surgery in late May in hopes that he would be back in action by the following rabbit season.

Larry's home town buddy from Florida, Dick Ohlson, accompanied us on the trip even though Larry couldn't. Walter McDuffie came along, and Judge Holdford (first recipient of the QDMA's Ambassador Award) from North Carolina was with us as well.

I inherited a fishing lure from my Father and was intent on putting that lure to its proper use — to fish with it. Most of my family and close friends were worried that I may lose the lure, so I photographed it from every angle prior to going to Canada just in case it was not retrieved. The lure was made by the Creek Chub Bait Company in Garrett, Indiana and was produced until the early-1950s. My Father probably purchased this lure in the mid- to late-1940s and I have cherished it along with its original cardboard box.

The first lake we fished was rather shallow and filled with debris — submerged trees and many limbs. I was advised by my host and guide not to use the lure there. On our second day we fished a lake that was much deeper and had a rocky bottom with accompanying grass beds. It was a perfect situation for the inaugural "launch" of my

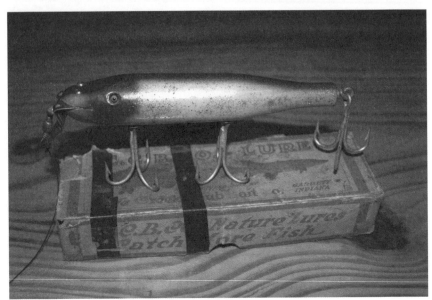

Creek Chub Huskie Pikie lure and its original box.

heirloom lure.

As a safety measure I attached an 18-inch woven-wire leader to the lure. Casting was a bit of a problem. The leader would tangle with the lure's hooks on almost every cast. A shorter leader was the solution, although I still had to learn how to "fly" the lure to avoid a tangle. This involved a high lob while maintaining slight pressure on the outgoing line with my thumb and forefinger. After several trial runs I had the routine worked out. On one of the early retrieves, Tom Brooke commented, "That's absolutely poetry in motion!" As the lure plowed at a depth of about 10 feet in crystal-clear water it swayed from side to side like a real minnow — a large one.

I lobbed the lure toward a buoy marking a rock outcrop and got a hit. The northern pike was on for a few seconds before sending the lure flying into the air. That was a close encounter, but the lure was retrieved. We moved to another buoy nearby and I resumed my lobbing — still can't call it casting. On my third or fourth lob the lure was less than 10 feet from the rod tip when I saw a large northern pike emerging quickly from the depths. In slow motion his opened mouth got larger and larger until the lure was engulfed. I immediately lowered the rod and loosened the drag. Tom shouted, "Don't horse him!" The hooked fish sounded and my drag whined as line was stripped from the reel. After his initial run, I raised the rod and began to turn him. Within minutes the great fish was brought alongside the boat. Phil Morlock, also a Shimano representative, looked over at the fish and said, "We need a bigger net!" What we had was appropriate and Tom gingerly moved the net under the fish and hoisted him aboard. In short order we weighed and measured the fish and took several photos. The prize fish was released back into the lake in hopes of thrilling other anglers. The great fish swam in a large circle and passed within feet of our boat. His gaze was one I'll always

296

Success!

remember. As a romantic, I'd rather think it was a look of appreciation for returning him to his aquatic environment. To others, the fish was simply retreating after a hard fought battle. For those, fishing is an activity — not a passion.

Phil called our buddies who were fishing nearby and uttered a one-word announcement — "Success!" They knew immediately that I had landed my quest and retrieved the lure. As we approached the other boat moments later, Walter McDuffie stood at the bow with tears in his eyes, pointed to the heavens and said, "Someone up there is smiling right now." Overcome by emotion, I could only nod in agreement. Dad would have been proud and envious!

The northern pike measured 36 inches and weighed 16 pounds! The lure, known as a Creek Chub Huskie Pikie, was officially declared "retired" and returned to its original cardboard box. The lure, box, and a photo of my prized northern pike have been framed and displayed as a constant reminder of following a dream and giving it an opportunity to come true. I seriously doubt that a future successful angler will experience the thrill of accomplishment that I had with that great fish, but at least I have provided the chance.

CHAPTER 10

EPILOGUE

This is my first encounter with a book that has Chapter One at both ends. In this instance the final chapter in my Firepot Stories book describes my initiation into the great outdoors as a three-year-old. Since I walked the sandy, two-rut roads on the beloved Sugar Loaf tract with my Father, I have had the distinct pleasure of not only knowing but hunting with four generations of hunters. Sugar Loaf has provided Chapter One in the lives of each of us.

Sugar Loaf on the Cape Fear River near Elizabethtown, North Carolina.

Chapter One

It was soon in the morning on this Saturday during turkey season in early April 2010. An old deer-hunting companion, Mr. Biddy McCulloch, always referred to the pre-dawn meeting time for a hunt as "soon" in the morning.

Time was flexible in those days. Arrival at the staging area, usually a local country store, could be an hour, 30 minutes, or even 15 minutes before the morning hunt was planned. But the earlier one arrived, the more stories could be heard and enjoyed. You just had to arrive before daybreak to put in your two cents worth on whether we were going to hunt east, west, or north of town — never south 'cause there were no deer in that portion of the county. Deer hunting, with dogs of course, was bitter sweet back then. There were no hunting leases and only three informal groups or clubs in the entire county, so there was plenty of elbow room. That was sweet. The bitter part was that huntable deer numbers occurred only in isolated and scattered pockets.

Sorry, but the term "soon" sent me on a tangent. Now, we'll return to the topic of turkey hunting.

This morning was special. It marked the spring turkey season's youth day. We gathered in pre-dawn darkness in the yard of the cabin, overlooking a "U" shaped bend in the Cape Fear River and the renowned sandbar historically known as Sugar Loaf. As a matter of fact, the sandbar's name was imparted to the land on both sides of the river. The atmosphere was tense, yet filled with excitement. There were two teams, each consisting of a caller, a father, and his son. One team was to hunt downriver and the other upriver. The decision of who was to go where occurred without incident — no jealousy, no privilege, and no expressed preference.

My team, Steve Guyton and his son Michael, headed upriver toward the Wright family cemetery. As we strolled along the two-rut sandy road I commented that my Father brought me here when I was only three years old — 60 years ago (at the time). Sugar Loaf was one of his favorite places in our home county, and it has remained high on my list too, for many reasons.

Before we reached our listening point, the simultaneous calls of a chuck-will's widow and a whip-poor-will were heard nearby. We had time for a brief ornithology lesson. I informed young Michael that the chuck-will's widow could be identified by a characteristic "chuck" at the beginning of each call and that it calls about 25 to 40 times a minute. The whip-poor-will, by comparison, calls incessantly about 50 to 65 times a minute. Although both species frequent the coastal plain, I found it unusual and noteworthy that we heard them calling together.

Our listening point was a high bluff overlooking the river's floodplain. The sky was battleship gray, yet bright enough to reveal wing marks left in the sandy road by a strutting gobbler. We knew they had been there in recent days, but would they return? Sign like this fuels anticipation. A barred owl sounded off to proclaim an avian change of the guard — its nocturnal shift had ended. An immediate response followed. That hair-raising call of a mature gobbler split the early morning air. He gobbled from his overnight perch in the hardwoods across the river. That's OK I whispered, I think we can entice him to fly down to our side of the river. I uttered the most seductive hen call

Black bear track and a wild turkey track at Sugar Loaf.

that I could muster and that gobbler interrupted me. He was lonesome! Our hopes were high until a cacophony of hen calling rang out between us at the bottom of the hill. Sure enough, that old gobbler crossed the river, but as soon as he joined the hens our hunt was over for that morning.

This was a monumental event for me. It was the first time I had ever heard a gobbler in my home county. I felt some degree of propriety in the occasion since I had been involved in the restocking of wild turkeys in North Carolina during the late-1980s and early-1990s from South Carolina where I worked as a wildlife biologist.

As we ambled along, somewhat dejected, back to the cabin to recount the morning's hunt we encountered bear tracks in the sandy road. In the mid-1970s I conducted a study of black bears and this property was within my study area. Black bear numbers were relatively low in those days, but they were on the rebound. These were back-to-back monumental events for me!

We were joined at the cabin by the other team of Stanley Sasser, Jake Puglia and his son Trebb. They were empty-handed as well, but their voices were obviously under the influence of an adrenalin rush from a close encounter with a gobbler. Neither hunt produced a gobbler, but lessons were learned, the father-son bond was strengthened, and memories were made.

This was an historic occasion of far-reaching significance. Just in my life there have been four generations of hunters that tramped the woods of Sugar Loaf in pursuit of game. This area has provided an integral building block in the lives of numerous hunters, many of which I have been privileged to hunt with and call my friends. In essence, the natural bounty and its associated experiences can be chronicled as CHAPTER ONE in the lives of these hunters.

Hanging on a wall in the cabin is a framed painting of great depth and significance (page 299). I had shared the story of a telephone conversation I had with Arthur Bentley, renowned "Father of the Deer" in Australia. He said, "Joseph, I had a dream recently that I was sitting at your firepot. You'll never guess who was sitting directly across from me — Al Brothers!" When Kenny White heard about Arthur's dream he took an artist's liberty of depicting an eclectic gathering of my mentors and fellow hunters in a firepot setting at Sugar Loaf along the Cape Fear River. I'm on the left wearing a deer stalker's hat secured during a visit to New Zealand in 1987. My faithful Labrador retriever, Brandy, accompanied me through graduate school in Georgia, my bear research project in North Carolina, and several years of deer research in South Carolina. Each person at the firepot provided guidance and meaning in my life, and each had a role in the creation of this *Firepot Stories* book. From left to right are: Dr. Larry Marchinton, Bob Hamilton (my Father), Arthur Bentley, Brian Murphy, Jonathan Jenkins, Simp Singletary, and Al Brothers.

When the morning turkey hunt was over and stories were told, I decided to spend the remainder of the day reminiscing in a rocking chair on the front porch of the cabin. Turkeys flew back and forth across the river throughout the day and a pair of wood ducks swam by. At roost time a turkey gobbled — signaling prospects for another day in the woods. Hunters should go to bed each night with this sense of hope, anticipation, and innate dedication to our role in life.

And the river slipped by quietly, but with a purpose as well. Its color, like creamed coffee, bears testimony of its origin — deep into the red clay hills of North Carolina. Its journey has been marked by constant flow for millennia. Its destination, drawn by gravity, has remained unchanged although the body of water never knew anything but to keep flowing in search of an ocean.

My day had been steeped in flavor by the calls of turkeys, chuck-will's widows, whip-poor-wills, barred owls and wood ducks. I headed back to civilization at dusk — in my Father's words, "…the shank of the evening." My truck windows were lowered so I could continue savoring nature's voices. A variety of amphibians including, spring peepers, narrow-mouthed toads, southern chorus frogs, and pine woods tree frogs extolled as many habitat types. To the casual observer there would be no obvious habitat changes along the three miles between the cabin and pavement. But, ah, to the student of anuran ethology (frog behavior), diversity existed throughout the journey. How can such tiny critters the size of the last digit of one's pinky be so finicky about home? Each has its niche with micro habitat characteristics. The answer — time — measured in millennia. Time put each species in its proper place, their niche.

Darkness is bracketed by the eight-hooter, the barred owl. He seems to say, "Who cooks for you, who cooks for y'all?" A writer would find it difficult to choose an animal voice as a definitive closing comment. There is a continuum to deal with: An owl proclaims the end of a night's hunt and prompts the turkey gobbler to announce another day of making a living.

To the person who is simply among nature without conviction, these are the sounds of the unknown, but to the student of nature it's the music of outdoor knowledge. This wisdom has no boundaries and is measured only by time and experience. Chapter One marks the beginning — there is no ending for the ardent naturalist, nor will there ever be a final exam.

If *Firepot Stories* builds a fire in your belly for adventures extolled within these pages, then the effort was worthwhile.

I would like to leave the reader with a poem written by my long-time friend, the late Arthur Bentley of Australia. His spirit will always grace the gatherings at our firepot.

Throwing In The Ends

How brightly burnt the fire then,
In those carefree days of spring,
The world was ours to conquer
Why care what the years might bring?

So, steadily burned the fire,
As the logs of life took hold,
Working towards our dreaming
With sorrows and joys untold.

Too soon we see the embers,
Rose-pink with snow-white ash,
The cooler breeze of evening
Stirs wisps of charred leaf trash.

But now, as we throw in the ends,
Flames lift our hearts, or so it seems,
Bright sparks swirling reach the stars
And memories take the place of dreams.

A.B.

Ian Gill

About the Author

R. Joseph Hamilton is a native of Elizabethtown, North Carolina with a Bachelor of Science Degree in Forest Resources (1971) and a Master of Science Degree in Wildlife Biology (1978) from The University of Georgia's School of Forest Resources. His Master's thesis, based on over two years of field research, was entitled: "Ecology of the black bear in southeastern North Carolina." In recognition for his research and public relations efforts, the North Carolina Wildlife Federation presented Joe with the 1975 Governor's Award as Wildlife Conservationist of the Year. This was the first and only presentation of this award to a college student.

Prior to joining The Nature Conservancy in February 2001, he was manager of Ducks Unlimited's Lowcountry Initiative for 3½ years, and was a wildlife biologist with the South Carolina Department of Natural Resources for nearly 19 years in the S.C. Lowcountry.

During his tenure as a wildlife biologist, Joe published several hundred newspaper, magazine, and technical articles. Joe received the Julian C. Greene Award in 1982 from the White Lake (N.C.) Chapter of Ducks Unlimited for successfully leading the opposition to the destruction of waterfowl habitat in a coastal blackwater river, South River. In 1984 the South Carolina Wildlife Federation presented Joe with the Harry Hampton "Woods and Waters" Conservation Memorial Journalism award for excellence in natural resource reporting. The Deer Committee of the Southeastern Section of The Wildlife Society honored Joe with the 2000 Deer Management Career Achievement Award for outstanding contributions to white-tailed deer management in the southeastern United States. Joe was the fifth recipient of this prestigious award. In 2004 Joe was inducted in Melbourne, Australia as a member of The Keepers of the Hunting Spirit. Only two Americans and four Australians have received this distinction. The South Carolina Chapter of The Wildlife Society presented Joe with The Professional Wildlife Management Award in October 2005 to recognize the important contributions and achievements made in the art and science of wildlife management. Outdoor Life Magazine selected Joe as the recipient of the 2005 Outdoor Life Conservation Award. In 2009 the South Carolina Wildlife Federation recognized Joe as the Wildlife Conservationist of the Year. Joe received the 2011 Budweiser Conservationist of the Year Award at an awards ceremony in Las Vegas in January 2011. He was inducted into Garry Mason's Legends of the Outdoors at an awards ceremony in Nashville, Tennessee in August 2012. In 2013 the governor, the General Assembly and the people of South Carolina, recognized R. Joseph Hamilton in for his extraordinary dedication to preserving and protecting South Carolina's environment and natural resources. The Warnell School of Forestry and Natural Resources, University of Georgia, recognized Joe as the 2015 Distinguished Alumnus.

He is the founder of the Quality Deer Management Association (QDMA), which had its birth in the ACE Basin, southeastern South Carolina, in 1988, and has gained international scope with nearly 63,000 members in 50 states, all Canadian provinces, and six foreign countries. Joe served on the board of directors of the QDMA until July 2006, when he began working with that organization as the director of Education and Outreach for the Southern Region (11 southeastern states). Joe continues to contribute to *Quality Whitetails*, Journal of the QDMA. From January 2012 to September 2014 Joe served as the director of development. Joe's title now is QDMA founder and senior advisor.

Professional and NGO memberships include: The Wildlife Society, the S.C. Chapter of The Wildlife Society, the Aldo Leopold Foundation, Ducks Unlimited, the National Wild Turkey Federation, the National Rifle Association, the S.C. Plantation Managers Association, The Nature Conservancy, and the Quality Deer Management Association.

Joe and his wife, Donna, are residents of Hendersonville in the lowcountry of South Carolina.